Kansai and the Asia Pacific

Economic Outlook 2022-23

APIR ASIA PACIFIC INSTITUTE OF RESEARCH

About APIR

The Asia Pacific Institute of Research (APIR) was founded in 2011, with the aim of supporting sustainable development in the Asia Pacific region and Kansai/Japan.[1] In the rapidly globalizing economic environment, APIR has been conducting timely macroeconomic forecasts, as well as research in various fields, such as economy, finance, business, etc. We have also been actively providing academic insights into both domestic and global issues. APIR has extensive connections with the academia, government, and industry, especially in the Kansai area. Many leading companies, organizations and universities are supporting APIR's activities. We are constantly striving to expand our global network through collaborative research, seminars and cooperative activities.

---

1) Kansai is an area located in the center of Japan and has a huge market with a population of approximately 21.45 million and a GRP of approximately JPY 85,820 billion.

Mission:

As a problem-solving think tank, we develop solutions for problems faced by the Asia-Pacific region and contribute to the creation of new vitality and the advancement of sustainable development in both Japan and the Asia-Pacific region.

1. Research that provides logical and factual evidence for developing policies and business strategies.
2. Research, that is accumulating for future forecasts and is being used as a frame for identifying issues and making policy suggestions.
3. Research, the results and data of which are used as a public property and foundational research.

Based on research results, we make practical suggestions and provide information for the economic, academic, and governmental communities at the appropriate time. We also develop excellent human resources for the future.

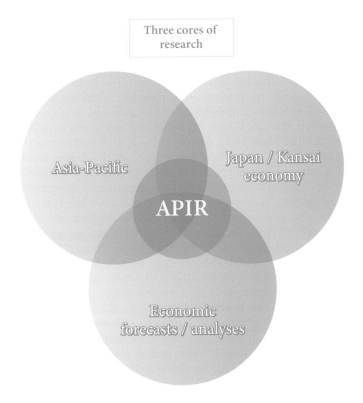

MESSAGE FROM THE RESEARCH DIRECTOR

Asia Pacific Institute of Research
Research Director *MIYAHARA, Hideo*

Similar to 2020, in 2021 the COVID-19 pandemic continued to affect the movement of people and goods worldwide. However, in 2021, the global economy began to recover as vaccination progressed, and the world started shifting toward 'life with corona'. In the first half of 2021, the global economy recovered significantly due in part to large-scale monetary easing and fiscal stimulus. In the second half, recovery stalled due to the increase of COVID-19 infections in emerging economies, disruptions in the global supply chain caused by semiconductor shortages, and surging energy and resource prices. Nevertheless, the global economy logged an overall growth of 6.0% in 2021 (IMF).

In February 2022, Russia invaded Ukraine, and the G7 and other advanced economies imposed economic sanctions on Russia. This had a very large impact on the world as energy and food prices skyrocketed, reminding us of the extent to which global economic interdependence has advanced. In China, COVID-19 infections spiked after the Winter Olympics, and lockdowns were imposed in Shanghai and other major cities. China's 'zero-COVID' policy brought about a decline in international trade. The Kansai region, which is highly dependent on trade with China, has been affected more severely than other regions in Japan.

In FY 2021, Japan's quarterly economic growth rate alternated between negative and positive, as emergency states and measures aimed at curbing the spread of the virus were repeatedly imposed and lifted. However, the recovery is still weak relative to the -4.5% slump in FY 2020. The soaring prices of raw materials, the protracted conflict in Ukraine, the impact of China's zero-COVID policy, and the resurgence of COVID-19 are expected to weigh heavily on growth.

In Japan, as in other countries, the BA.1 Omicron variant of COVID-19 spread rapidly at the beginning of 2022, causing a sixth wave of infections. Although the number of new infections subsided, the BA.5 Omicron variant triggered a seventh wave of infections in the summer, far exceeding the number of infections during the sixth wave. Fortunately, the number of severe infections was lower than the fifth and sixth waves, and no restrictions were imposed on economic activities. In October, after the seventh wave of infections had subsided, the restrictions on entry into Japan from overseas were lifted, which was good news for the tourism industry in the Kansai region. However, as new variants of COVID-19 are being identified (BQ.1, BQ1.1, XBB, etc.), we need to keep a close watch on the trends in infection numbers.

The Osaka-Kansai Expo will be held in 2025. The theme of the Expo is "Designing a Future Society for Our Lives," and its purpose is to be "a place for co-creating a future society," "an online platform for sharing issues and solutions from around the world," and "a place for creating and disseminating new ideas". "People, things, and wisdom" will gather from around the world to solve a variety of issues. We believe that those "people, things, and wisdom" will keep being utilized long after the Expo, and that this is precisely the legacy of the Expo. We also believe that one of the factors for the success of the Expo will be to conduct activities not only in Yumeshima, the site of the Expo, but also in the entire Kansai region.

Osaka is preparing to host an integrated resort (IR), which will be developed on the land adjacent to the Osaka/Kansai Expo site. The Expo and the IR are expected to attract many visitors both domestically and internationally. If domestic and foreign tourists from the Expo and IR can be channeled into tourism in the wider Kansai region, an economic ripple effect can be expected for the entire Kansai region.

In light of these circumstances, this year's Economic Outlook has two themes: "The Asia Pacific at a Historical Turning Point for the World Order" and "Kansai's Role and Future Challenges Seen through the COVID-19 Pandemic." The former focuses on the challenges and prospects of the Asia-Pacific region in 2022 from an international political and economic perspective. The latter analyzes how the economic crisis caused by the COVID-19 pandemic has affected income distribution in the Kansai region, especially the decrease in the middle class which had been observed even before the pandemic. In addition, demographic trends and local fiscal issues are analyzed from various perspectives. Finally, we discuss the economic ripple effects of the Osaka-Kansai Expo, as well as aspirations for the rebranding of Kansai as a tourist destination. This year, the Economic Outlook features a new section, Part III, which is dedicated to the Osaka-Kansai Expo 2025.

At the Asia Pacific Institute of Research (APIR), we will keep putting the results of our research into practice, and we will keep aiming to be a frontrunner in contributing to the economic development of the Asia Pacific, Japan and Kansai.

I would like to express my sincere gratitude to all those involved in the publication of this Economic Outlook.

H. Miyahara

February 2023

TABLE OF CONTENTS

EDITORS & CONTRIBUTORS

Editor in Chief	HONDA, Yuzo
Associate Editors	INOKI, Takenori; INADA, Yoshihisa; MATSUBAYASHI, Yoichi; GOTO, Kenta
Production Editors	IMAI, Ko; OSHIMA, Hisanori; NOMURA, Ryousuke; YAMAMORI, Nobuhiro

Contributors

HONDA, Yuzo
Director of Research, APIR
Professor, Faculty of Economics, Osaka Gakuin University
Professor Emeritus, Osaka University
Ph.D. in Economics (Princeton University, 1980)
Preface; Chapter 1, Section 2

INOKI, Takenori
Research Advisor, APIR
Professor Emeritus, Osaka University;
Professor Emeritus, International Research Center for Japanese Studies
Ph.D. in Economics (Massachusetts Institute of Technology, 1974)
Chapter 1, Section 1

INADA, Yoshihisa
Director of Research & Director of Center for Quantitative Economic Analysis (CQEA), APIR
Professor Emeritus, Konan University
Ph.D. in Economics (Kobe University, 1992)
PartII Introduction; Chapter 2, Section 1,3; Chapter3 , Section 3, Column B; Chapter4 , Section 1,2

MATSUBAYASHI, Yoichi
Senior Research Fellow, APIR
Professor, Graduate School of Economics and Faculty of Economics, Kobe University
Ph.D. in Economics (Kobe University, 1991)

GOTO, Kenta
Senior Research Fellow, APIR
Professor, Faculty of Economics, Kansai University
Ph.D. in Area Studies (Kyoto University, 2005)
Chapter 1, Section 5

KAJITANI, Kai
Senior Research Fellow, APIR
Professor, Graduate School of Economics, Kobe University
Ph.D. in Economics (Kobe University, 2001)
Chapter 1, Section 3

KIMURA, Fukunari
Senior Research Fellow, APIR;
Chief Economist, Economic Research Institute for ASEAN and East Asia
(ERIA)
Professor, Faculty of Economics, Keio University
Ph.D. in Economics (University of Wisconsin-Madison, 1991)
Chapter 1, Section 4

MORIYA, Takashi
Senior Research Fellow, APIR;
Professor, College of Business Administration, Ritsumeikan University
Ph.D. in Sociology (Ritsumeikan University, 2002)
Chapter 1, Section 6

SHIMODA, Mitsuru
Director & Chief Researcher, Applied Research Institute, Inc.
Master of Economics (Tezukayama University, 1999)
Chapter 2, Section 1; Chapter 4, Section 3

IRIE, Hiroaki
Associate Professor, Junior College Division, Kindai University
Ph.D. in Economics (Kwansei Gakuin University, 2012)
Chapter 2, Section 2; Chapter 4, Section 2

KINOSHITA, Yusuke
Lecturer, Faculty of Economics Osaka University of Commerce
Ph.D. in Economics (Kobe University, 2022)

Chapter 2, Section 3; Chapter 3, Section 1; Chapter 4, Section 2

FUJIWARA, Yukinori
Senior Research Fellow, APIR
Professor, Osaka University of Economics and Law
M.A. in Law (Osaka University, 1986)
B.A. in Economics (Osaka University, 1980)
Chapter 3, Column A

SHIMOJO, Shinji
Senior Research Fellow, APIR
Director and Professor, Cybermedia Center, Osaka University
Ph.D. Engineering Science (Osaka University, 1986)
Chapter 3, Section 2

ISHIHARA Yasuyuki
NEXT Kansai 2025 Policy Planning Office, Kansai Bureau of Economy,
Trade and Industry
Chapter 4, Column A

SHIMOYAMA, Akira
Professor, Faculty of Economics, Osaka University of Economics
Ph.D. in Economics (Kwansei Gakuin University, 2010)
Chapter 4, Section 3

TAKABAYASHI, Kikuo
Senior Research Fellow, APIR
Professor, Osaka University of Economics and Law
Professor Emeritus, Kwansei Gakuin University
Ph.D. in Economics (Kyoto University, 1989)
Chapter 4, Section 3

NAKAYAMA, Akira
Chief Program Officer and Research Fellow, APIR
Guest Professor, Fukuoka University
Seconded from Sumitomo Electric Industries, Ltd.
Chapter 1, Section 6

KARAVASILEV, Yani
Research Fellow, APIR
Lecturer, Kyoto Bunkyo University
Ph.D. in International Public Policy (Osaka University, 2017)
Chapter 1, Section 7

YOSHIDA, Shigekazu
Staff, APIR
M.A. in Economics (Kobe University, 2009)
Chapter 2, Section 3, Column A

TERADA, Kenji
General Manager,Outreach Department, APIR
Seconded from Osaka Gas.,Ltd
Part III EXPO 2025 Chronology

IHARA, Wataru
Chief Program Officer, APIR
Seconded from Hitachi,Ltd
Part III EXPO 2025 Chronology

TOKOYAMA, Kuriko
Senior Advisor, APIR
Part III EXPO 2025 Chronology

TANAKA, Mika
Former Staff, APIR
Part III EXPO 2025 Chronology; Part IV Statistical Annex

IMAI, Ko
Chief Program Officer and Research Fellow, APIR
Seconded from Resona Bank, LTD
Part I Summary

OSHIMA, Hisanori
Chief Program Officer and Research Fellow, APIR
MBA in General Management (Kobe University, 2003)
Seconded from DAIKIN INDUSTRIES, LTD
Chapter 3, Section 2; Chapter 3, Column B ; Part IV Statistical Annex

NOMURA, Ryosuke
Research Fellow, APIR
M.A. in Economics (Konan University, 2014)
Part II Summary; Chapter 2, Section 3; Chapter 3, Section 1, 3, Column B;
Part III EXPO 2025 Chronology

YAMAMORI, Nobuhiro
Program Officer & Research Fellow, APIR
Seconded from Takenaka Corporation
Part I Summary; Chapter 1, Section 1; Part III EXPO 2025 Chronology;
Part IV Statistical Annex

(As of March 31, 2023)

PREFACE:
THE J-CURVE EFFECT

HONDA, Yuzo

The US Federal Reserve Board (FRB), which had embarked on an expansionary monetary policy to fight the coronavirus recession since March 2020, quickly changed its stance in the beginning of 2022, and vigorously started squeezing the monetary base and raising interest rates to curb the high inflation. Unfortunately, however, Russia's invasion of Ukraine in February 2022 brought about a global surge in energy and food prices, which in turn exerted further upward pressure on inflation in the US. As a result, the US inflation rate hit 9.1% in June 2022. Thanks to the restrictive monetary policy measures, it gradually declined to 7.1% as of November 2022. However, the aggressive contractionary monetary policy in such a short time period has posed a threat to financial markets of a possible recession in 2023. Stock markets stagnated throughout 2022, which suggests investors are divided as to whether the US economy will be able to make a successful soft landing or fall into a recession in 2023.

The solid appetite for spending by US consumers and companies, as seen during the past 6 years under the Trump and Biden administrations, seems to provide support for the cautiously optimistic view that the US economy might not enter a recession in year 2023. Even if it does, it is likely to be a mild one.

In contrast to the relatively optimistic US economy, China's abandonment of its so-called "Zero COVID-19 Policy" is now creating social unrest in many of its cities. The widespread turmoil will certainly have an adverse effect on both spending and production. In addition to this ongoing problem, there are some other factors which decelerate the Chinese economic growth trend in the future.

First, the Trump administration in the US imposed higher tariff rates on imported goods from China in 2019, and the Biden administration is sticking to this policy. In addition, the US government has also imposed restrictions on exports to China with regard to AI technology, telecommunications, semiconductors and other products. They are also imposing the same restrictions on foreign manufactures, which make use of US technology. All these measures are making technological spillovers to China increasingly difficult.

Second, the US and other G7 members have been getting increasingly cautious toward China. For example,some manufactures in the US and other G7 countries have reduced their direct investments in China and have started diversifying their production bases. This will decrease employment and income in China.

Furthermore, the average income of Chinese people has already dramatically increased as a result of China's remarkable economic growth in the 21st century. The higher income erodes China's global labor cost advantage. All of the above is likely to cause a deceleration in China's economic growth rate.

Turning to the next major economy, the Eurozone is facing the same problem as the US - severe inflation and a possible future recession at the same time. Additionally, EU members are determined to reduce their reliance on energy from Russia for security reasons, implying that they have to pay higher prices for energy from now on. Although certainly understandable, this decision will put a heavy burden on their economic growth.

As explained in the above, the overall economic environment surrounding Japan is not good. However, the US contractionary monetary policy since the beginning of 2022 has led to a depreciation of the yen against the US dollar. The exchange rate dropped from 115 yen per dollar at the end of 2021 to 132 yen per dollar at the end of 2022, corresponding approximately to a 15% depreciation.

Generally, currency depreciation initially worsens a country's trade balance and its production. However, with some time lag, net exports and production improve significantly, provided that net exports are sufficiently elastic with respect to changes in the exchange rate. This empirical macroeconomic phenomenon is called the "J-curve effect".

In 2022, the initial unfavorable phase of the J-curve effect has dominated, as seen by the Japanese trade balance. However, we expect that the second favorable part of the J curve will start taking effect in 2023 or 2024, and it will boost the Japanese economy.

Part I of this year's Economic Outlook discusses the economic status quo in the major countries along the Pacific Rim surrounding Japan. Part II outlines the performance of the Japanese economy in general, as well as that of the Kansai area in particular. Given that Osaka-Kansai Expo is going to be held in 2025, we have added a chronology of events related to the Expo in Part III for your convenience. Although this Economic Outlook is an abridged English-language version of the original Economic Outlook 2022 published by APIR in Japanese, some of the authors have updated their manuscripts in order to provide readers with the latest information.

Part

I A HISTORICAL TURNING POINT

IMAI, Ko; YAMAMORI, Nobuhiro

Part I summarizes the status quo of the world's major countries which are facing a historical turning point. We analyze the challenges major economies at a historical turning point in the world order, with a particular focus on the Asia-Pacific region.

Section 1 discusses the destabilization of the world economy. First, we discuss the political instability caused by the inequality of income distribution in China and the U.S. We then analyze the vulnerabilities of global supply chains in the semiconductor industry, as well as the geopolitical challenges in the energy market from the viewpoint of economic security.

Section 2 analyzes the causes of high inflation in the U.S. economy, and discusses the past and future measures taken by the Federal Reserve with regard to inflation. We elucidate the impact of trends in the U.S. economy on the Japanese economy, and we discuss the inflation outlook for Japan.

In the first half of Section 3, we discuss the status quo of China's zero-COVID policy and the challenges China is facing with regard to its fiscal and monetary policies. In the second half, we provide an outline of China's 'Common Prosperity Policy' by making reference to past policies.

Section 4 addresses two challenges facing the so-called "Factory Asia". In the first half, we analyze empirically the impact of the COVID pandemic on East Asia's international production networks. In the second half, we outline the future challenges and prospects for Japan and East Asia, including growing geopolitical tensions.

Section 5 discusses human rights issues in business. It explains how companies should respond to human rights issues and reflect them in their activities in the age of globalization. Finally, it discusses human rights responses and future challenges in Japan and around the world.

Section 6 discusses the characteristics of human resource development in major Asian countries. The analysis is situated within the framework of the Quadrilateral Security Dialogue (the Quad), a strategic security dialogue between Australia, India, Japan, and the US. We also analyze the possibility of developing "bridge human resources" as a way of promoting economic cooperation based on a questionnaire survey of foreign engineers working for Japanese companies.

Section 7 explores the rise of Asia's middle class from three different per-spectives – income, education-occupation and social values. By juxtaposing the size and characteristics of middle classes in Asia-Pacific countries with those of middle classes in developed Western democracies, the section aims to provide an insight into the extent to which major developing economies in the region have progressed in becoming middle-class societies.

Chapter 1

MAJOR ISSUES IN THE ASIA-PACIFIC REGION IN 2022–2023

Section 1
THE DESTABILIZATION OF THE GLOBAL ECONOMY

YAMAMORI, Nobuhiro; INOKI, Takenori

Some Destabilizing Factors

Many research papers analyzing the equality of income distribution have shown that the income distribution in many developed countries became more polarized in the 1990s and the first decade of the 21st century. Milanovic (2016), who published collective research results, examined the changes in the global income distribution over a 20-year period through painstaking statistical work and pointed out the following noticeable phenomenon regarding each country's income distribution and income growth rate. That is, globally, the world has become divided into two groups in the past approximately 20 years: those who experienced income growth and those who experienced almost no income growth. The former, of people who enjoyed a dramatic increase in incomes, are the middle classes in developing countries (e.g., Southeast Asian countries) and the wealthy in developed countries, while the latter, of those who saw almost no increase in their incomes, are the middle classes of developed countries. Japan belongs to the latter group.

The shrinking of the middle classes in developed countries, especially after the increase in the degree of inequality of income distribution in the two major economic powers of the US and China, shows no sign of improvement, and people belonging to the poor segment increased due to intensifying economic competition. It is undeniable that these are factors contributing to social instability in the global economy. It goes without saying that the above-mentioned progress of inequality and shrinking of the middle classes have a great impact on politics. Other than the above, we cannot underestimate the fragile nature hidden in the trade structure called the "global supply chain" due to the cross-national spread of advanced technologies, especially IT, into production activities. Furthermore, we must pay close attention to several important risk factors and destabilizing factors, such as the geopolitical changes taking place in the global energy supply system due to Russia's invasion of Ukraine.

1. Inequality of Income Distribution

There is no great difference among the world's major countries in that economic activities are basically carried out under the so-called capitalist system based on market economies. Even while capitalism can take different forms, widening income disparities, poverty, and political corruption are factors causing instability both domestically and internationally under any form of capitalism. Milanovic (2019) discussed this point by classifying capitalism broadly into the US style and the Chinese style as follows.

The reason why the US-style liberal meritocratic capitalism has shown stability so far at any rate is that labor unions have had a certain amount of power and contributed to the equalization of income, and that fiscal policies have contributed to economic and political order and stability by redistributing income through a highly progressive tax burden and an income transfer policy.

But nowadays, this environment has changed significantly. For example, the labor union membership rate has declined significantly in developed countries (with the exception of Scandinavia countries), and unionized workers account for only about 10% of workers in the US and France. Although Japan boasted a labor union organization rate of around 50% when the Labor Union Act was enacted after World War II, it has now fallen to 16%. The organization rate for part-time workers, whose number continues to rise, has not yet reached 10%.

The wealthy in developed countries, who did not like the conditions that had supported the global economic system after the Cold War, disliked the high burden and the influx of immigrants and proceeded to withdraw from the system by transferring their income and assets to other countries.

The reason why the US-style liberal meritocratic capitalism has just about prevented political corruption from becoming as severe as in China is because the self-purification effects of freedom of speech and the press work in liberal democracies.

(1) Background of China's "Common Prosperity" Policy

In the Chinese-style political capitalism, an efficient technocratic-bureaucratic system controls the private sector under the one-party autocratic state with lax legal restrictions. Here, the mechanism that rapidly expands income disparities is also activated, creating a maldistribution of wealth and political corruption.

China's rapid economic growth has created an expansion of income disparities, which has forced the government to launch the slogan of "common prosperity" out of a dire need to narrow the gap between the rich and the poor as much as possible and pursue common prosperity for society as a whole. It can be said that the fact that the world's second largest economic power has caused the same maldistribution of income and wealth as the US, the world's largest economic power, is evidence for the validity of Milanovic's discussion that such maldistribution is due to the capitalist system that is common to both countries. It is easy to infer that this slogan comes from President Xi Jinping's strong will for political power as he sought a third term in office at the party congress in the fall of 2022. In analyzing the true aim of this aggressive redistribution policy under the slogan of "common prosperity," Chapter 1, Section 3 of this Economic Outlook points out that the target is successful IT companies and their managers by overlapping this campaign with the anti-corruption campaign of 10 years ago.

A survey paper by Junsen Zhang (2021) is helpful to understand the changes in China's income distribution since 1978, and we will briefly introduce part of it (especially, by social group and by region). Zhang (mainly using income distribution figures at the household level as data) emphasizes the following stylized facts.

1) For the past 40 years, the Gini coefficient, which indicates the degree of inequality (the greater the coefficient, the less even the income distribution), for households has risen at the regional level as well as the urban and rural levels.

2) For the past 10 years, income inequality has remained high, with only a slight decline observed. This phenomenon can be seen in both official statistics and informal estimates.

3) The gaps between urban and rural incomes and inequality in regional distribution were extremely closely correlated with the rise in inequality in China as a whole in the 1980s, 1990s, and early 2000s. However, no such correlation has been observed in the most recent 10 years.

4) The contribution of the gap between urban and rural incomes and regional inequality to national-level inequality has been less important in the most recent decade than in the three decades up to the early 2000s.

5) As a new trend, the contribution of capital income inequality to national-level inequality is found to be increasing, albeit not dramatically.

The following points should be noted. There is a clear negative correlation between the index of the degree of income inequality and the intergenerational income mobility (the degree of movement between income brackets). The so-called Great Gatsby Curve, which illustrates the transmission of income inequality across generations, was observed, indicating an increase in class stratification by assets and income in Chinese society. In the first 30 years of observations, the gaps in incomes between urban and rural areas and between regions were large, but the income inequality stabilized in recent years is no longer a regional problem. The main cause for the overall income disparities is the rise in the income of the highly educated, prime-age male labor force. Privatization, trade and investment liberalization, and technological progress with a bias toward high technologies have widened the wage and salary gap in the labor force. Income disparities arising from these causes will not be resolved spontaneously. Social discontent will continue to accumulate, leading to social instability. This is why economic policies need to be carried out under the slogan of "common prosperity" to improve income disparities.

(2) Political Destabilization

Studies to confirm from data the fact that the US and Chinese socioeconomic systems no longer provide the basis for daily life for 'good citizens,' let alone those with a low level of education, are helpful in considering how the existence of such income disparities and the poor leads to political instability. (Case and Deaton (2021))

For example, among white non-Hispanics (WNHs) in the US between the ages of 45 and 54, the three causes of death that were rising most rapidly were suicide, drug overdose, and alcoholic liver disease (the mortality from these three causes was 34–37 per 100,000). These three causes were also rising quickly for WNHs in every 5-year age group from 30–34 to 60–64.

In the US, while the suicide rate almost doubled from 1992 to 2019 among WNHs aged 25–74 (without an undergraduate degree), increasing from 17.6 to 31.1 per 100,000, there was almost no increase among those with a degree.

If the majority of Americans are failing to thrive while a minority prospers, why does the democratic process not work to improve their material and health outcomes?

Less-educated whites see policies such as safety nets and health provision as favoring minorities at their expense and vote for conservative candidates who oppose such welfare programs. In contrast, blacks and more educated whites react in the opposite direction, widening political polarization, which on net favors the right and provides an opening for populist politicians. (Woolhandler et al. (2021))

Until around 1970, the Democratic Party supported many of the workers' demands. The rate of organization of private-sector unions declined, but even so, with the support of the Democratic Party, the unions had political power, such as raising real wages. However, since 1970, a split has occurred between Democrats and the white working class. Especially after the 1968 Democratic Party Convention, the Party slowly oriented itself away from its traditional working-class and union base toward what it is today, a coalition of minorities and educated professionals.

For example, the voters in Pennsylvania, Michigan, and Wisconsin who voted for Trump in the 2016 presidential election had already moved away from Obama of the Democratic Party in the 2012 election. The trend that average life expectancy at age 25 is lower in states with a higher percentage of voters for Republican candidates has become increasingly clear since 2000. (Case and Deaton (2021) Figure 2)

The interstate correlation was +0.42 when Gerald Ford was the Republican candidate in 1976, and the healthier states voted for Ford of the Republican Party, but it changed to high negative correlations of –0.69 and –0.64 in the 2016 and 2020 presidential elections, respectively. The least healthy states voted for Trump and against Biden.

These recent votes were surely not made for a president who will dismantle safety nets, but rather show that working-class whites are against a Democratic Party that previously supported their rights but now represents an alliance between minorities and an educated elite that has benefited from globalization and from the soaring stock prices of firms that have increasingly denied jobs to working-class whites. In other words, the political structure of the US is changing dramatically because the white middle class, which has fallen into a difficult economic situation, has changed its party affiliation.

2. Vulnerabilities in the Technological Structure—Global Supply Chains

The second destabilizing factor lies in changes in the technological system. Advances in IT have enabled the separation of production and management. Changes in capital movements and the trade structure that have become conspicuous in recent years do not mean the relocation of companies themselves, but rather a shift to a thorough subdivision of production processes within a company, both from operational and management perspectives, as well as a shift to a division of labor on an international scale. Production processes are scattered geographically according to the expertise level, low wages, and other factors, which has given rise to the formation of so-called global supply chains. It goes without saying that changes in production technologies and advances in data analysis technologies and information and communication technologies in the manufacturing industry have made these major changes possible. In fact, the semiconductors that work as the brains of Apple's iPhones are designed in the US, but its semiconductor factory is not located in the US and the manufacturing is outsourced mainly to Taiwan Semiconductor Manufacturing Company (TSMC), a major semiconductor manufacturer in Taiwan.

The basis that has enabled this technological shift lies in the technology and production capacity for semiconductor manufacturing. Therefore, the US and China, as well as many other countries including emerging Asian countries, are developing strategies for how to support and foster the semiconductor industry as a key challenge for their national economic policies.

How to deal with the vulnerabilities hidden in the global trading system based on the global supply chain structure will be one of the central issues of each country's economic policy in the future. This is a typical example of the so-called "economic security" issue. It is a noticeable phenomenon that Taiwan's TSMC is said to be a key strategic item for East Asian security.

In the past, security was a concept covered by foreign policy centered on military and diplomacy, but in recent years, the focus of security has shifted to the relationship with national security, being regarded as an issue of vulnerability in the economic and technological fields (especially in infrastructure). In short, when considering economic sanctions as a means of conflict resolution, economic measures can serve as a kind of weapon. This is also clearly shown in the economic sanctions imposed by the countries that are aiding Ukraine, including Europe and the US, following Russia's recent invasion of Ukraine.

What does this situation mean? Russia's invasion of Ukraine shows once again that "war potential" is no longer limited to traditional military means such as missiles, other weapons, and military force, as well as economic sanctions. Cyber-attacks, including virus attacks, on computer systems, may expose global supply chains to the risk of damage.

The COVID-19 pandemic has severely impacted the structure of production, consumption, and trade, resulting in the shortage of supply of semiconductors in many countries. To analyze the cause of such a situation, we would like to discuss the technological nature of semiconductors, their production and distribution structures, and shortage status, while showing the structure of supply chains and their inherent vulnerabilities.

(1) Semiconductor Shortage Problem

Semiconductors are used as core components for a vast array of electronic devices devices—everything from smartphones and cloud servers to automobiles, industrial automation, critical infrastructure, and defense systems. The global structure of the semiconductor supply chain developed over the past three decades has enabled the industry to deliver continual leaps in cost savings and performance enhancements, which made possible the explosive spread of information technologies and digital services. In the past few years, however, several new factors have emerged that could put the successful continuation of this global model at risk.

In the automotive industry, the shortage of semiconductors has caused serious delays of from six months to a year in the deliveries of some new cars[1]. Toyota Motor Corporation's domestic production in September 2021 fell to 136,750 vehicles, down 44.7% year-on-year (Figures 1-1-1 and 1-1-2). The impact of the semiconductor shortage has not yet been fully resolved, and on May 24, 2022, Toyota announced that it would cut its global production plan by 100,000 to roughly 850,000 vehicles in June.

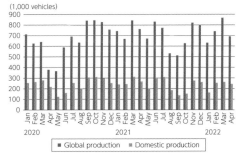

Figure 1-1-1   Changes in Toyota Motor Cooperation's production volume (January 2020 to April 2022)

Source: Created by the author based on Toyota's Sales, Production, and Export Results for April 2022 (May 30, 2022)

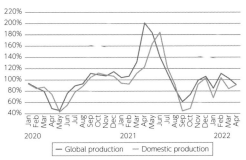

Figure 1-1-2   Year-on-year changes in Toyota Motor Cooperation's production volume (January 2020 to April 2022)

Source: Created by the author based on Toyota's Sales, Production, and Export Results for April 2022 (May 30, 2022)

1) Nihon Keizai Shimbun (October 30, 2021)

The impact of the semiconductor shortage has not been limited to the automobile industry, but has spread to companies in many other industries (Table 1-1-1). According to Fujitsu's financial results briefing on January 27, 2022, delays in the supply of parts and materials due to semiconductor shortages resulted in a sales decline of JPY 39.7 billion and a negative impact on operating income of JPY 19 billion for the first nine months from April to December 2021. For the third quarter alone (October to December 2021), sales decreased by JPY 24.8 billion and the negative impact on operating income was JPY 11.9 billion on a non-consolidated basis[2].

Table 1-1-1   Questionnaire on the impact of the semiconductor shortage

Company name	Impact
NEC	Delays in the supply of parts and materials due to semiconductor shortages resulted in a sales decline of JPY 16 billion and a negative impact on operating income of JPY 7 billion for the first nine months from April to December 2021. The negative impact on operating income is expected to expand to JPY 8 billion for the full year.
ITOCHU Techno-Solutions	There is a risk that approximately JPY 10 billion in sales will slide into the next fiscal year (fiscal year ending March 31, 2023) due to delays in delivery and construction.
BIPROGY(former Nihon Unisys)	The impact on sales amounted to more than JPY 1 billion.
Fujitsu	Delays in the supply of parts and materials resulted in a sales decline of JPY 39.7 billion and a negative impact on operating income of JPY 19 billion for the first nine months from April to December 2021. For the third quarter alone, sales decreased by JPY 24.8 billion and the negative impact on operating income was JPY 11.9 billion on a non-consolidated basis.

Source: Excerpts from Nikkei CrossTech (xTECH) (March 4, 2022)

(2) The Global Supply Chain for the Semiconductor Industry[3]

Semiconductors are products that are highly complex to design and manufacture. The need for deep technical know-how and production scale has resulted in a highly specialized global supply chain, in which regions perform different roles according to their comparative advantages. The US leads in the most R&D-intensive activities—electronic design automation (EDA), core intellectual property (IP), chip design, and advanced manufacturing equipment—thanks to its world-class universities, vast pool of engineering talent and market-driven innovation ecosystem. East Asia is at the forefront of wafer fabrication, which requires massive capital investment supported by government incentives, as

---

2) Nikkei CrossTech (xTECH) (March 4, 2022)
3) This subsection relies primarily on Varas et al. (2021).

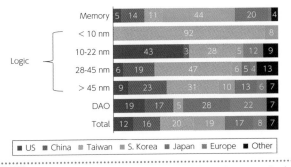

	US	China	Taiwan	S. Korea	Japan	Europe	Other
Memory	5	14	11	44	20		4
Logic < 10 nm			92				8
Logic 10-22 nm	43	3	28	5	12		9
Logic 28-45 nm	6	19	47	6	5 4		13
Logic > 45 nm	9	23	31	10	13	6	7
DAO	19	17	5	28	22		7
Total	12	16	20	19	17	8	7

Figure 1-1-3   Breakdown of the global wafer fabrication capacity by region, 2019 (%)

Note: DAO means discretes, analog and others (including optoelectronics and sensors)
Source: Varas et al. (2021)

well as access to a robust infrastructure and skilled workforce. China is the leader in assembly, packaging and testing, which is relatively less skill- and capital-intensive. All countries are interdependent in this integrated global supply chain, relying on free trade to move each manufacturing process around the world to the optimal location for performing each activity.

The establishment of a global supply chain by locating the right processes in the right places, based on such comparative advantages, has promoted productivity improvements in the semiconductor market, leading to continued cost reductions and performance improvements. For example, according to Varas et al. (2021), many suppliers of key materials, such as silicon wafers, photoresist, and other specialty chemicals, which account for about 75% of semiconductor manufacturing capacity, are concentrated in China and East Asia. Furthermore, all of the world's semiconductor manufacturing capacity for nodes below 10 nanometers is currently located in South Korea (8%) and Taiwan (92%) (Figure 1-1-3). However, by building a production system where specific production processes are limited to specific regions, such regions may be single points of failure.

If such single points of failure are disrupted by natural disasters, infrastructure shutdowns, or international conflicts, severe interruptions may arise in the supply of semiconductors. Table 1-1-2 shows historical examples of disruptions to semiconductor supply.

Such single points of failure are not limited to manufacturing facilities, but the same can be said for raw materials. As an example, C4F6 is a critical process gas used to make 3D NAND memory and some advanced logic chips. It is essential for the etching process during chip fabrication, allowing etching to be completed 30% faster than the next fastest alternative. Furthermore, once a

Part I

Part II

Part III

Part IV

Table 1-1-2   Historical examples of disruption to semiconductor supply

Date	Case	Outline and Impact
July 4, 1993	An explosion at Sumitomo Chemical's Ehime plant	This explosion impacted 60% of the global supply of epoxy resin, and spot prices for DRAM memory chips in the US market spiked from an average of USD 30/megabyte to around USD 80/megabyte.
September 21, 1999	A strong earthquake in the center of Taiwan	This earthquake caused a six-day shutdown of the Hsinchu Science Park due to power outages. As a result, memory-chip prices tripled and shares of electronics companies around the world fell sharply, with IBM, Hewlett Packard, Intel, and Xerox, all part of the Fortune 100 at that time, losing 18 to 40% of their value in the month after the earthquake.
March 11, 2011	The Great East Japan Earthquake	A major earthquake struck Japan, followed by a tsunami and nuclear power-plant melt down. 25% of the global production of silicon wafers and 75% of the global supply of hydrogen peroxide was affected by the disaster. Several plants were shut down for several months.
July 1, 2019	Japan's export controls on semiconductor materials against South Korea	The export controls impacted approximately USD 7 billion in semiconductor exports per month.
December 3, 2020	A power outage at a memory plant in Taiwan	This power outage impacted 10% of global DRAM supply.
October 28, 2020 February 4, 2021	Two fires at a package substrate plant in Taiwan	These fires aggravated the global capacity shortage for assembly, packaging and testing services, making it impossible to meet the surge in semiconductor demand in the last few months of 2020.
February 15, 2021	Widespread power failures following a polar vortex in Texas	The global chip supply shortage, especially for the automotive market, was further exacerbated.
March 19, 2021	A fire at a plant of a subsidiary of Renesas in Japan	The global chip supply shortage, especially for the automotive market, was further exacerbated.

Source: Prepared based on Varas et al. (2021) and materials from relevant sources

manufacturing plant is calibrated to use C4F6, it cannot be substituted. Sales of C4F6 were approximately USD 250 million in 2019, with the top three suppliers located in Japan (40% of the global supply), Russia (25%), and South Korea (23%). Varas et al. (2021) predicts that if any of these top three producers are severely disrupted, the loss of USD 60–100 million in C4F6 supplies could lead to about USD 10 to 18 billion in lost revenue for NAND alone downstream in the semiconductor chain, an amount almost 175 times higher than the direct impact. It also speculates that if such disruption in a portion of the C4F6 supply were to become permanent, NAND production levels would potentially be constrained for 2 to 3 years until alternative locations could introduce new capacity ready for mass production. There is no doubt that the impact of Russia's invasion of Ukraine, which began on February 24, 2022, has added pressure on the semiconductor industry to address this challenge.

(3) Risk Response Scenarios

To address these risks, the concepts of semiconductor "self-sufficiency" are being discussed as potential desirable national policy goals. It is helpful to understand what level of investment would be needed if most countries or regions were to re-shore or nearshore production capacity to reduce exposure to these risks and to protect their national interests. Varas et al. (2021) analyzes the following two scenarios.

i) A scenario where each region pursues complete semiconductor self-sufficiency

Figure 1-1-4 presents a hypothetical extreme scenario, where each major region in the world looks to construct their semiconductor "self-sufficiency" in a strict sense, across all layers of the supply chain. Aside from any considerations of execution feasibility, such an extreme scenario of regional independence would require a staggering amount of upfront investment totaling of USD 900 to 1,225 billion in order to cover each region's 2019 consumption levels, while any future growth in domestic consumption would require further investment in additional capacity in each region. This amount is equivalent to about six times the combined R&D investment and capital expenditure of the total semiconductor value chain in 2019. In addition, even assuming that semiconductor companies across the supply chain could maintain their current cost structure despite the loss of global scale, the industry is estimated to incur USD 45 to 125 billion in incremental recurrent annual operational costs (Figure 1-1-5).

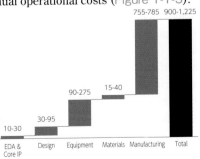

| Figure 1-1-4 | Scenario of complete semiconductor self-sufficiency: Upfront investment (USD 1 billion) |

Source: Varas et al. (2021)

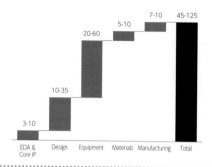

Figure 1-1-5 Scenario of complete semiconductor self-sufficiency: Operational costs (USD 1 billion)

Source: Varas et al. (2021)

At least a portion of this total estimated USD 900 to 1,225 billion in upfront investment and USD 45 to 125 billion in incremental annual operating costs would necessarily have to be passed on to device makers in the form of higher prices for the semiconductors they purchase. If fully charged to customers, it would amount to an average increase of 35 to 65% in the price of semiconductors. This may result in higher prices of the electronic devices for end users. Furthermore, it is also likely that siloed domestic industries shielded from foreign competition and deprived of global scale would suffer a loss of efficiency and ability to innovate. In conclusion, full semiconductor self-sufficiency appears to be more of a theoretical concept than an attainable policy goal.

ii) Market-driven alternative approach scenario focused on key strategic risks

As shown in Figure 1-1-3 above, all of the world's manufacturing capacity of chips for nodes below 10 nanometers is currently located in South Korea (8%) and Taiwan (92%). The US has identified chips as a vulnerability that could pose a national security risk. Advanced logic chips account for about 34% of US total semiconductor consumption. A significant portion of that figure actually comes from consumer-driven applications, such as smartphones, PCs, consumer electronics, and automobiles.

However, merely 9% of the US consumption of advanced logic chips is associated with critical infrastructure applications, including aerospace and defense systems, core telecommunications networks, supercomputers and data centers for essential sectors such as government, energy, transportation, healthcare and financial services. A hypothetical disruption in the supply of these chips could have a severe impact on the economy and national security, so maintaining at least a minimum viable manufacturing capacity located onshore could significantly enhance the resilience of the US electronics supply chain.

Varas et al. (2021) estimates that covering the expected domestic consumption of advanced logic chips for critical infrastructure applications by 2030 would require building just two or three new state-of-the-art plants in the US[4]. This additional new capacity is less than 5% of the new advance logic capacity that needs to be added globally to keep up with the expected demand growth in the next 10 years.

(4) Japan's Semiconductor Strategy

Against the backdrop of the US-China trade friction and Russia's invasion of Ukraine, and also from the perspective of strengthening competitiveness and economic security in the semiconductor industry, countries around the world are promoting industrial policies, including attracting production bases to their home nations using huge subsidies (Table 1-1-3).

The Japanese government allocated JPY 617 billion for the FY 2021 supplementary budget for the purpose of securing domestic production bases for advanced semiconductors. In addition, on March 1, 2022, the amended act to encourage the establishment of domestic production facilities for advanced semiconductors came into effect. If a company's plan to develop a production facility in Japan meets particular requirements, it can receive subsidies covering half of the necessary construction costs. The TSMC plant will be the first to receive support under the Act. TSMC is constructing a new production plant in Kumamoto Prefecture, with shipments scheduled to begin in December 2024. Attracting production plants for future growth industries to Japan will lead to the creation of jobs and have a positive effect on the economy. However, as mentioned above, from the standpoint of economic security and market competitiveness, the construction of production facilities alone is not enough, and it is also necessary to strengthen research and development facilities. In 2021, TSMC established a research and development facility in Tsukuba, Ibaraki Prefecture.

In addition to government subsidies, the National Institute of Advanced Industrial Science and Technology (AIST) played a central role in attracting companies by establishing a framework for collaboration between Japanese companies and universities. In order for Japan to survive in this unstable semiconductor industry supply chain in the future, industry-government-academia collaboration will be essential.

---

4) The new plants are assumed to have a production capacity between 20,000 and 35,000 wafers per month.

Part I
Part II
Part III
Part IV

Table 1-1-3	Trends in the semiconductor industry policies of major countries and regions

Country/Region	Major Trends in Industrial Policies
US	• The National Defense Authorization Act (NDAA 2021), which includes subsidies of up to JPY 300 billion per project and the establishment of the Multilateral Semiconductors Security Fund, was passed. • The House and Senate are in session on the America COMPETES Act (China Competition Bill) including a budget of USD 52 billion (approx. JPY 6 trillion) to subsidize semiconductor industry. (April 2022)
China	• The National Integrated Circuit Industry Investment Fund was established (2014, 2019) and made major investments totaling over JPY 5 trillion in semiconductor-related technologies. • In addition, local governments have funds totaling over JPY 5 trillion for the semiconductor industry (total fund amount: over JPY 10 trillion).
Europe	• Digital strategy for 2030 was announced, including an investment of €134.5 billion (approx. JPY 17.5 trillion) in digital transition (logistic semiconductors, HPC, quantum computers, quantum communication infrastructure, etc.) • The European Commission announced the European Chips Act, which aims to make €43 billion of investments by 2030. (February 2022)"
Taiwan	• Subsidies and other preferential measures were launched to attract investments back to Taiwan. A total of JPY 2.7 trillion investment applications were approved, mainly in the high-tech sector. (January 2019) • A plan was announced to inject a total of JPY 30 billion in subsidies to the semiconductor sector by 2021. (July 2020) • Prospects for Semiconductor R&D and Talent Deployment under the US-China Science and Technology War were announced, which includes human resource development and factory area expansion (NT$27.3 billion). (April 2022)
South Korea	• An investment of JPY 100 billion was approved for AI semiconductor technology development. (December 2019) • An investment plan was announced to intensively inject more than JPY 500 billion in technological development in the materials, parts, and equipment industries, including semiconductors, by 2022. (July 2020) • The K-Semiconductor Strategy was formulated to turn South Korea into a comprehensive semiconductor powerhouse. (May 2021)

Source: Prepared based on "Semiconductor and Digital Industry Strategy" formulated by the Ministry of Economy, Trade and Industry (METI) and other media sources

3. Situation of Interdependence in the Energy Markets

The war in Ukraine has dragged on longer than Russia expected as the Ukrainian army has fought hard against its invasion and Western powers have provided Ukraine with effective military support. As long as Ukraine's war potential depends on Western military support, the West's economic relations with Russia will undoubtedly be a major factor in determining the course of the war. The most important factor in the economic relations would be the degree of energy dependence of the West (especially Europe) on Russia.

Figure 1-1-6 shows the changes in the energy import dependency of major countries from 1990 to 2019. Negative values indicate that energy production exceeds domestic energy supply, i.e., exports exceed imports. Japan's import dependence reached 83% in 1990 and increased to 88% in 2019, while Russia

increased its share of exports in production from –47% in 1990 to 2000 (–58%),
2010 (–85%), and 2019 (–98%).

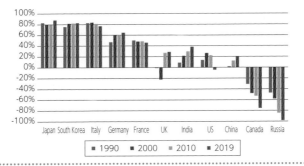

Figure 1-1-6 Changes in the energy import dependency of major countries (1990 to 2019)

Source: Prepared based on the IEA Data and Statistics

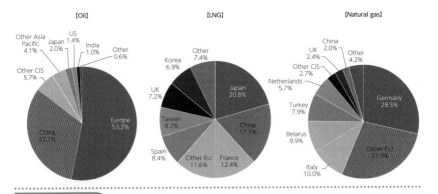

Figure 1-1-7 Share of Russian energy importers: Crude oil, LNG, and natural gas

Source: Prepared by the author based on the BP Statistical Review of World Energy (2021)

Looking at the shares of the major energy importers from Russia (in 2020),
Europe and China account for 53.2% and 32.1% of crude oil, respectively. Japan
(20.8%) accounts for the largest share of liquefied natural gas (LNG), followed
by China (17.1%) and France (12.4%). It can be seen that the majority of natural gas exports via direct pipelines are to Europe, mainly due to geographical
factors (Figure 1-1-7). Among others, exports to Germany account for 28.5%,
indicating that exports to Europe generally account for a major proportion.

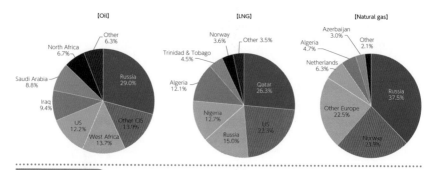

Source: Prepared by the author based on the BP Statistical Review of World Energy (2021)

Figure 1-1-8   Share of energy exporters to EU: Crude oil, LNG, and natural gas

Changing the perspective, looking at the share of energy exporters to the European region (in 2020), Russia ranks first for crude oil and natural gas, with 29% and 37.5% of the totals, respectively. As for LNG, 15% is imported from Russia, despite the fact that abundant natural gas supply networks are available through pipelines (Figure 1-1-8). In particular, Germany's share of natural gas imports from Russia via pipelines is as high as 55.2%. As can be seen from these data, it will be extremely difficult for Europe to replace natural gas from Russia in the short term. However, even if zero dependence cannot be achieved immediately, it would be possible to gradually reduce the dependence towards zero over three to four years. If such a policy continues in the medium term, it is expected that Russia will suffer significant economic damage.

References

BP, *Statistical Review of World Energy 2021*

Case, Anne and Angus Deaton, *Deaths of Despair and the Future of Capitalism*, Princeton University Press, 2020

Case, Anne and Angus Deaton, "The Great Divide: Education, Despair and Death," NBER WORKING PAPER 29241, September 2021

Daniel Yergin, *The New Map: Energy, Climate, and the Clash of Nations*

INOMATA, S., *Value Chains: A New Look at the North-South Problem* (Japanese title: *Gurobaru Baryu Chein: Shin Nanboku Mondai e no Manazashi*), Nihon Keizai Shimbun Publishing, 2019

JETRO Business Brief, "Strengthening R&D and Human Resource Development to Maintain the Competitiveness of the Semiconductor Industry" (Japanese title: *Handotai Sangyo no Kyosoryoku Iji no Tame Kenkyu Kaihatsu Jinzai Ikusei o Kyoka*), April 23, 2021

JETRO Business Brief, "European Commission Announces Legislation Aimed at Strengthening Regional Semiconductor R&D and Production and Stable Supply" (Japanese title: *Oshu Iinkai Ikinai deno Handotai no Kenkyu Kaihatsu Seisan no Kyoka to Antei Kyokyu o Mezasu Hoan o Happyo*), February 10, 2022

JETRO Business Brief, "U.S. Congress Announces Joint Committee Members for a Consensus on the China Competition Bill (America COMPETES Act)" (Japanese title: *Beigikai Taichu Kyosohoan Chosei no Ryoin Godoiinkai Menbaa o Happyo*), April 11, 2022

Junsen Zhang, "A Survey of Income Inequality in China," Journal of Economic Literature 2021, 59 (4), 1191-1239

METI news release, "Review of Export Controls for the Republic of Korea (ROK)" (Japanese title: *Daikan Minkoku Muke Yushutsu Kanri no Unyo no Minaoshi ni Tsuite*), July 1, 2019

Milanovic, Branko, *Capitalism, Alone: The Future of the System that Rules the World*, Harvard University Press, 2019

Milanovic, Branko, *Global Inequality: A New Approach for the Age of Globalization*, Harvard University Press, 2016

METI, "Semiconductor and Digital Industry Strategy," June 2021

Nihon Keizai Shimbun, "Excessive Return to Domestic Market Lead to Weak Supply Chain: Economic Security Focus" (Japanese title: *Kado na Kokunai Kaiki, Kyokyumou Yowaku: Keizai Anzen Hoshou no Shoten*), March 9, 2022

Nihon Keizai Shimbun, "Shortage of New Cars and Delayed Deliveries: Popular Cars May Take 6 Months to Ship due to Production Cuts" (Japanese title: *Shinsha Busoku, Okureru Noki: Gensan de Ninkisha wa Hantoshi Machi mo*), October 30, 2021

Nihon Keizai Shimbun, "Toyota under Scrutiny over Whether It can Stick to Its Annual Production Target of 9.7 Million Units; Production Decline due to Semiconductor Shortage" (Japanese title: *Toyota, Nen 970 mandai Iji ga Shoten ni: Handotai Busoku de Seisangen*), May 24, 2022

Renesas Electronics Corporation Press Release "Renesas Electronics Announces Fire at Semiconductor Manufacturing Plant (Naka Plant) (3rd Report)" (Japanese title: *Handotai Seizo Kojo (Naka Kojo) no Kasai Hassei ni Kansuru Oshirase (Dai Sanpou)*), March 21, 2021

SUZUKI, K. *The Increasing Severity of the Semiconductor Shock and Its Impact on the Eight Leading IT Services Companies* (Japanese title: *Shinkokusa Masu Handotai Shokku, IT Saabisu Ote Hassha e no Eikyo wa*), Nikkei CrossTech (xTECH), March 4, 2022

Varas, Antonio, Raj Varadarajan, Ramiro Palma, Jimmy Goodrich, and Falan Yinug, "Strengthening the Global Semiconductor Supply Chain in an Un-

Part I

Part II

Part III

Part IV

certain Era," Boston Consulting Group, April 1, 2021

Woolhandler, S. et al. "Public Policy and Health in the Trump Era," The Lancet 397, 2021 (10275): 705-53.

Section 2
THE US ECONOMY UNDER HIGH INFLATION

HONDA, Yuzo

1. The US Economy: Why Are Prices Soaring in the US?

As of May 2022, production and employment in the US have been recovering steadily from the COVID-19 recession. Production already exceeded the pre-pandemic level by mid-2021 and has kept increasing. Likewise, in the labor market, the unemployment rate has been declining rapidly since mid-2021 and reached the low rate of 3.6% in May.

Prices are rising, however, and the recovery in production and employment are fraught with the risk of economic overheating. Based on the Consumer Price Index (CPI), inflation rates (12-month percentage change) in March, April, and May 2022 were as high as 8.5%, 8.3%, and 8.6%, respectively, well above the 2% target (see Figure 1-2-1). The Federal Reserve Board (FRB), which had initially interpreted the rise in prices as transitory and kept the expansionary monetary policy in response to the COVID-19 crisis, has changed its stance to a neutral at first, and then to a contractionary monetary policy since the end of 2021. The primary focus as of May 2022 has now shifted to whether the FRB's continued monetary tightening will allow the US economy to make a soft landing on its growth trajectory.

To examine the various aspects described above, it is necessary to understand why the current inflation rate is high in the US, whether it will continue to rise, how the FRB has responded to high inflation, and how it intends to deal with it in the future. In this report, we also discuss how these movements in the US economy will affect the Japanese economy.

Why is the US currently experiencing high inflation? The following six points are important in explaining the current high inflation rate: (1) the government's massive fiscal stimulus and the FRB's bold monetary easing to counter the COVID-19 pandemic; (2) the surging prices of resources such as crude oil, natural gas, nickel, and others, as the economy recovers from the COVID-19 recession; (3) the disruption of the supply chain of goods and services as a result of the global spread of the COVID-19 pandemic; (4) the shortage of workers in the US; (5) the further rising prices of resources and food as a result of Russia's invasion of Ukraine; and (6) the statistical bias caused by the use of 12-month percentage change comparisons.

Part I
Part II
Part III
Part IV

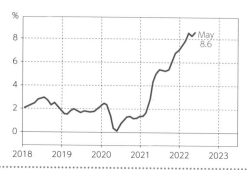

Figure 1-2-1   US Consumer Price Inflation (% change from the same month of the previous year)

Source: Federal Reserve Bank of New York

First, we will start with (6) the statistical bias which is easy to understand. When the COVID-19 broke out widely in the US in March 2020, total spending fell sharply, especially in the service industry, and the CPI inflation rate plummeted from around 2% to near 0% (see Figure 1-2-1). Then the CPI inflation rate remained well below 2% throughout the year 2020. Therefore, the CPI inflation rate for the year after March 2021 was calculated based on the low price levels during 2020, resulting in a higher inflation rate. (This might be one of the reasons why the FRB initially thought that the inflation spike was transient.) This bias, however, was and will be eliminated after March 2022, and it is not necessary to consider this problem (6) to any great extent as of May 2022.

To consider the impact of the remaining five factors, it is easier to understand them by using the framework of an aggregate demand and supply analysis (see Chapter 1, Section 2 of the "Kansai and the Asia Pacific Economic Outlook 2020" for more information). According to this analytical framework, the COVID-19 pandemic shifts the aggregate demand curve when it affects people's spending behavior and shifts the aggregate supply curve when it affects firms' production activities. In the case of the COVID-19 pandemic, the decrease in people's spending due to the COVID-19 disaster shifts the aggregate demand curve downward to the left, and as a result, prices fall and output also declines. On the other hand, a disruption in the production-supply network shifts the aggregate supply curve upward to the left, and as a result, prices rise and output declines.

The first blow of the COVID-19 pandemic to the economy was at aggregate demand. The service and other related industries have experienced large declines in their sales. Many countries around the world, however, adopted appropriate expansionary fiscal and monetary policies, and the global economy began to recover quite quickly. As global aggregate demand started to come back, the prices of resources such as crude oil, natural gas, and nickel soared.

A sharp rise in resource prices raised the cost of production, shifting the aggregate supply curve upward. As a result, prices went up (see (2) above).

The COVID-19 pandemic has been spreading around the globe from place to place and time to time. At the same time, the global supply chain, as the name "chain" implies, is multi-layered and easy to be disrupted due to an infectious disease. A disruption occurs even if one chain is broken in this supply chain network. Therefore, supply shortages are likely to occur (Grossman, 2022). Supply chain disruptions shift the aggregate supply curve to the upper left, causing prices to rise (see (3) above).

Because the US government and the FRB's COVID-19 recession counter-measures were extremely swift and extensive, the US economy recovered quite quickly from its initial serious unemployment rate of 14.7%. Bailouts, especially by fiscal policy, have been massive and seamless, beginning with the former President Trump and continuing under the current President Biden. With these generous government bailouts, an increasing number of people left the labor market. Numerous workers did not return to their jobs when the economy recovered, including those who did not want to return to the jobs that were susceptible to COVID-19. Partly due to the recovery from the COVID-19 recession, the labor market is getting tighter, which puts upward pressure on wages (see (4) above).

Russia invaded Ukraine on February 24, 2022. Currently, as of the end of July 2022, the war between Russia and Ukraine is still ongoing. The Russian invasion of Ukraine resulted in global shortages of resources and foodstuffs, including crude oil, natural gas, wheat, and nickel, and their prices have skyrocketed. Shortages in the supply of these goods also shift the aggregate supply curve upward to the left in the US, pushing up prices. Gasoline and wheat price hikes, in particular, have hit consumers hard (see (5) above).

Each factor in the above contributes to explain the current sharp rise in prices in the US economy. However, the most fundamental cause of inflation is the bold monetary easing measures taken by the FRB and the expansionary fiscal policy of the US government, both of which were implemented as counter-measures against the COVID-19 recession. Expansionary fiscal and monetary policies shift the aggregate demand curve to the right. As a result, prices rise (see (1) above). Although the FRB initially believed that the rapid rise in prices would be transient, it clearly recognized the risk of persistent high inflation over the medium to long term in the future, and therefore has drastically changed its policy stance since the beginning of 2022. We will explain this point in the next section.

Part I

Part II

Part III

Part IV

2. Shift from Monetary Easing to Tightening

(1) Countermeasures against COVID-19 Recession

The U.S. government has provided a series of fiscal stimulus against COVID-19 recession under both the Trump and Biden administrations to protect people's daily life. In March 2021, the congress has approved the Biden's American Rescue Plan Act, amounting to approximately USD 1.9 trillion. With no supports from Republicans, Democrats, who have decision-making power both in the House and Senate, have passed the Act, which is now being implemented as of May 2022. This Act focuses largely on supporting households. The bailout plan consists of USD 400 billion in cash benefits, USD 250 billion in unemployment benefits, USD 400 billion in COVID-19 measures, and USD 850 billion in other benefits.

On March 3, 2020 when the COVID-19 was spreading widely, the FRB lowered its target for the short-term market interest rate from a range between 1.5% and 1.75% to between 1.0% and 1.25%, and further lowered it to between 0% to 0.25% on March 15. Simultaneously, it continued to use a variety of monetary easing measures to provide liquidity. Specifically, the FRB has continued to supply a large quantity of monetary base by purchasing large amounts of government bonds and mortgages issued by government-related agencies (known as Quantitative Easing (QE)). To understand the FRB's series of monetary easing policies, see Figure 1-2-2.

(2) FRB's Shift to a Tighter Monetary Policy

Figure 1-2-2 shows that the supply of monetary base was skyrocketing in March 2020, when COVID-19 exploded in the U.S. The base money continued to increase at a rapid pace after that as well. Recognizing the risk that the surge in prices might not be transient but could last in the medium to long term, however, the FRB shifted its policy toward decelerating monetary easing, and ended its QE policy in March 2022. Now the FRB has been rapidly tightening its monetary policy because the seriousness of the inflation has become increasingly clear.

Specifically, in response to the very high CPI inflation rate of 8.5% of March 2022, the FRB raised its target for short-term market interest rate from a range between 0% and 0.25% to between 0.25% and 0.50% at the Federal Open Market Committee (FOMC) meeting in March. At the subsequent FOMC meeting in May, it further raised the target range to between 0.75% and 1.00%.

It also raised the interest rate on reserve deposits from 0.15% to 0.4% on

Figure 1-2-2 Monetary Base (Jan 2000 to Mar 2022: before seasonal adjustment)

Source: Federal Reserve Bank of St. Louis

March 17, 2022, and again further to 0.9% on May 5. In addition, in June, the FRB started Quantitative Tightening (QT), which is a decrease in the monetary base. As a result of the FRB's policy shift described above, Figure 1-2-2 shows that the monetary base balance has reversed its course and is now declining. The most important message obtained from Figure 1-2-2 is that the monetary easing policy in response to the COVID-19 recession was implemented in a very short period of time and on a very large scale compared to previous easing policies. These facts on monetary policy contribute to the current sharp inflation.

3. Outlook for Inflation in the US Economy

(1) Experience of High Inflation in the 70s and early 80s

When we think of high inflation, we recall the high inflation after the first oil shock in 1973 in Japan, but in the US, it is the high inflation of the late 1970s. Excessive monetary easing policies continued from the mid-1960s, and as a result, inflation and expected inflation rates continued to rise, peaking at about 13%. Just as in the case of the current inflation, the rise in oil and food prices and the expansion of fiscal spending (due to the Vietnam War) also contributed to the high inflation at that time.

Paul Volcker, who became FRB Chairman in 1979, demonstrated leadership and overcame this inflationary crisis. His bold restrictive monetary policy was successful in subsiding the high inflation rate to 3% to 4% and stabilizing the economy. This tightening process, however, also caused the real economy to fall into a serious recession at the same time. This bitter experience taught us an important lesson. Once people's expectations of high inflation become embedded in their productive and spending behavior, it is highly costly to remove them. For example, if wages are negotiated on the assumption of high inflation,

Part I

Part II

Part III

Part IV

even higher inflation will certainly come out. If the even higher inflation comes out, then the next year's wage negotiations will take place based on the assumption of this even higher inflation rate. Hence inflation persists.

A rise in the price level is not the same as a continuing (or accelerating) high inflation rate. Price increases are a matter of level, whereas continued high inflation is a matter of growth rate. For example, if the price of oil increases at a given point in time, the price increase pushes up the inflation rate for the year in question but does not in itself lead to a higher inflation rate in the second and subsequent years. High inflation will continue only when people change their behavior based on the assumption of high inflation. Whether high inflation continues or not depends on people's expectations on the future course of inflation rates.

(2) Expected Inflation Rate

How do we measure people's expected inflation rates? We introduce two types of indicators. The first type comes from a survey conducted by the University of Michigan, called the University of Michigan Surveys of Consumers. The second one is the statistical data of the breakeven inflation rate (BEI). We use these two to report the current expected inflation rate for the United States.

Figure 1-2-3 and Figure 1-2-4 are the results on the consumers' expected inflation rates over the next year and the next five years, respectively, obtained by the University of Michigan monthly survey.

Figure 1-2-3 shows that the expected inflation rate over the next year began to increase rapidly in April 2020, rose sharply to 4.6% in May 2021, and then reached 5.3% as of May 2022, the most recent month available. It is rising rapidly, reflecting the actual increase in the current inflation rate.

The expected inflation rate for the next five years, however, provides a somewhat different picture, as shown in Figure 1-2-4. The expected inflation rate over the next five years was found to be relatively stable, standing at around 3.0% as of May 2022. This suggests that many people believe that, based on the current inflation rate, inflation will remain somewhat high next year, but that high inflation will eventually subside in the medium to long term. One reason is that the current high inflation rate is mainly caused by the shortage in the supply of resources and foodstuffs at the global level, which people take as transient. Above all, the US economy has been successful in avoiding high inflation for the past 40 years by taking appropriate monetary policies. This successful experience is the key element in keeping medium- and long-term inflation expectations largely unchanged. These results could be interpreted as a reflection of people's confidence in the FRB. The results on the five years expected

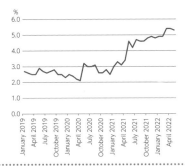

| Figure 1-2-3 | University of Michigan Surveys on Consumers' Expected Inflation Rates for the Next 12 Months (January 2019 to May 2022) |

Source: University of Michigan

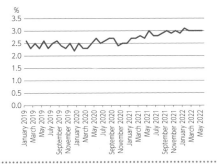

| Figure 1-2-4 | University of Michigan Surveys on Consumers' Expected Inflation Rates Over the Next Five Years (January 2019 to May 2022) |

Source: University of Michigan

inflation rates also indicate that the high expected inflation rate has not yet been incorporated into people's economic behavior.

These are the results of the survey conducted by the University of Michigan. To reinforce this interpretation, we also present the results of one more indicator, the expected inflation rate based on the BEI. Figure 1-2-5 shows the BEI index over a five-year horizon.

Government bonds that promise the real interest rate, which is the nominal interest rate minus the inflation rate, are called inflation-indexed bonds. Holders of inflation-indexed bonds receive a real interest income in line with changes in the inflation rate. Interest rate arbitrage works between the market for these inflation-indexed bonds and the market for regular government bonds. For example, as more investors expect higher inflation in the future, more investors will buy inflation-indexed bonds that earn more interest in response to higher inflation. In this case, the price of an inflation-indexed bond becomes higher

Part I

Part II

Part III

Part IV

Figure 1-2-5   Five-Year Breakeven Inflation Rate (May 2017 to May 2022)

Source: Federal Reserve Bank of St. Louis

than the price of a regular government bond (The market yield of the infla-tion-indexed bond decreases). Conversely, if more investors expect inflation to decline in the future, the price of the inflation-indexed bond will fall (The market yield of the inflation-indexed bonds will rise). Interest rate arbitrage is at work between the observed yield on the 5-year inflation-indexed bond and the yield on the regular 5-year bond, and the result determines the respective bond prices (i.e., their yields).

BEI refers to the expected inflation rate such that the yields of the two types of government bonds with the same maturity will have the same (breakeven) yield due to interest rate arbitrage between the yield on a regular government bond and the yield on an inflation-indexed bond that promises the real rate of interest. Therefore, the BEI of a five-year government bond can be interpreted as an indicator of the expected inflation rate over the next five years by market participants.

The BEI differs from the University of Michigan survey in that the University of Michigan survey is based on questionnaires, whereas the BEI is calculated as the difference between the yields of two government bonds. The former is a measure of consumers' expected inflation, while the latter is a mea-sure of financial market participants' expected inflation. They are different in this respect as well.

Despite these differences in nature between the BEI and the University of Michigan survey's expected inflation, Figure 1-2-4 and Figure 1-2-5 show very similar results. Even though the current inflation rate has remained in the 8% range, the five-year BEI has also been relatively stable, remaining around the 3% range. In fact, reflecting the FRB's shift in monetary policy since the beginning of 2022, the five-year BEI peaked in March 2022 and has since fallen to just below 3%.

These results indicate that, at least as of May 2022, the medium- to long-term expected inflation rate is relatively stable. This finding suggests that the recent sharp increase in inflation has not yet been significantly built into people's economic behavior.

(3) Trends in the Global Resources and Food Markets

The medium- to long-term expected inflation rate has not risen much as of May 2022. However, it will eventually rise if the current high inflation rate continues for some time. Once the expected inflation rate rises, people's economic behavior is likely to change, causing high inflation to continue or accelerate. Once high inflation persists or accelerates, we will have to pay the high price of a severe recession in the future.

At present, possible factors to cause high inflation in the future are the surging prices in foodstuffs, such as wheat, and in resources such as crude oil. Please take a look at Chapter 1, Section 1 of this report, discussing the trends in energy markets, especially of crude oil. Here in this Section, we only briefly examine the West Texas Intermediate (WTI) crude oil price as a sample of these markets (Figure 1-2-6).

COVID-19 has spread widely since the beginning of 2020, leading to a decrease in spending at the global level. As a result, energy prices initially collapsed. The WTI crude oil price in Figure 1-2-6 shows a sharp drop to a level of USD 16 per barrel in April 2020. The WTI price subsequently began to rise as the global economy recovered.

The WTI price has surged further with Russia's invasion of Ukraine on February 24, 2022. In addition to crude oil, the EU has decided to stop buying natural gas from Russia in order to reduce its energy dependence on Russia.

Part I

Part II

Part III

Part IV

Figure 1-2-6   WTI Crude Oil Price (USD: 1 barrel) (January 2005 to May 2022)

Source: Federal Reserve Bank of St. Louis

This also reduces energy supply in the West in the short run, thus raising energy prices. The growth rate of energy price in 38 OECD countries remains high at 32.5% (12 month percentage change; OECD: April 2022).

Food commodities, including wheat, continue to trade at high prices at the global level, as do energy prices. Soaring food and resource prices are another important factor contributing to the current high inflation in the US economy.

(4) Three Risks

As discussed, the US economy has been expanding steadily in terms of production and employment. The medium- to long-term expected inflation rate is also quite firmly anchored near the 2% inflation target. Political risks aside, however, the US economy faces at least three risks.

The first risk is the Russian-Ukrainian war. As noted above, the war has caused shortages of resources and foodstuffs at the global markets. In the aggregate demand and supply diagram, the supply shortages of resources and foodstuffs imply a shift of the aggregate supply curve to the upper left, pushing prices to up and real GDP to down. In addition, trade restrictions imposed on Russia by Western countries and the withdrawal of local subsidiaries from Russia also provide negative impacts on the U.S. economy.

The second is the risk of a recession due to the sharp monetary tightening by the FRB. The FRB is currently mobilizing all of its policy tools in an effort to calm down high inflation. If the current high inflation rate were to continue, it would increase the likelihood of higher expected inflation in the medium to long term as well. Hence, there is certainly a need to put the current high inflation under control as soon as possible. At the same time, however, if the FRB tightens monetary policy too much and/or too aggressively, it might invite a serious recession within the next two years.

Rapid monetary tightening over a short period of time does not merely lower consumption spending on automobiles and other consumption goods, and investment spending on equipment and housing. Bondholders also might incur capital losses due to higher interest rates. Because stocks, land, and houses are also (imperfect) substitutes for currencies, holders of these assets might also incur capital losses. Individuals or institutions incurring capital losses might reduce their spending, which could lead to a downturn in the real economy. In fact, the stock market, concerned about such future risks, has now turned around from its previous uptrend and has been bearish since the beginning of 2022. If capital losses should become so large that their impacts spread further to the point where they shake the solvency of financial institutions, the turmoil might become even greater.

The third risk is the re-emergence of COVID-19 infections, which still requires an appropriate response.

(5) Summary of the US Economy

For now, the five-year expected inflation rate is anchored quite firmly in the 3% range, even though the actual US inflation rate is hovering over the 8% range. In the future, however, there is a risk that the medium- to long-term expected inflation rate might rise if the prices of natural resources, such as crude oil and natural gas, or foodstuffs like wheat should keep rising. The FRB has been striving to prevent such a situation from occurring by tightening monetary policy and calming the overheated economy. The policy change to monetary tightening has been so boldly implemented in a relatively short span of time that it might lead to a recession in the near future. Given there is a considerable time lag before the effects of the monetary policy change are transmitted to the real economy, it will be necessary to continue to monitor closely developments in the real economy.

4. Impact on the Japanese Economy

(1) Current State of the Japanese Economy

Production began to fall in mid-2019 due to the US-China trade friction. Japan's consumption tax hike in October 2019 also caused a significant drop in production. The spread of COVID-19 infections exacerbated these economic downturns. Despite all these headwinds, the Japanese production at one time approached near to the level before the pandemic, thanks to the appropriate responses by the government and the Bank of Japan. However, production subsequently deteriorated again, partly because the fifth wave of the COVID-19 pandemic coincided with the summer Olympics and Paralympic Games in Tokyo. The production level in the Japanese economy as of May 2022 is still lower than that in February 2020 before the COVID-19 outbreak. Japan's economic recovery has been slower and weaker than that of the United States.

The unemployment rate, which temporarily exceeded 3% due to the COVID-19 wide outbreak in March 2020, has been slowly recovering, and falling to 2.5% as of April 2022. However, the level before the pandemic has not been reached yet.

As for prices, as shown in Figure 1-2-7, spending has been weak mainly in the services sector, and service prices have kept falling. The headline CPI fell sharply in the wake of the spread of COVID-19 after March 2020, due to a decline in consumption expenditures (especially in the services sector).

In 2021, the prices of goods rose sharply as shown in Figure 1-2-8 for

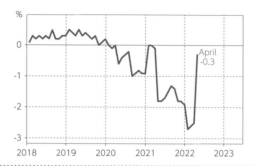

Figure 1-2-7 Services Prices in the Japanese Economy (12 month percentage change)

Source: Federal Reserve Bank of New York

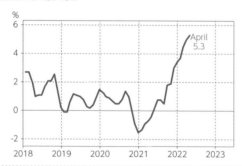

Figure 1-2-8 Goods Prices in the Japanese Economy (12 month percentage change)

Source: Federal Reserve Bank of New York

four reasons: (a) energy prices began to soar as the US and European economies recovered to some extent from the COVID-19 disaster; (b) the COVID-19 disaster disrupted the global production supply chain, driving up the prices of imported goods; and in 2022, (c) the FRB's change in monetary policy weakened the yen, driving import prices even higher; and (d) Russia's invasion of Ukraine led to a further surge in resource and food prices.

(2) The Immediate Impact of FRB Monetary Tightening on the Japanese Economy

In 2022, the FRB has changed its monetary policy stance from monetary easing to tightening. This section explains how this change in monetary policy in the US is affecting the Japanese economy, and prices in particular.

The FRB's policy transition has an immediate impact on the Japanese economy through at least three channels. The three paths are through stock prices, interest rates, and foreign exchange rates. The FRB's rapid shift to a tighter monetary policy has raised the US interest rates, lowered bond prices, and made bearish the US stock market (despite a strong real economy). The weak stock market is caused by investors' concerns about the risk of a future recession and/or a possible asset market turmoil in the US due to the FRB's monetary tightening. The bearish movements in the US stock market seem to transmit to the Japanese stock market immediately.

The FRB's shift to monetary tightening has been accompanied by an increase in the interest rate, thus adding upward pressure to the term structure of the Japanese interest rates through arbitrage. Taking that the Japanese economy is not strong enough to withstand upward pressure on interest rates from abroad, however, the BOJ has maintained its policy of guiding the long-term interest rate at around 0 percent. This has resulted in widening the interest rate differential between the Japanese yen and the US dollars, creating a tendency for the yen to depreciate and the dollar to appreciate. The FRB's monetary tightening is expected to continue for some time, and the BOJ's monetary easing policy, including its guidance of long-term interest rates, is also expected to continue for the foreseeable future. Consequently, yen has depreciated from the middle of the 100 yen per USD 1 at the beginning of 2021 to the 133 yen per USD 1 as of June 7, 2022.

This depreciation of the yen is one of the factors pushing up import prices in Japan. The yen depreciation together with the sharp rises in resource and food prices at the global market had pushed the CPI upward to 2.5% by April 2022. The core core CPI excluding energy and food, however, has remained at 0.1% at the same point in time, even though the headline CPI has already exceeded the 2% target inflation rate.

This reflects the current weakness of the Japanese real economy. As noted above, production in the Japanese economy has not yet reached the levels seen before the COVID-19 outbreak. The core core CPI is rising, but its level is still low at the current point in time. However, this indicator should continue to be monitored closely because Japan's 10-year BEI has been gradually rising, mainly due to overseas factors.

References

Bernanke, B. 2012, The Federal Reserve and the Financial Crisis, Federal Reserve Board of Governors, Lecture 2 (The Federal Reserve after the World War II).

Grossman, G., 2022, "Q&A: Economist Gene Grossman Analyzes Supply Chain Challenges" (by Julie Bonette), Princeton Alumni Weekly, March 2022 Issue.

Section 3
UNCERTAINTY IN THE CHINESE ECONOMY: FROM "COMMON PROSPERITY" TO "ZERO-COVID"

KAJITANI, Kai

1. The Adverse Effects of the Zero-Corona Policy Becoming More Serious

In Shanghai, where the number of people infected with COVID-19 had been increasing since the beginning of 2022, a complete lockdown was implemented for two months from March 28 to the end of May. Through social media, people outside China have become aware that food procurement has become difficult due to logistics disruptions and that many residents have become increasingly stressed due to the uncertainty about the future during the lockdown.

Even if a complete city blockade has not been imposed, many cities have implemented a dynamic zero-corona policy in which even a single infected person within an apartment building results in the whole residents being prohibited from going outside until the number of new cases becomes zero. The Xi Jinping administration's adherence to a zero–corona policy, in which it is unable to break away from its past successes even against the highly infectious and less severe Omicron variant, has been questioned not only overseas but also domestically. In this report, I would like to discuss the future of the Chinese economy, which faces many uncertainties in addition to the zero-corona policy, with a focus on three risks that are confronting it.

The negative effects on the overall economy of the lockdown of major cities brought about by the adherence to the zero-corona policy became apparent in the economic statistics for April 2022, released in mid-May. The largest impact was on consumption, with retail sales in April falling 11.1% year-on-year, the first decline since March 2020 (Figure 1-3-1). On the production side, industrial production in April declined 2.9% year-on-year and the cumulative amount of investment in fixed assets in the period from the beginning of the year until April increased 6.8% year-on-year, a significant drop from a 9.3% increase in the period from the beginning of the year until March. Reflecting these declines in both demand and supply, the nation's surveyed unemployment rate worsened to 6.1% in April, surpassing 6% for the first time in two years since April 2020.

It is assumed that the repeated strict and prolonged blockades of major cities such as Xi'an, Changchun, and Shanghai since the beginning of 2022 have not only depressed production and consumption in those cities but have also

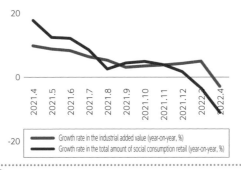

| Figure 1-3-1 | Trends in the industrial added value and the retail consumption amount |

Material)"National database" https://data.stats.gov.cn/easyquery.htm

affected the entire economy through the suspension of logistics.

In a paper published in April this year, Zheng Song and his colleagues at the Chinese University of Hong Kong analyzed the impact of an urban lockdown on economic activity using GPS information records of long-distance trucks from April 2020 to January 2022 (Chen et al, 2022). According to Song and his colleagues, a total blockade of a city for one month reduces truck traffic to and from that city by almost half. If China's four largest cities (Beijing, Guangzhou, Shanghai, and Shenzhen) were to be completely blockaded for one month, real income in the four blockaded cities would decline by 61%, and the nation's real gross domestic product (GDP) would decline by 8.6%. 11% of these effects are spillover effects to other regions. The negative effects are even larger when the long-term effects of reduced savings and investment are included.

When Song was interviewed by the economic journal Caixin Weekly (April 18, 2022 Logistics Security), he projected that if any one of the four major cities were to go on lockdown for a month, it would result in a loss of roughly 0.7% of GDP.

Additionally, the lockdown of cities that have the world's leading container handling capacity, such as Shenzhen and Shanghai, has a direct impact on the global supply chain through the stagnation of cargo transport to overseas destinations. According to a survey conducted by a research firm targeting 1,500 companies engaged in overseas trade, 90% of them stated that they were unable to ship as scheduled and 50% of them stated that their shipments were overdue by 15 days or more (Caixin Weekly May 9, 2022 "Why exports have slowed down"). Additionally, the rising cost of raw materials is also serious, with more than 70% of companies experiencing a 20% or more increase in the costs of raw materials. As a result of these rising logistics costs, more than 90% of companies have been forced to reduce production and almost half of them have halved their production volume.

2. Insufficient Fiscal Stimulus

As noted in the previous section, even though it is evident that the adherence to the zero-corona policy has damaged the entire economy, the government has been unable to come up with an effective macroeconomic policy to counter this, especially an aggressive relief measure through fiscal stimulus. This reluctant attitude of the government undeniably makes the future of the Chinese economy even more uncertain.

In retrospect, in February 2020, when urban blockades were implemented nationwide, starting with the city of Wuhan, the Chinese government quickly initiated bold monetary easing as a post-corona economic policy (Tsuyuguchi, 2020). On the other hand, unlike other major countries, they have rarely provided relief measures through fiscal stimulus, such as the provision of benefits to individuals and companies. Even though measures such as the reduction of social insurance premiums or tax breaks were put in place for companies, most of these measures had ended by 2021, which led to the economic recession that began in the latter half of 2021.

The government has consistently emphasized policies to improve efficiency on the supply side rather than stimulating the demand side, as represented by its aggressive fiscal policies. In March 2020, the Chinese Communist Party issued a document entitled "Opinion on the Establishment of a More Complete Arrangement System and Mechanism for the Production Factor Market." In this opinion, the Chinese government emphasized the direction of (1) developing an efficient arrangement based on the market mechanism and (2) promoting the establishment and development of the factor market by eliminating institutional factors that hinder the smooth movement of production factors regarding the five major production factors, including land, labor, capital, technology, and data; in other words, the direction of reforming the situation in which state-owned companies and local governments have monopolized access to land, capital, and data (China Research Office, Research and Advisory Department, 2020).

As the continuation of this policy, in January 2022, the State Council released the General Bill on Comprehensive Reform Trial Points for Factor Marketization and revealed specific plans for the marketization of production factors, including the efficient use of land resources through markets, the mobilization of labor markets through systems that can evaluate workers' skills and technologies, and the development of rules and systems for the protection of intellectual property rights of new technology and data distribution.

Furthermore, in the Opinion on Accelerating the Construction of a National Unified Great Market released by the Central Party and the State Council on April 10, 2022, the development of the above factor market, along with the creation of unified market systems and rules, as well as the consolidation of the infrastructure supporting the market, is listed as one of the six goals to be pursued in order to construct a national unified market for more efficient resource allocation.

These series of reforms are only aimed at improving the efficiency of the supply side and do not cover the other aspect brought by the thorough implementation of the zero-corona policy of the sharp drop in demand. However, even in 2022, when the zero-corona policy led to subsequent lockdowns in major cities, the government was slow to act to underpin demand. On May 20, the five-year loan prime rate (LPR), which is the benchmark for mortgage rates, was finally lowered from 4.6% to 4.45%, but the one-year LPR, which is practically the base rate for lending, was left unchanged. It seems that the fears of an asset bubble since last year and the continuing depreciation of the yuan in the foreign exchange markets are the main factors behind this decision.

In addition, with regard to fiscal policy, the government revealed a return to its pre-corona balanced budget policy of limiting the budget deficit to 2.8% of GDP (3.6% in 2020) in the Government Activity Report of the National People's Congress held in March this year. In late May, the State Council announced additional stimulus measures (comprehensive policy measures to firmly stabilize the economy), including a 140 billion yuan increase in the scale of tax refunds, but it has not shown any tolerance for expanding the budget deficit.

3. Excessive Reliance on Monetary Easing and Its Side Effects

As mentioned in the previous section, the fact that the Chinese government consistently failed to implement sufficient fiscal stimulus and instead tended to rely exclusively on monetary easing for the economic recovery from the Corona shock is thought to have subsequently caused various distortions in the Chinese economy. The first issue is the rapid growth of private sector debt, which has exacerbated concerns about corporate bond defaults. According to the statistics on the outstanding debt of each country released by the Bank for International Settlements (BIS) (Figure 1-3-2), the outstanding debt of the corporate sector, which had been kept at a level of 149.3% of GDP as of the end of 2019 through the aforementioned deleveraging policy, has increased to 163.3% of GDP as of

Part I

Part II

Part III

Part IV

the end of September 2020 due to the increased corporate debt, reflecting the monetary easing triggered by the COVID-19 pandemic. This situation has led many to point out that the issue of excessive debt in the corporate sector may be reproduced.

As if to confirm this, the deterioration in the cash flow of major government-affiliated companies has become apparent, as exemplified by the emergence of cash-flow difficulties at Tsinghua Unigroup, a government-affiliated semiconductor giant, in early November 2020 and the reported credit crisis at the China Huarong Asset Management Co., Ltd., a bad debt disposal company in which the Ministry of Finance of China holds a 60% stake, in April 2021. Furthermore, in the summer of 2021, there were widespread concerns that a default on corporate bonds might occur due to the financial instability of the Evergrande Group, China's real estate giant, which sparked speculation that this could lead to global credit instability.

The Evergrande Group has continued its risky management by raising short-term funds in the corporate bond market and making long-term investments in various businesses, including the electric vehicle industry. Therefore, when the government tightened regulations on financing for real estate companies in August 2020, its financial position deteriorated drastically. The restrictions on the total amount of real estate-related loans that were imposed on financial institutions in January 2021 are also believed to have exacerbated the situation.

The increase in outstanding debt as a result of the measures against COVID-19 is a worldwide phenomenon and by itself it is not an immediately pressing issue. But as discussed in the previous section, what characterizes China compared to other countries is that the debt of the government sector has not expanded sufficiently in comparison with the corporate sector.

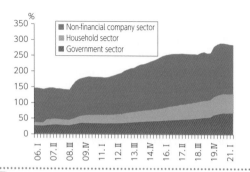

Figure 1-3-2   Change in debt outstanding (vs. GDP)

Material) Source: BIS website (https://www.bis.org/)

The situation in which bold monetary easing is implemented while fiscal spending is restrained is similar to that of the Japanese economy, which relied on monetary easing to overcome the strong yen recession brought about by the Plaza Accord in 1985 and is prone to the emergence of asset bubbles. In fact, when the Chinese economy gradually recovered from the impact of COVID-19, the real estate market showed signs of prosperity at an early stage.

The Xi Jinping administration's stance of emphasizing that housing is for living, not for speculation led to a tightening of the real estate market as represented by the three red lines mentioned above, which caused real estate prices to stagnate in many cities (Figure 1-3-3). In the case of the Evergrande Group, the debt that ballooned as a result of the tightening of the real estate market turned immediately into bad loans, and it is fair to say that many companies have the potential to experience similar problems.

In December 2021, it was reported that the Evergrande Group aims to repay its debt, including foreign currency-denominated debt estimated at about USD 19.5 billion (JPY 2 trillion), under the supervision and guidance of the Guangdong Provincial Government, PBC, and other entities. Prior to this, on October 23, the National People's Congress announced the pilot introduction of a real estate tax, equivalent to a fixed property tax, in some cities. Although the introduction of this real estate tax is a desirable long-term measure to curb skyrocketing real estate prices and correct disparities, its introduction has been actually stalled by the subsequent economic downturn because of its potential to dampen local economies that have been dependent on the enthusiasm for real estate development.

Another issue with the lack of sufficient fiscal stimulus has been the apparent deterioration of the financial situation of some local governments

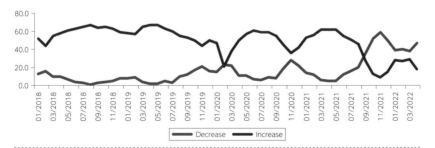

Figure 1-3-3 Changes in real estate prices (70 cities nationwide, compared to the previous month)

Note: The graph shows the number of cities where the price index for new houses increased or decreased from the previous month among 70 cities nationwide.
Material) CEIC Data

Part I
Part II
Part III
Part IV

(Cheng 2022a). In late December 2021, the municipal government of Hegang, Heilongjiang Province, in the northeast of China, announced that it would cancel its staff recruitment plan and implement a financial restructuring plan, which led to reports that the municipal government had become de facto financially bankrupt (Cheng, 2022b).

It was also reported that in some areas, public officials are experiencing pay cuts due to a lack of financial resources. Originally, a local government's finances depend largely on the proceeds of the sale of land titles, such as agricultural land accommodated by the local government. It is said that the direct reason for the lack of financial resources is that this income has fallen sharply due to the tightening of the real estate market in 2020 (Nakazawa 2021). One of the major backdrops for this shortfall in local government funds is that the main sources of local government revenue, such as the value-added tax and corporate income tax, declined due to tax exemptions and deferrals for companies brought about by the spread of COVID-19, yet such declines were not adequately compensated for by central government finances.

The severe financial situation surrounding local governments is continuing even in 2022. It is said that some local governments have issued strict orders for frugality, such as prohibiting the purchase of new computers and other equipment and requiring the use of cafeterias in government buildings for business entertainment (Nihon Keizai Shimbun, May 26, 2022 "Real estate recession hits China, Strict orders for thrift spreading among local governments"). It is fair to say that the financial difficulties of local governments are a major obstacle to supporting the recovery of the Chinese economy, which is suffering from weakening demand due to the series of lockdowns.

4. Implementation of Forcible Redistribution Policies

Finally, I would like to mention that another cause for concern regarding the future of the Chinese economy is the widening economic disparity and the implementation of forcible redistribution policies as its countermeasure. The Central Finance Committee of the Communist Party held in August 2021 emphasized common prosperity as an essential requirement of socialism and proposed tertiary distribution (redistribution of the means of production is defined as primary distribution, redistribution through fiscal expenditure is defined as secondary distribution, and redistribution through other means is defined as tertiary distribution), in which individuals and organizations voluntarily donate as a means of achieving common prosperity.

In response to this policy, the Alibaba Group and Tencent have successively pledged to contribute the large sums of 100 billion yuan (about JPY 2 trillion) by 2025. The abruptness of this series of policies raised concerns that they might be a return to traditional socialist policies, which were settled by a single word from President Xi. Some experts and China-watchers have viewed this situation as the resurgence of the Cultural Revolution (Cultural Revolution 2.0). However, this view is clearly mistaken. The Cultural Revolution developed into a cultural and political conflict under the guise of promoting further socialism after the thorough public ownership of the means of production through the preceding reforms toward socialism. In contrast, Xi's leadership has not rejected capitalist means of production and has not fundamentally changed the management of the economy. In fact, as mentioned above, his administration is trying to introduce market mechanisms into the production factors, the very foundation of socialism, to promote fluidity and efficiency. As if to confirm this, the term "common prosperity" appeared only once in Premier Li Keqiang's government activity report at the National People's Congress in March 2022.

Rather, it seems that the current administration has recognized that the series of factor market reforms will be inevitably accompanied by a further increase in disparities and has brought common prosperity to the forefront as a preventive measure, or as a kind of vaccine, to prevent criticism from being directed at the administration. To equate the emphasis on common prosperity with a vaccine, a second and third round of vaccinations is necessary. Along with this, it is inevitable that there will be some sorts of side effects, such as the devastating blow to the education industry brought by the ban on the establishment of new tutoring schools, as well as the imposition of non-profit status and delisting of current tutoring schools by the Chinese government's notification.

The successful experience of the anti-corruption campaign is recalled in the implementation of common prosperity. In 2012, at the Second General Conference of the 18th Central Commission for Discipline Inspection, President Xi Jinping announced a large-scale anti-corruption campaign that would strike both "tigers" (high-level cadres) and "flies" (low-level cadres). About 1.34 million party members nationwide, including "big tigers" such as Zhou Yongkang, a former senior leader of the Chinese Communist Party, and Xu Caihou, a former vice-chairman of the Central Military Commission, were punished.

Xi Tian Yang and his colleagues, who examined which government officials were targeted by this anti-corruption campaign, made the interesting point that the anti-corruption campaign conducted by the Xi administration symbolized a shift in China's growth model from the rent model of the Jiang Zemin and Hu Jintao administrations to the loyalty model centered on the Communist Party (Xi=Yao=Zhang, 2018).

Part I

Part II

Part III

Part IV

According to them, under the rent model of the Jiang Zemin and Hu Jintao administrations, (1) economic growth is the primary goal and (local) governments lead it, (2) local government leaders support the market economy by utilizing local information under a decentralized system, and (3) the Communist Party and central government induce growth competition among local governments through personnel management. In other words, the model is characterized by the combination of high growth in the regions and the expansion of bureaucratic authority.

In 2012 when the Xi Jinping administration began, the widening of economic disparities and criticism from the public about the illicit accumulation of wealth grew, which led to higher costs of maintaining the existing rent model. It seems that because of this, the Xi administration has shifted to the loyalty model that emphasizes trust in the ideological line of the Xi administration party and loyalty to the leaders' policies.

Xi=Yao=Zhang (2018) have verified that the loyalty model is seen in actual corruption detection patterns through empirical research that connects information on the profiles and promotions of city-level administrative division heads, as well as lists of targets of corruption investigations released by the Communist Party Central Technical Committee.

As a result of this research, it became clear that officials who were able to ascend the ladder as competent and at the same time amass considerable financial resources up to the time of the Hu Jintao administration were more likely to be targeted for prosecution. The approach of this anti-corruption campaign to ease the resentment of the general public by penalizing competent, wealthy, and socially prominent local executives is similar to the current approach of targeting successful IT-related companies and their managers in the name of common prosperity.

5. Conclusion

What attitude should the Japanese business community take toward the Chinese economy that is facing such risks? First, we need to reaffirm that the relationship between companies and the government in China is not a simple one. The Alibaba Group, for example, has under its umbrella a public welfare foundation fund to address poverty issues. The large donation of 100 billion yuan is in fact only a promise to give back to the poor through this fund, and the Alibaba Group has the right to decide whether or not to implement it. Looking at this alone, seeing the current situation simply as a return to traditional socialism does not correspond to the actual situation, in which the corporate side readily accepts and implements measures that conform to the government's grandiose slogan of common prosperity. It is dangerous for Japanese companies doing business with Chinese companies or conducting investment projects to easily accept the major policies of the Chinese government and assume the direction of the country. Nevertheless, it should not be forgotten that doing business in China always carries the risk of being greatly affected by domestic political trends. The Chinese Communist Party is about to hold its Party Congress this fall. In order for the Xi Jinping administration, which is expected to enter its third term, to solidify its power base, it will be difficult to change the zero-corona policy at least until the party congress is successfully completed.

With China's economic growth entering a downward phase and the current situation in which abuses of the zero-corona policy are having unpredictable downside effects on the economy, it is conceivable that dissatisfaction among the general public is gradually building up, and headwinds against the implementation of the factor market reforms, which were originally supposed to be the centerpiece of a growth strategy, are expected to become stronger. If this situation continues, no matter how much the government stresses the importance of supply chains, foreign companies may inevitably leave China.

Nevertheless, from a long-term perspective, it will be essential for both the public and private sectors in Japan to discuss how far they can cooperate with China in promoting decarbonization policies, sharing data across borders, and creating rules for this purpose. Therefore, I would like to emphasize again that it is more necessary than ever to ascertain the actual situation, which is the premise for discussion.

References

China Research Office, Research & Advisory Department (2020), *Marketization Reform of Production Factor Allocation Begins in China: Smoothing Factor Mobility to be a New Driver of Economic Growth*, MUFG Bank (China) Economic Weekly Report, No. 452, May 12, 2020

Cheng Siwei (2022a), *Pressure on Local Fiscal Balance Intensifies,* Caixin Weekly, No. 7, 2022

Cheng Siwei (2022b), *Where is the Way out of Hegang?*, Caixin Weekly, .No. 12, 2022

Jingjing Chen, Wei Chen, Ernest Liu, Jie Luo, and Zheng (Michael) Song (2022), *The Economic Cost of Locking Down like China: Evidence from City-to City Truck Flows*, Mimeo

Katsuji Nakazawa (2021), *Chinese Civil Servants Suddenly Notified of 25% Salary Cut. The Land ATM is in Bankruptcy,* Nihon Keizai Shimbun, Decem-

Part I

Part II

Part III

Part IV

ber 29, 2021, https://www.nikkkei.com/article/DGXZQODK272YX0X-21C21A2000000/, Accessed on May 26, 2022

Xi, Tianyang, Yao,Yang and Qian Zhang (2018), *Purifying the Leviathan: The Anti-Corruption Campaign and Changing Governance Models in China*, Mimeo

Yosuke Tsuyuguchi (2020) ,*Financial Policy against the Novel Coronavirus*, Science Portal China, February 28, 2020, https://spc.jst.go.jp/experiences/tsuyuguchi/tsuyuguchi_2002.html, Accessed on May 26, 2022

Section 4
THE INTERNATIONAL DIVISION OF LABOR IN EAST ASIA IN THE POST-PANDEMIC ERA

KIMURA, Fukunari

1. Two Challenges

Since the late 1980s, East Asia, including Northeast Asia and Southeast Asia, has constructed Factory Asia by expanding and deepening International Production Networks (IPNs) (Ando and Kimura, 2005) or the second unbundling (Baldwin, 2016), i. e., the task-by-task international division of labor, mainly in the machinery industry, ahead of the world, leading to rapid economic growth and the eradication of poverty. Japan and Japanese companies have consistently contributed to the development of Factory Asia as major players and have made its development a source of their own international competitiveness. Factory Asia's presence in the global economy is particularly significant in the general machinery and electrical machinery sectors.

In the last few years, however, Factory Asia has been faced with two major challenges. The first is the emergence of COVID-19. The movement of people stopped due to infection control measures, imports of parts and finished products from China were interrupted, and the supply chain for personal protective equipment such as masks was disrupted, which fueled people's anxiety. At one time, it was even speculated that the emergence of COVID-19 would bring about the end of globalization. However, as will be discussed below, IPNs in the machinery industry, a particularly sophisticated part of the supply chain, provided an opportunity to demonstrate their robustness and resilience, contrary to most expectations.

The second is rising geopolitical tensions. The U.S.-China confrontation began as a relatively simple tariff war but has gradually turned into a technological competition between the superpowers and a fight for supremacy. As COVID-19 spread, Western countries' distrust of China has grown rather strong and geopolitical tensions have further intensified due to human rights issues. The Russian-Ukrainian war broke out in February 2022, which resulted in even more extensive trade controls. The era of tacit acceptance of the separation of politics and economics was over. However, as Lamy and Köhler-Suzuki (2022) point out, while the political dispute has escalated, economic activity continues to be vigorous. What is the future of Factory Asia?

This section below examines how Factory Asia is maintaining its vitality in

Part I

Part II

Part III

Part IV

the face of these two challenges.

2. Factory Asia and the International Trade Order

Global Value Chains (GVCs) and Global Supply Chains (GSCs) are generic terms for international industrial linkages, among which IPNs, the international division of labor based on production processes and tasks, and the supply chain called the second unbundling, refer to those with a particularly high degree of sophistication. The difference between general GSCs and IPNs lies in the importance of service links between production blocks that are placed at a distance (Jones and Kierzkowski, 1990). International trade in the past was primarily concerned with raw materials or finished goods. Trade in these goods was usually not so strict in terms of time and reliability, and being held up at a port for a few days for some reason did not cause serious problems. However, as trade in components and intermediate goods brought about the international division of labor in production processes or task units, time-accurate and reliable service links became indispensable. The cost of service links is highly dependent on the transportation infrastructure and policy environment. Therefore, emerging and developing countries other than East Asian countries that can participate in IPNs are limited to only a few countries in Central and Eastern Europe and Mexico, even if there is a significant wage gap between them and developed countries.

Developing IPNs requires good location advantages and stable connectivity, and companies must also defray sunk costs to build their business networks. That is why companies try to retain IPNs even if they are hit by shocks in the upstream or downstream as long as the shocks are considered temporary. IPNs are robust to shocks brought about by natural disasters or economic crises. The fact that trade within IPNs, especially trade in machinery parts, is less likely to be disrupted (which means it is robust) and more likely to be restored (which means it is resilient) than other trade has been demonstrated through trade data during the Asian economic crisis, the global financial crisis, and the Great East Japan Earthquake (Obashi, 2010, Ando and Kimura, 2012, Okubo, Kimura, and Teshima, 2014).

IPNs in the machinery industry are concentrated in three regions of East Asia, North America, and Europe. Table 1-4-1 shows the trade matrix for machinery (HS84-92) in the three regions and the rest of the world as of 2019 (Ando, Kimura, and Yamanouchi, 2022). The rows represent the export side and the columns represent the import side. In addition to the actual trade values, projected trade values based on the gravity model estimation using trade data

Table 1-4-1	Matrix of Machinery Trade in the Three Main Regions of the World: Projected Values Based on the Gravity Model and Actual Values (2019)

Exporting/ Importing Country	Amount (Million USD, %)	East Asia	North America	Europe	Rest of World	World Total
East Asia	Actual value (A)	874,958	607,050	434,667	897,997	2,814,672
	Projected value (B)	564,700	284,701	298,778	567,605	1,715,783
	(A)/(B) (%)	155	213	145	158	164
North America	Actual value (A)	158,443	617,230	161,678	192,226	1,129,577
	Projected value (B)	233,376	591,802	291,501	362,368	1,479,047
	(A)/(B) (%)	68	104	55	53	76
Europe	Actual value (A)	277,206	286,773	1,517,637	461,516	2,543,132
	Projected value (B)	262,974	318,751	1,298,753	581,866	2,462,344
	(A)/(B) (%)	105	90	117	79	103
Rest of World	Actual value (A)	204,942	109,694	192,904	258,272	765,812
	Projected value (B)	375,111	268,660	431,686	520,561	1,596,019
	(A)/(B) (%)	55	41	45	50	48
World Total	Actual value (A)	1,515,549	1,620,747	2,306,885	1,810,011	7,253,193
	Projected value (B)	1,436,160	1,463,914	2,320,719	2,032,400	7,253,193
	(A)/(B) (%)	106	111	99	89	100

Note: East Asia includes China, Japan, Korea, and ASEAN countries.
Source: Ando, Kimura, and Yamanouchi (2022)

for 176 countries are also shown. The ratio of actual values to projected values indicates how much larger or smaller the actual trade value is compared to the "standard" trade value calculated by taking into account factors including the economic size of each country and the distance between the two countries. East Asia has a high ratio of actual values to projected values at 164% for exports to the world, 106% for imports, and 155% for intra-regional trade within East Asia, far ahead of that of North America and Europe. Although not shown in the chart, East Asia has a particular advantage in general and electrical machinery. A closer look within East Asia shows that the Association of Southeast Asian Nations (ASEAN) countries have particularly high ratios of actual values to projected values, reflecting their high level of commitment to IPNs.

The diffusion of digital technology is also expanding the third unbundling in the international division of labor, namely, the person-to-person international division of labor (Baldwin, 2016), resulting in a clear increase in international trade in digitized services. However, it has yet to quantitatively account for a large part of the international division of labor between North and South so far. The importance of IPNs, especially in the manufacturing industry, will not be lost for a while.

The preconditions that made possible the expansion and deepening of IPNs in East Asia were the long-lasting peace and rules-based international trade order in the region. The question now is whether these preconditions can be maintained even in the post-corona era.

3. Overcoming COVID-19

The novel coronavirus pandemic that began in China in 2019 quickly spread throughout the world, and the lockdown and other measures to restrict people's activities introduced to fight against the disease have significantly impacted our production and consumption activities. Economic growth rates for most countries were negative in 2020, leading to a pessimistic view of the future of globalization. Among GSCs, however, particularly IPNs, which form the core of the East Asian economy, once again proved their robustness.

The impact of COVID-19 on GSCs can be divided into three types of shocks: negative supply shock, negative demand shock, and positive demand shock (Ando, Kimura, and Obashi, 2021). The first shock, negative supply shock, hit various countries in February and March 2020 when imports of components and finished goods from China stopped. However, this was resolved after only two months. As the infections spread to other countries since then, negative supply shocks have occurred in different places and at different times, but their impact was only temporary.

The second negative demand shock of a decline in economic activity that might hurt financial institutions and lead to a major recession was initially the most feared. However, the impact of the negative demand shock was limited due to the unprecedented scale of mitigating policies implemented by each country.

The third, the positive demand shock, has two aspects. Firstly, demand for personal protective equipment such as masks as anti-infection measures and, in some countries, food and other so-called essential goods suddenly increased. In addition, some exporting countries imposed export restrictions, leading to a temporary state of panic. However, this was also largely resolved within a few months, with the exception of the vaccines, as the production sites were quickly replaced. Secondly, demand for personal computers, displays, electric dishwashers, electric hand drills, etc., has increased because telecommuting and home

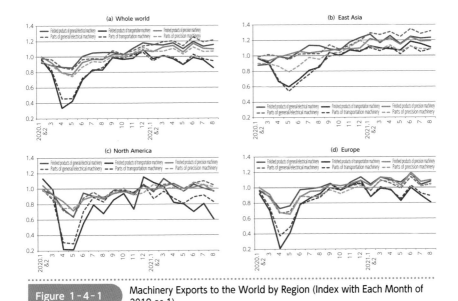

Figure 1-4-1 Machinery Exports to the World by Region (Index with Each Month of 2019 as 1)

Note: For the countries included here and detailed data compilation methods, refer to the source.
Source: Ando and Hayakawa (2021)

isolation have become established in many countries around the world. The fact that East Asia is an exporter of these commodities, combined with the fact that the outbreak was relatively minor, helped the East Asian economies to recover quickly.

Figure 1-4-1 shows exports of finished goods and parts of general/electrical machinery, transport equipment, and precision machinery to the world by region, with the index set at 1 for each month in 2019 (Ando and Hayakawa, 2021). Looking at (a) Worldwide exports, we can see that exports have declined with the spread of the infection but bottomed out in April or May 2020. The decline was particularly large in transportation machinery, which dropped 60% year-on-year, while general/clectrical machinery and precision machinery fell by more than 10% and 20%, respectively. After that, it returned to the level of the same month of the previous year by around September. (b) Export in East Asia shows that the decline in transportation machinery is obviously small. In February and March 2020, exports of general/electric machinery and precision machinery finished products decreased year-on-year, but subsequently quickly increased. The impact of the positive demand shock can be seen here.

The Economic Research Institute for ASEAN and East Asia (ERIA) conducted an internet-based questionnaire survey of companies located in 10 ASEAN countries and India and received responses from nearly 2,000 companies (including local and foreign companies) (Oikawa, Todo, Ambashi, Kimura, and Urata, 2021, Todo, Oikawa, Ambashi, Kimura, and Urata, 2021). It was found there that many Asian companies fought against COVID-19 by reconfiguring their upstream and downstream supply chains. It also revealed that in more than half of the responding companies, profits increased even in 2020, despite some sampling bias. This may indicate the dynamism of Asian companies in contrast to the status quo-focused behavior of Japanese companies.

The COVID-19-related issues are not over yet. With the emergence of new mutant variants, East Asian countries, which had initially been the best at controlling the spread of infections, have been forced to respond, while China has implemented a lockdown based on its zero-corona policy. It will take time for the tourism industry and the industry providing face-to-face services, which were adversely affected by the restrictions on human mobility, to recover. However, it is clear that the GSCs, especially IPNs being developed in East Asia, have not suffered a major setback.

4. Rising Geopolitical Tensions

When the former US President Donald Trump and his administration abandoned its previous policy of engagement with China and embarked on a path of confrontation, the confrontation between the US and China took the form of a tariff war in which both sides imposed tariffs on each other. This alone was considered disruptive to the rules-based international trade order because it meant lifting tariffs above the most-favored-nation (MFN) tariffs promised by the World Trade Organization (WTO). The tariff system itself is a relatively transparent policy tool. Not only U.S. and Chinese companies but also companies in third countries have taken it into account in their actions. As the theory suggests, trade between the U.S. and China has shrunk. On the other hand, some third countries, such as Vietnam and Mexico, have enjoyed a certain degree of positive effects of trade diversion.

The U.S.-China confrontation gradually intensified into a struggle over technologies and hegemony between the superpowers. The U.S. strengthened its security trade controls, blocked Chinese companies from government procurement, and tightened its screening of inward foreign direct investment, among other measures. In particular, various measures targeting specific companies, such as Huawei, proved to be immediately effective. Export controls for specific companies require that not only exports from the U.S. but also exports of products manufactured outside the U.S. using U.S. technologies and software have to be approved by the U.S. authorities. This extra-regional application measure has a direct impact on Japanese companies and others. The U.S. aims to decouple supply chains for strategic goods.

The first-stage agreement between the U.S. and China was signed in January 2020, promising to promote imports of U.S. products to China and structural reforms in various areas on the Chinese side. However, they could not agree on the reform of China's industrial policy and the issues of subsidies, and the agreement was characterized by a tone of managed trade. Afterwards, sentiment toward China worsened not only in the U.S. but also in Western countries as a whole as COVID-19 spread. Democracy and human rights issues have also emerged. In the U.S., customs began to suspend imports involving forced labor, and the Uyghur Forced Labor Prevention Act came into effect in June 2022. In both the U.S. and the EU, responses to human rights issues are becoming institutionalized.

The Chinese response was also very harsh. They introduced a series of trade and investment controls modeled after U.S. policies, making their confrontational stance clear. The high-pressure diplomatic stance known as "wolf warrior diplomacy" also caused friction here and there as well.

Even before the emergence of COVID-19, Japan had already proposed stricter export controls, a review of research integrity, and tighter regulations on inward investment. The Law for the Promotion of Economic Security was enacted in May 2022 to encompass these measures and is scheduled to go into effect in 2023. This law consists of the following four pillars: (i) A system to ensure the stable supply of critical goods, (ii) A system to ensure the stable provision of critical infrastructure services, (iii) A system to keep patent applications confidential, and (iv) A system to support the development of cutting-edge critical technologies. How the scope of specified critical goods will be defined will become an important issue in the future.[1]

The Russian-Ukrainian war that broke out in February 2022 has further intensified geopolitical tensions, forcing Western countries to strengthen their export and foreign direct investment control systems. So far, export and foreign direct investment controls have proven more effective in undermining Russia's ability to pursue war than macro-financial measures, such as restrictions on remittances abroad.

Only geopolitical tensions are being discussed on the political scene these days, but the real economy is still moving. We must not forget that there is a big gap between geopolitical tensions and the real economy. Hayakawa, Ito, Fukao,

Part I

Part II

Part III

Part IV

---

1) Matsumoto (2022) clearly describes the security shift in trade policy under the COVID-19 crisis.

and Deseatnicov (2022) analyzed the impact of trade controls on Japan's exports using monthly trade data. The tentative conclusion indicates that there is no statistically observable impact of the Japanese government's tightening of export controls on trade, and that the U.S. government's Huawei-related restrictions have had a significant negative impact on Japan's exports to China and other countries. Todo (2022) showed that despite the tightening of export controls by both the U.S. and China, U.S.-China trade, including trade of semiconductors, has rather been expanding since 2020 and that Japan's export of high-tech products to China is also not shrinking. The supply chain decoupling between the U.S. and China, or between the West and China, is currently occurring only in relation to high-tech products and rare earths, which are particularly important for security, and it is not necessarily progressing in the economy as a whole.

Asian countries, for example, ASEAN countries, are also anxious about the rise of geopolitical tensions. However, the direct impact has so far been minor. The economies of Asian countries are running almost as usual and are closely connected to both the West and China. They also want to somehow avoid a situation in which they are under pressure of decoupling from both sides and forced to choose one side over the other. They are also becoming increasingly wary because they may have their own problems with regard to democracy and human rights.

5. How to Maintain Economic Vitality

Factory Asia has weathered the raging waves of COVID-19 and remains strong despite heightened geopolitical tensions. On the other hand, for the sake of security in the broad sense, it is anticipated that trade and investment controls will be further enhanced in the future. Close economic relations with Asian countries, especially ASEAN countries, will remain important for Japan. How to reconcile their responses to geopolitical risk with vigorous economic activity will be a major challenge for Japan and East Asia in the future.

I would like to emphasize the following three points. Firstly, the scope of trade and investment controls, etc., should be as clearly defined as possible to minimize uncertainty and keep compliance costs for companies as low as possible. The Japanese authorities need to be clearly aware of this point when designing the detailed system for the implementation of the Law for the Promotion of Economic Security, which the Japanese government is currently working on. In addition, Japanese companies will need to consider the intentions of the U.S. and other Western countries in their actions, including measures for the extraterritorial application of the decoupling implemented by the U.S. and human rights. This part must rely largely on the efforts of individual companies. However, the Japanese government may be able to do something, such as collecting the necessary information and disseminating it to the public. The cost of complying with trade and investment controls is particularly burdensome for small and medium-sized companies and Asian local companies. Tailored treatment is required to ensure that economic vitality is not greatly reduced.

Secondly, trade, investment, and economic activities outside of strictly decoupled sectors should be kept under the rules-based international trade order. If decoupling remains partial, then vigorous economic activity should be allowed in other areas. This will require the restoration of the World Trade Organization (WTO) and the effective utilization of the Free Trade Agreements (FTAs). At the 12th WTO Ministerial Conference (MC12) held in June 2022, a ministerial declaration was adopted for the first time in six and a half years, confirming the importance of restoring WTO. In particular, it is urgent to restore confidence in the WTO for dispute settlement, and it was promised that discussions would be held to overcome the issues by 2024. The issue of so-called "appeal into the void" has arisen because the Appellate Body is no longer functioning. It is necessary for Japan to participate in the Multi-Party Interim Appeal Arbitration Arrangement (MPIA) for partial and temporary resolution of the issue. It is also desirable to use the Regional Comprehensive Economic Partnership (RCEP) Agreement, of which China is a member, and other agreements to mitigate policy risks (Kimura, 2022).

Thirdly, Japan should strategically develop a vision for the future of its economic relations with Asian countries, especially with ASEAN. There is no chance in the short term that the US will return to the Trans-Pacific Partnership Agreement (TPP). The Indo-Pacific Economic Framework (IPEF) was launched in May 2022 under the leadership of the United States with the participation of 14 countries, including Japan and the United States. It outlines four pillars: trade, supply chains, clean energy, decarbonization, and infrastructure, as well as tax and anti-corruption. If the logic of security is too much at the forefront, Asian countries will not be on board with it. What economic benefits can be delivered to Asian countries without market access to trade in goods, which the U.S. stubbornly rejects? Japan needs to be active in listing up well-accepted agenda items.

The Russian-Ukrainian war has accelerated food and energy price spikes that had begun even before then, and many countries are entering a phase of cost-push inflation for the first time in decades. It is highly likely that the global economy, which was expected to enter a post-corona boom period, will be slowed down by interest rate hikes by the major economies. This could have a negative impact on East Asia as a whole. Japan and East Asia must not forget the strength

Part I

Part II

Part III

Part IV

of IPNs and continue to enhance their own international competitiveness.

References

Ando, Mitsuyo and Hayakawa, Kazunobu (2021), "Global Value Chains and COVID-19: An Update on Machinery Production Networks in East Asia," *ERIA Policy Brief,* No. 2021-04.

Ando, Mitsuyo and Kimura, Fukunari (2005), "The Formation of International Production and Distribution Networks in East Asia." In T. Ito and Rose, A. K., eds., *International Trade in East Asia, (NBER-East Asia Seminar on Economics, Volume 14)*, The University of Chicago Press: 177–213.

Ando, Mitsuyo and Kimura, Fukunari (2012), "How Did the Japanese Exports Respond to Two Crises in the International Production Networks? The Global Financial Crisis and the Great East Japan Earthquake," *Asian Economic Journal*, 26 (3): 261–87.

Ando, Mitsuyo; Kimura, Fukunari; and Obashi, Ayako (2021), "International Production Networks Are Overcoming COVID-19 Shocks: Evidence from Japan's Machinery Trade," *Asian Economic Papers*, 20 (3): 40–72.

Ando, Mitsuyo; Kimura, Fukunari; and Yamanouchi, Kenta (2022), "East Asian Production Networks Go beyond the Gravity Prediction." *Asian Economic Papers*, 21 (2): 78-101.

Baldwin, Richard (2016), *"The Great Convergence: Information Technology and the New Globalization,"* Cambridge, MA: The Belknap Press of Harvard University Press.

Hayakawa, Kazunobu; Ito, Keiko; Fukao, Kyoji; and Deseatnicov, Ivan (2021), "The Impact of the U.S.-China Conflict and the Strengthening of Export Controls on Japanese Exports," IDE Discussion Paper, No. 852 (May).

Jones, Ronald W. and Kierzkowski, Henryk (1990), "The Role of Services in Production and International Trade: A Theoretical Framework." In R. W. Jones and Krueger, A. O., eds., *The Political Economy of International Trade: Essays in Honor of Robert E. Baldwin*, Oxford: Basil Blackwell: 31–48.

Kimura, Fukunari (2022), "Significance and Role of RCEP," In Kimura, F. and Nishiwaki, O., eds., *Structural Transformation of International Trading Regime: The US-China Confrontation WTO, Regional Economic Integration, and Japan*, Keiso Shobo: 207–228. In Japanese

Lamy, Pascal and Köhler - Suzuki, Nicolas (2022), "Deglobalization Is Not Inevitable: How the World Trade Organization Can Shore Up the Global Economic Order," *Foreign Affairs*, June 9

Matsumoto, Izumi (2022), "Trade Policy under the With/After the COVID-19 Crisis." In Kimura, F. and Nishiwaki, O., eds., *Structural Transformation of*

International Trading Regime: The US-China Confrontation WTO, Regional Economic Integration, and Japan, Keiso Shobo: 229–259. In Japanese
Obashi, Ayako (2010), "Stability of Production Networks in East Asia: Duration and Survival of Trade," *Japan and the World Economy*, 22(1): 21–30
Oikawa, Keita; Todo, Yasuyuki; Ambashi, Masahito; Kimura, Fukunari; and Urata, Shujiro (2021), "The Impact of COVID-19 on Business Activities and Supply Chains in the ASEAN Member States and India," *ERIA Discussion Paper Series*, No. 384
Okubo, Toshihiro; Kimura, Fukunari; and Teshima, Nozomu (2014), "Asian Fragmentation in the Global Financial Crisis," *International Review of Economics and Finance*, 31: 114–27.
Todo, Yasuyuki (2022), "Decoupling of the U.S.-China Economy and Restructuring of Global Supply Chains." In Kimura, F. and Nishiwaki, O., eds., *Structural Transformation of International Trading Regime: The US-China Confrontation WTO, Regional Economic Integration, and Japan*, Keiso Shobo: 121–145. In Japanese
Todo, Yasuyuki; Oikawa, Keita; Ambashi, Masahito; Kimura, Fukunari; and Urata, Shujiro (2021), "Robustness and Resilience of Supply Chains during the COVID-19 Pandemic: Findings from a Questionnaire Survey on the Supply Chain Links of Firms in ASEAN and India," *ERIA Discussion Paper Series*, No. 407

Part I

Part II

Part III

Part IV

Section 5
"BUSINESS AND HUMAN RIGHTS" IN THE ERA OF GLOBALIZATION

GOTO, Kenta

1. Introduction

When the second Kishida administration took office in November 2021, there was one particular appointment that attracted attention. This was the newly created post of Special Advisor to the Prime Minister for International Human Rights Issues, and former Defense Minister Gen Nakatani was appointed to this post. The public may have perceived the government's emphasis on human rights as abrupt, but this development was not a one-time, ad hoc effort by the Kishida administration and in the background to it lies major international geopolitical dynamics.

When the Biden administration took office in the United States in January of the same year, a major shift was made to multilateralism, which was an about-face from the inward-looking stance that the Trump administration took to its international relationships. To counter the escalating confrontation with China, the strategy that was clearly chosen was to solidify the bonds of "like-minded countries" that share values such as freedom, democracy, and the rule of law, and build an encircling net. At the heart of this axis of values are human rights. Human rights have become one of the most crucial factors in defining the international position of the Japanese government, and this trend is having a significant impact on the business world.

As such, this paper reviews the significance and challenges of "business and human rights" in Japan from the perspective of businesses in the age of globalization.

2. Human Rights Issues in Business

What are human rights issues in business? This question is often asked. There is a strong impression that human rights are generally perceived as a vague concept or idea in Japan and often it is treated as an issue in a specific context, such as Buraku discrimination. Human rights, however, are clearly delineated, well-defined, universal rights that all people are born with. That is a universal value system that humanity has developed through repeated trial and error over a long period of time (Human Rights Bureau, Ministry of Justice, 2020). In 1948, the United Nations General Assembly adopted the Universal Declaration of Human Rights, which became the International Covenants on Human Rights in 1966, and human rights became a common value standard for the international community. This is clearly stipulated also in the Constitution of Japan.

The protection and promotion of human rights have traditionally been regarded as the responsibility of the state. Since the beginning of this century, however, in addition to the state, firms have been expected to play an active role in respecting human rights through their businesses and have been required to mainstream human rights into their business practices. In fact, several international rules and frameworks already exist regarding corporate activities and human rights. It should be noted that these human rights issues specified in these conventions are based on global norms, such as international treaties.

For example, an important international norm closely related to companies is the International Labour Organization's (ILO) Core Labour Standards. These include eight conventions in four standards; freedom of association and the effective recognition of the right to collective bargaining, the elimination of all forms of forced and compulsory labour, the effective abolition of child labour, and the elimination of discrimination in respect of employment and occupation[1]. The standards are positioned as fundamental rights that must be complied with at a minimum in order to simultaneously achieve social progress and economic development by promoting decent work in an increasingly globalized world. In principle, labor-related guidelines should be developed with reference to these standards to ensure consistency.

In actual business settings, specific human rights risks are diverse. These include insufficient or unpaid wages, excessive or unreasonable working hours, inadequate occupational health and safety, and various types of harassment, such as power harassment and sexual harassment. Violations of the right to social security, the rights of foreign workers, and discrimination based on race, ethnicity, gender, or sexual orientation are also considered to be human rights issues. Firms are required to respect these business-related human rights risks more than ever before. In an era of advanced globalization, it is essential for businesses to reflect intrinsic changes in their business practices to respond to these requirements.

Part I

Part II

Part III

Part IV

---

1) A resolution was adopted at the International Labour Conference in June 2022 on the inclusion of a fifth standard—namely, a safe and healthy working environment—in the ILO's framework of fundamental principles and rights at work.

3. "Business and Human Rights" in the Age of Globalization

"Business and human rights" is both an old and new issue. The beginning of this development dates back to the 1970s. The expansion of multinational enterprises (MNE's) and their impact on the world economy, especially in developing countries, were already evident in those days. In response to this, the Organisation for Economic Co-operation and Development (OECD) formulated the OECD Guidelines for Multinational Enterprises in 1976, and the ILO formulated the Tripartite Declaration of Principles concerning Multinational Enterprises and Social Policy (MNE Declaration) in 1977. These two guidelines have served as basic principles when considering business and human rights in subsequent years.

Since the rise of neoliberalism in the 1980s through the post-Cold War era in the 1990s, economic globalization has flourished. The development of complex cross-border production and distribution systems, or so-called global value chains, also accelerated around this time and spread to all corners of the world. As the influence of these value-chain-driven MNEs on society grows, so does the focus on responsible corporate practices. In particular, the negative impact of globalization on the "social dimensions," i.e., the relationship between corporate activities and global issues such as widening inequality and environmental destruction, has been discussed, and the nature of Responsible Business Conduct (RBC) has been questioned.

At the 1999 Davos Conference, Kofi Annan, then Secretary-General of the United Nations, called for the establishment of a "United Nations Global Compact" in partnership with the private sector to achieve sustainable growth, and this was enacted the following year. In Japan, a local network for this framework (Global Compact Network Japan, GCNJ) was launched in December 2003, and as of June 2022 when this report was written, it has become a major organization with 489 member businesses and organizations. Participating companies are required to adhere to and practice the 10 principles in four areas; human rights, labor, environment, and anti-corruption.

The most considerable influence on the "business and human rights" movement has been the Guiding Principles on Business and Human Rights (hereinafter referred to as the Guiding Principles)[2] that were unanimously endorsed by the United Nations Human Rights Council in 2011. The Guiding Principles were formulated because of the influence of MNEs and their growing

---

[2] The official name is Guiding Principles for Business and Human Rights: Implementing the United Nations "Protect, Respect and Remedy" Framework.

impact on the economies and societies of developing countries. In particular, as they improved their competitiveness through global value chains, firms in developed countries, including in Japan, were increasingly seen as facilitating or complicit in human rights abuses.

Following the adoption of Agenda 2030 at the United Nations General Assembly in 2015, the world began to focus on Sustainable Development Goals (SDGs). In this context, the "excitement" about SDGs in Japan is noteworthy (Goto, 2019). In 2016, the Abe administration swiftly set up the SDGs Promotion Headquarters in the Cabinet, and in the following year, Keidanren revised its Charter of Corporate Behavior with "Achieving the SDGs through the realization of Society 5.0" as its main pillar. Since then, many firms have begun to link their existing businesses to the individual goals of the SDGs and to publicize them on their websites. The SDGs were also strongly promoted in the bid to host the international exposition to be held in Osaka in 2025. Despite the fact that the SDGs have become an everyday topic in various situations, the fact that there is a lack of specific discussions on human rights as a central theme in the business world has caused a deep sense of discomfort. Agenda 2030 also clearly states that the realization of the SDGs is predicated on respect for human rights. Human rights are the common basis for all 17 goals and it is impossible to implement the SDGs while leaving human rights on the sidelines.

4. Global Trends on Business and Human Rights

The Guiding Principles, which describe the human-rights responsibilities of states and corporations, have three main pillars. The first pillar is the obligation of states to respect, protect and fulfill human rights and fundamental freedoms (Protect); the second pillar is the responsibility of businesses to comply with all applicable laws and regulations and to respect human rights (Respect); and the third pillar is the requirement to have adequate and effective remedy mechanisms and to guarantee access to them in the event of a violation of human rights or non-compliance with them (Remedy). It is important to reiterate that they specify the responsibilities of states as well as businesses for the protection or extension of human rights.

The Guiding Principles are not enforceable against governments or businesses, so in order to give them a certain degree of effectiveness, each country is encouraged to develop a national action plan. The Japanese government responded by formulating the National Action Plan on Business and Human rights (NAP) in October 2020. The plan's period is five years, from 2020 to 2025, with subsequent revisions being scheduled. It became the 24th national action plan in the world.

While these Guiding Principles are the focus of global efforts, developed countries (especially in the EU) are also formulating related legal systems to promote even stronger respect for human rights in business. A precursor to this, for example, is the Modern Slavery Act that came into force in the UK in 2015. The law requires businesses that are operating in the UK and are meeting certain conditions to publicly disclose their efforts to prevent human rights violations, including those of their business partners. Similar laws are already in force in France, Australia, Germany, and California in the United States. In the EU, there is a move toward legislation that will require businesses operating in the region to conduct human rights and environmental due diligence and to establish a complaint handling and problem-solving mechanism (see Table 1-5-1). Many of these legal frameworks also cover Japanese businesses operating in the respective country or that are involved in the value chain for the target market.

5. Global Value Chains and Human Rights

As discussed so far, the global trend regarding business and human rights is moving from voluntary compliance with human rights norms by companies to compliance legally mandated by states. Global frameworks such as the Guiding Principles, the OECD's Guidelines for Multinational Enterprises, and the ILO's MNE Declaration serve as guidelines in this regard as well. The Guiding Principles call for companies to implement the following three items in order to realize the ten principles in the four areas mentioned above. The first is to formulate a human rights policy and to express its commitment as a company. The second is that ongoing human rights due diligence must be implemented. The third is to provide remedies in the event of human rights violations. Among these items, human rights due diligence has recently become a topic of discussion in the media and the push toward legislation related to this has been gathering momentum, particularly in Europe.

As mentioned earlier, human rights due diligence is an ongoing process by which companies fulfill their responsibilities to respect human rights in their day-to-day activities. Its focus is preventing and mitigating human rights violations after identifying human rights risks according to the characteristics of each industry and company. Based on this process, remedying the victim(s) is the next requirement. More specific guidelines for implementing procedures can be found, for example, in the OECD Due Diligence Guidance for Responsible Business Conduct. According to this, human rights due diligence includes the

Table 1-5-1   Legal systems related to human rights (selected excerpts)

Country	Applicable Laws	Contents
UK	Modern Slavery Act	Enforced in 2015. Strengthens legal regulations against slave labor and human trafficking. Requires companies with annual sales over a certain size and operating in the UK to publish a statement that there is no slave labor or human trafficking in their supply chain.
France	Obligation of duty of care for parent and ordering companies (Duty of Care Act)	Enforced in 2017. Stipulates the duty of care (due diligence) with respect to human rights. It legally requires companies of a certain size located in France to prepare and implement a duty-of-care plan.
Australia	Modern Slavery Act	Enforced in 2019. A law similar to the UK's Modern Slavery Act. Requires companies that operate in Australia and exceed certain revenue levels to assess, analyze, and report on the risk of modern slavery in their supply chains. Applies also to Japanese companies.
Netherlands	Child Labor Due Diligence Act	Enacted (not yet enforced) in 2019. Covers all companies (including Japanese companies) that offer or sell products or services on the Dutch market. Makes mandatory the submission of a statement indicating that due diligence has been conducted in the supply chain to prevent child labor.
Germany	Supply Chain Due Diligence Act	Enacted in June 2021 and scheduled to come into effect in January 2023. Obliges companies above a certain size (including Japanese companies) to pay attention to human rights and environmental risks related to all domestic and foreign companies in their supply chain, including indirect business partners.
USA	California Transparency in Supply Chains Act	Enforced in 2012. Companies (including Japanese companies) operating in California and above a certain size are required to disclose their actions to eradicate slavery and human trafficking in their supply chains.
USA	Uyghur Forced Labor Prevention Act	Enacted in 2021 and enforced in June 2022. This act prohibits, in principle, the import of products produced in the Xinjiang Uyghur Autonomous Region of China (including products in which parts produced there are incorporated) unless the products meet requirements, such as proof that they were not produced by forced labor.
EU	Directive on corporate sustainability due diligence	Announced in February 2022. Makes it mandatory to conduct due diligence in the supply chain. This was preceded by the publication in July 2021 of guidance on conducting due diligence to address forced labor risks in the supply chain.
EU	EU Conflict Minerals Regulation	Enforced in 2021. Makes it mandatory for EU operators to ensure that their handling of minerals from designated areas does not contribute to conflicts or human rights abuses.

Source: Prepared by the author from JETRO (2021a, b, c, d) and JETRO (2022a, b).

Part I
Part II
Part III
Part IV

following actions (OECD, 2018).

1) Embed responsible business conduct into policies and management systems
2) Identify and assess actual and potential adverse impacts associated with the enterprise's operations, products or services (6) Provide for or cooperate in

remediation when appropriate
3) Cease, prevent and mitigate adverse impacts
4) Track implementation and results
5) Communicate how impacts are addressed

In an era of globalized corporate activities, it is not easy to conduct the human rights due diligence described above. The reason is that many business activities are embedded in global value chains that connect across boundaries of firms and countries. In short, a business' respect for and compliance with human rights in its activities are not limited to its own sphere of activity but must extend throughout its entire value chain.

A global value chain refers to a production and distribution network consisting of complex inter-firm relationships. The forms of governance are also diverse. From the point of view of the business that organizes and governs this, the essence of its strategy is to externalize and reorganize peripheral processes and functions other than the core functions (core competence) that enable the business to demonstrate its international comparative advantage. This externalization is deployed on the two basic strategic axes of 1) offshoring and 2) outsourcing. Offshoring in 1) is the process of transferring the relevant processes and functions to outside of Japan. A common case is the transfer of a process to a developing country with lower income levels in response to a decline in its comparative advantage due to higher wage levels in Japan. Outsourcing 2) is the process of transferring the relevant processes and functions outside the firm. A case in point is outsourcing a specific function or process. The part that remains within the firm is the competitive domain (core competence) that constitutes the core function. The four quadrants (strategies) created by the combination of these two axes form the global value chain (Table 1-5-2). Whether it is an electronic or an apparel product, its value chain is basically a combination of these four strategies (Goto, 2019).

The Guiding Principles require that due diligence be performed not only

| Table 1-5-2 | Two strategic axes of externalization |

		1) Offshoring axis	
		None	Yes
2) Outsourcing Axis	None	(1) Core competitive domains (own capabilities)	(2) Own overseas offices (FDI)
	Yes	(3) Domestic outsourcing	(4) Overseas outsourcing

Source: Goto (2019).

for the company's own domestic offices, including its headquarters, but also for its overseas offices, as well as for its domestic and overseas suppliers with whom it has no capital relationship. Furthermore, the scope of human rights due diligence is not limited to "direct business partners" with whom the firm has a direct contractual relationship, but also includes a responsibility for "indirect business partners" with whom the firm has no business contract. This means, for example, that lead firms that govern the value chain must take responsibility for the employment and human rights issues of the subcontractors with whom their overseas suppliers do business, as well as their own subcontractors. There is also the development of extensive informal economies in Southeast and South Asian countries (Endo and Goto, 2018; Goto, 2021). If a firm's value chain extends to such sectors, it is also subject to due diligence.

6. Current Status of Human Rights Response by Japanese Companies

Amid the accelerating global movement towards "business and human rights," the Japanese government has established the Business and Human Rights Policy Office in the Ministry of Economy, Trade, and Industry (METI) to promote its response to human rights risks in global value chains, including the afore-mentioned Special Advisor to the Prime Minister. Furthermore, the Ministry of Foreign Affairs (MOFA) also established the post of the Senior Coordinator for Human Rights Violations. In February 2022, METI announced the formulation of the Guidelines on Respecting Human Rights in Responsible Supply Chains. In some cases, the private sector has taken the lead, such as by including provisions for respect for human rights in the Corporate Governance Code (corporate governance guidelines) for companies listed on the Tokyo Stock Exchange in June 2021. In addition, the Japan Textile Federation, with the support of the ILO and backed by the METI is developing its Guideline for Responsible Business Conduct for the Textile and Clothing Industry of Japan through dialogues with stakeholders (at the time of drafting this paper).

There have been several studies conducted regarding the current state of business and human rights in Japan. METI conducted a Questionnaire Survey on Human Rights Initiatives in the Supply Chain of Japanese Companies (760 valid responses, 27.3% valid response rate) from September to October 2021. The survey revealed that about 70% of the responding companies have formu-lated human rights policies and more than 50% are conducting human rights due diligence. Of the companies conducting human rights due diligence, 25% include indirect business partners in their due diligence process. As a general trend, the results also showed that the larger the sales volume, the more likely it is that the firm is responding to human rights issues.

The Japan External Trade Organization (JETRO) conduced a similar survey from November to December 2021. This Questionnaire on Overseas Business Development of Japanese Companies for FY 2021 (1,745 valid responses, 13.0% valid response rate) showed that 38.1% of the surveyed businesses have a human rights policy in place, but that 60% have not yet formulated one. Concerning the percentage of businesses that have formulated human rights policies, 64.3% of large companies have such policies compared to 32.7% of small and medium-sized companies. Of the companies that have human rights policies, 65.4% also require their own suppliers to comply with human rights. Among them, 81.6% of the companies request compliance from their domestic suppliers, but only 26.0% request compliance from their overseas suppliers. Only 10.6% of the companies require their suppliers' suppliers to comply with their human rights policies. On the other hand, 31.3% of the surveyed companies are required by their domestic and foreign customers to comply with a policy of respect for human rights. Although the Japanese government and related organizations have finally begun to act on human rights, the efforts of the industry as a whole and individual companies are still limited.

7. Future Issues

As the UN Guiding Principles indicate, it might be virtually impossible to completely eliminate human rights risks that may arise in business. As such, it is necessary to ascertain conditions in the entire value chain, including in indirect business partners, on the premise that human rights-related problems may occur, and therefore it is essential to identify the risks in each process and function according to the level of severity. Continuous human rights due diligence can only be effective through active engagement with stakeholders of these value chains. In such cases, it is important to disclose the efforts and results in a transparent manner.

In January 2021, some of the products of a major Japanese apparel company were blocked from being imported into the United States. The US authorities gave the reason that an organization in Xinjiang Uyghur Autonomous Region of China, where forced labor is suspected, may be involved in the production of the raw materials for these products. Although the apparel company appealed, it appears that the US authorities decided that the evidence presented were not convincing enough.

Finally, when Japan addresses human rights and business on a national level, the issue of foreign technical intern trainees should not be avoided. The system of foreign technical intern trainees is positioned as a scheme for Japan's "international cooperation" centering on "human resource development" that encourages the transfer of skills, technology, or knowledge to developing countries. There must be cases in which the transfer of skills and technology to developing countries has been effectively advanced through this system, thereby contributing to their economic development. In reality, however, it is a well-known fact that Asian workers dispatched under this system have become simply a labor force to meet the labor needs of firms and industries suffering from labor shortages. As such, this foreign technical intern trainees program has long been subject to international criticism. For example, in its Trafficking in Persons Report, the United States has repeatedly pointed out that the system allows the exploitation of foreign workers and encourages forced labor.

Sustainability and SDGs are not merely "fashionable trends." If Japan is serious about promoting "sustainable development" and leading the world through it, all of its efforts must be based on a respect for human rights. Now is the time to have a real discussion and to implement concrete measures that embrace the essence of sustainability.

References

Endo, T. and Goto, K. (2020), "Informalizing Asia: Another Dynamism of the Asian Economy." In Goto, K; Endo, T; and Ito, A (eds), *The Asian Economy: Contemporary Issues and Challenges*, London and New York: Routledge, pp. 169-187.

Goto, K., (2019), *What is the Asian Economy? The Dynamics of Breakthroughs and Japan's Path Forward* (Japanese title: *Ajia Keizai toha Nanika? Yakushin no Dainamizumu to Nihon no Katsuro*) (Chuko Shinsho), Chuokoron-shinsha.

Goto, K., "SDGs and Global Value Chains", *Kansai and the Asia Pacific Economic Outlook (2019)*, Asia Pacific Institute of Research, pp. 75-78.

Goto, K. (2021), "Asian Labor Markets and Informal Economies in the Corona Disaster", *Kansai and the Asia Pacific Economic Outlook (2021)*, Asia Pacific Institute of Research, pp. 53-59.

Japan External Trade Organization (JETRO), (2021a), *Overview of California's Transparency in Supply Chains Act*, Overseas Research Department, Los Angeles Office.

Japan External Trade Organization (JETRO), (2021b), *The United Kingdom Modern Slavery Act 2015*, Overseas Research Department, London Office.

Japan External Trade Organization (JETRO), (2021c), *Australia Modern Slave Law 2018*, Overseas Research Department.

Japan External Trade Organization (JETRO), (2021d), *Republic of France Law No. 2017-399 (1) of March 27, 2017 on Obligations to Monitor Parent Companies and Companies Controlling Their Management (1)*, Paris Office, Overseas Research Department.

Japan External Trade Organization (JETRO), (2022a), *Law Concerning Due Diligence Obligations of Companies in the German Supply Chain*, Overseas Research Department Berlin Office.

Japan External Trade Organization (JETRO), (2022b), *Policies on Supply Chains and Human Rights and Examples of Application and Responses to Companies (Revised 2022 Edition)*, Overseas Research Department.

Organisation for Economic Co-operation and Development (OECD). (2018), *OECD Due Diligence Guidance for Responsible Business Conduct*, OECD.

The Human Rights Bureau of the Ministry of Justice, (2020), *Response to Business and Human Rights Required of Companies Today, Research and Study on Business and Human Rights, Report (Detailed Version)*, Center for Human Rights Education and Training

Section 6
CHALLENGES AND PROSPECTS FOR A COOPERATING SOCIETY WITH ASIAN HUMAN RESOURCES

MORIYA, Takashi; NAKAYAMA, Akira

1. Introduction

This section introduces the challenges and prospects for Japan and Japanese companies from the perspective of "cooperating" with Asian human resources based on research that was conducted over a year by the Cooperating with Asian Human Resources Study Group of the Asia Pacific Institute of Research in FY 2021.

First, we will analyze and introduce the characteristics of human resource development in Asia with a focus on India. The reasons for focusing on India include analyzing from a comparative perspective with China and from the perspective of the Quadrilateral Security Dialogue (the Quad), and the security framework formed by Japan, the US, Australia, and India. Then in the following section, we will explain how and why Japan and Japanese companies should work together with Asian human resources, particularly Indian firms, based on previous research reports and the questionnaire survey and interview survey originally conducted by the Cooperating with Asian Human Resources Study Group.

2. Characteristics of Human Resource Development in Asia

(1) Developing human resources adaptable to the Fourth Industrial Revolution in Singapore, Vietnam, and India

Asian countries have been actively developing highly adapted human resources and promoting the digital industry since the IT revolution occurred at the beginning of the 21st century. The purpose of this section is to introduce the development of human resources with digital capabilities and the prosperity of the digital industry adapted to the Fourth Industrial Revolution in Singapore, Vietnam, and in particular, India as case studies.

Singapore, which has a national policy to be a brainpower nation, has been gathering the world's best scientists, particularly in the area of pharmaceuticals, since the 21st century, thereby building an education and research system adapted to the Fourth Industrial Revolution and promoting the digital industry.

Vietnam has attracted much attention as a destination for production bases

Part I

Part II

Part III

Part IV

and has established itself as a production base in Asia in place of China where labor costs have already soared. Vietnam has also been proactively educating human resources well versed in digital technologies and developing the digital industry.

Similarly, in India, the current Modi Administration has been promoting Digital India and has attempted to transition to become a digitally empowered society and knowledge economy. Digital India's vision is to provide all citizens with digital infrastructure (e.g., high-speed internet) to digitize identification and bank accounts, to make administrative services on-demand, to enhance digital literacy, and to use cloud storage for administrative documents.

Each of these countries in Asia of Singapore, Vietnam, and India have developed education adapted to the Fourth Industrial Revolution and are providing practical education such as internships with companies.

It is a critical challenge for Japan and Japanese companies to ensure "cooperation" with human resources from the Asian countries adapted to the Fourth Industrial Revolution and various Asian companies such as those in the digital industry. In particular, the partnership with India is a major challenge for the future in terms of the aspects to be discussed below. The reasons why India was chosen are the following points: India is a country nurturing excellent science and math human resources, the characteristics of India's distinctive industrial structure and digital industry, and the need to build cooperative relations in the new Cold War era between Japan, the US, Australia, and India in the future.

(2) Distinctive science university education and digital industry policy in India

In the digital industry, India's greatest strengths are its capability to produce IT engineers each year and the use of English as a common language.

Tertiary education in India is characterized by the increasing popularity of science and engineering, especially IT majors, which offer good remuneration prospects after graduation. Highly qualified graduates from prestigious tertiary education institutions such as the Indian Institutes of Technology (IITs), the Indian Institutes of Science (IISc), the Indian Institutes of Management (IIMs) and the University Institute of Chemical Technology (UICT), are particularly attracting attention worldwide.

The famous Indian Institutes of Technology are not a single university and each campus is independent, while there is a common system among the Indian Institutes of Technology. These institutes are similar to the University of California in the USA, with 23 institutes and 13,000 students. Each institute has 500 to 600 students per academic year. The backgrounds to entrance examinations in India differ from Japan, as a student passes the entrance examination in India if he or she has excellent ability in one subject, such as mathematics and physics. Computer science and electrical engineering are the two most popular disciplines.

3. Contrasting Industrial Liberalization Policies in India and China

(1) India's digital industry liberalization and China's industrial liberalization

China's industrial liberalization policy has opened up the industrial sector to foreign-invested enterprises and actively attracted them, whereas its digital industry sector has been monopolized by and restricted to Chinese firms. In addition, China has adopted a policy of digital isolation to Chinese digital companies listed in the US, delisting them in some cases, and instead limiting listings only to the Hong Kong market.

India has long had a protectionist policy in the industrial sector, partly because of its history as a British colony. In contrast, India's digital industry sector has been open and welcoming to American companies in the US digital industry.

Table 1-6-1   Contrasting industrial liberalization policies in India and China

	Manufacturing Industry	Digital Industry
China	Liberalized	Closed
India	Closed	Liberalized

Source: Prepared by the author

It is generally accepted that the major development of India's IT industry began in response to the Year 2000 problem when US IT companies needed many IT engineers to carry out simultaneous software modifications and because there was a large demand for human resources in India. As Indian IT engineers responded successfully to that problem, the Indian IT industry grew rapidly, starting from being subcontractors for the US ICT industry. Various US IT giants such as Google, Yahoo, Amazon, Microsoft, and IBM have since

Part I

Part II

Part III

Part IV

expanded and set up R&D centers in Bengaluru (Bangalore), India[1].

Indian companies are strong in IT consulting, which promotes operational efficiency through the use of information technology. Specifically, by looking at the leading Indian IT consulting firms in terms of sales size, first is Tata Consultancy Services (TCS), the second is Infosys Limited, and the third is Mphasis. India has also allowed Indian IT companies to list on the US stock market since 2019. Sales for FY 03/2021 showed that Infosys' customers are mainly from developed regions, with the USA accounting for 61.5%, Europe 24.1% and India 2.6% of sales by region. The company offers high levels of customer satisfaction to customers in developed countries in Europe and the US, using its state-of-the-art IT technology standards as a weapon. It also has achieved stable growth, with many of its operations being managed by cost-competitive engineers and staff residing in India. Its average annual growth rates between FY 03/2009 and FY 03/2021 were high, at 13.6% for sales and 10.2% for profit after tax.

(2) Differences in industrial policy between India and China and future projections

India did not follow the path of development from primary to secondary to tertiary industries as in Japan, but instead it shifted from the primary to the tertiary ICT industry as a result of natural evolution. In addition, India has moved in the opposite direction vis-a-vis China that has opened up its manufacturing industry to the rest of the world and protected its ICT industry. It has been pointed out that China has pursued an "open industrialization, closed digitalization strategy," whereas India has followed a "closed industrialization, open digitalization strategy"[2].

The comparison between India and China based on World Bank data for 2018 showed that China's manufacturing sector accounted for 29.4% of its GDP, whereas India's manufacturing sector accounted for 15% of its GDP, which was significantly lower than that of China. World Bank data for 2018 showed that the share of agriculture in GDP was significantly higher in India at 14% compared to 7% in China.

In addition, if we look at the industrial structure of India in 2020 based on the Gross Value Added (GVA) of India from the statistics of the Indian

1) Hayashi, Yukihide (ed.), Higuchi, Takehito and Nishikawa, Yuji (2016), The Science and Technology Situation in India: Can a Human Resources Superpower Take Off?, Maruzen Publishing, p. 27, Reference
2) Ito, Asei (2020), Digitalizing Emerging Countries: Beyond the Developed Countries or the Coming of Surveillance Society, Chuokoron-sha, p. 108. Reference

government, agriculture, which is the primary industry, accounted for 20% and was the main industry, whereas manufacturing and construction in the secondary industry were stagnant at 15% and 7.3%, respectively, due to the closed type of industrialization.

India's open digitalization strategy has inevitably deepened its relationship with its partners of US corporate behemoths, and at the same time as this, India and the US began sharing information technology and a range of information. Therefore, India and the US are expected to reinforce their mutual collaboration in the future by accelerating the highly sophisticated international division of

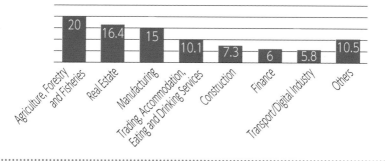

Part I

Figure 1-6-1   The industrial structure of India

Note: Industry categories are representative and values are percentages.
Source: Percentage of gross value added (GVA) in FY2020 from Ministry of Statistics and Program Implementation (Ministry of Statistics, Government of India) data

Part II

labor through the information industry, including research and development.

In contrast, China is intensifying trade friction relating to exports to the US in the industrial sector, while at the same time adopting a policy of separation and closure in the digital industrial sector. Therefore, the conflict between the US and China is expected to deepen in the future.

Part III

India's emerging digital companies are expected to go public in financial securities markets as their Chinese counterparts did in the past and to use this as leverage to acquire share of global markets and massive amounts of capital and to grow rapidly. At the same time, it is considered that the US and US companies and India's emerging digital companies will likely build even closer relationships. In 2021, India will have the third largest number of unicorns in the world (26 companies) after China (122 companies), and the number of unicorns is expected to increase year by year as Indian digital start-ups will replace Chinese digital companies and be listed on US Stock Exchanges.

Part IV

On the other hand and in stark contrast, China's emerging digital companies have not only been forced to delist from the US stock markets in some cases, but they also are subject to making huge donations to the Chinese government, regulations such as antitrust laws, and penalties, all of which are imposed in the name of "common prosperity."

In light of this situation and future predictions, it is important for Japan and Japanese companies to give careful thought to building future relationships with the governments and companies of Asia's two largest economies, China, and India.

4. The Role of India in the New Cold War Era and the Importance of Economic Co-operation between India and Japan

(1) Reasons for focusing on India: building cooperative relationships between Japan, the US, Australia, and India in the New Cold War Era

Japan, the US, Australia, and India form the Quad as a cooperative partnership of liberal countries that share fundamental liberal principles and values. The Quad is a framework for a relationship of security and economic cooperation between Japan, the US, Australia, and India, with the combined military expenditure of the four countries surpassing that of China. The Quad was started as a result of a four-party strategic dialogue initiated by former Prime Minister Shinzo Abe in 2006. Although it is not a military alliance like NATO, it already conducts joint military exercises.

The foreign ministers of the Quad's four member states issued a statement criticizing Russia's invasion of Ukraine.

Russia's invasion of Ukraine has thrown into sharp relief the dichotomy in a new Cold War era between liberal states on the one hand that share basic liberal principles and values and controlling and surveillance nations on the other, such as Russia and China.

The progress of the Quad is shown in Table 1-6-2.

Within this Quad, India maintains a non-aligned and neutral position, and for Japan, the US and Australia, building close relations with India is a major political, economic and security challenge for the future. Therefore, Japan, the US and Australia have been actively trying to attract India's initiative-taking participation and co-operation in the Quad through economic bilateral cooperation and partnerships.

Also, in the Asia-Pacific region, Japan, China, and other countries have a noticeably ageing population with a declining birthrate and are expected to

Table 1-6-2	Progress of the Quad

Progress in cooperation between Japan, the US, Australia, and India	
2006	Then-Prime Minister Shinzo Abe proposed a framework for dialogue
November 2011	Director-General-level meeting in the Philippines
September 2019	Foreign Ministers' meeting in New York, US
October 2020	Foreign Ministers' meeting in Tokyo. Confirmation of regular holding of meetings
November 2020	Joint exercises by SDF and US-India-Australia

Source: Compiled from the Nihon Keizai Shimbun, March 13, 2021.

experience a population decline in the future, whereas India has a large youth population and is extremely attractive for its potential future economic growth.

Japanese companies are faced with the management challenge of the absolute shortage of IT, engineering, and other science-based human resources due to the declining birthrate and ageing population. As such, it is a critical issue for Japan and Japanese companies to tap into the sophisticated human resources and corporate vitality in India's growing IT sector through collaborations with Japanese companies and employment in Japanese companies and Japanese companies overseas.

(2) The importance of economic agreements and economic cooperation between Japan and India—using the example of Japan's Manufacturing Skills Transfer Promotion Program in India

In November 2016 at the Japan-India summit meeting, Japan's Minister of Economy, Trade and Industry Hiroshige Seko and India's Ambassador to Japan Sujan R. Chinoy signed a Memorandum of Cooperation on the Manufacturing Skills Transfer Promotion Program in order to develop the high-quality human resources required by Japanese companies in India and to meet India's demand for the development of its stagnant secondary industry. In this Manufacturing Skills Transfer Promotion Program, the plan is to develop 30,000 manufacturing personnel in 10 years.

Two important parts of the program are (1) the Japan-India Institute for Manufacturing (JIM) and (2) the Japanese Endowed Courses (JEC). This program is in line with Prime Minister Modi's Make in India and Skill India programs.

The content of the Japanese-style manufacturing school in this program includes discipline (preparedness for factory work), manufacturing spirit (kaizen), the 5S (Seiri (Sorting), Seiton (Setting-in-Order), Seiso (Shining), Seiketsu (Standardizing), and Shitsuke (Sustaining the Discipline)), skills (practical techniques), thinking ability (problem analysis and solution proposals), and

Part I

Part II

Part III

Part IV

practical factory training, namely practical on-site education (parts, assembly, etc., at the factory). The duration of training ranges from one to three years. Specifically, Suzuki and Toyota have opened schools as Japanese-style manufacturing schools.

In addition, the Japanese Endowed Courses (JEC) aim to provide the practical, specialized education practiced in Japanese companies to groups of excellent Indian students who have the potential to become managers and engineers in India in the future. In doing so, the JEC aims to develop Indian industrial human resources for future employment by Japanese companies, and also to develop industrial human resources in the IT sector, not limited to manufacturing.

The development of the Manufacturing Skills Transfer Promotion Program has helped Japanese manufacturing and IT companies in India to cultivate excellent Indian human resources who are adapted to Japanese manufacturing, which has been a bottleneck for the development of Japanese companies in the country.

It is also significant for India to cooperate with Japan and Japanese companies that excel in manufacturing because India's development of the secondary industry has been stagnant.

In particular, the current Modi Administration launched the Make in India program in September 2014, which aims to promote the development of the manufacturing sector. The building of relations between Japan and India through manufacturing is an important initiative to facilitate the development of political and military relations such as the Quad.

5. Nurturing Human Resources to Bridge the Indo-Japan Bilateral Relationship and its Challenges for Promoting Economic Cooperation between India and Japan

The last part of this section looks at nurturing human resources in Japan who can bridge the bilateral relationship in order to promote political and economic cooperation in Asia, particularly between Japan and India, from the perspective of "cooperating" with Indian human resources.

(1) Implications from the preceding research reports

JETRO's Survey Report on Indian Highly Skilled Human Resources in Japan (2020) pointed out two particular challenges in recruiting and utilizing Indian highly skilled human resources. The first is understanding the thinking and tendencies unique to Indian personnel and closing the gaps in terms of the recognition of length of service and performance indicators, and the second is the importance of designing, introducing and implementing internal communication and appropriate evaluation systems to further increase retention rates after recruitment.

Furthermore, with regard to specific initiatives, this survey report pointed to the importance of company-wide agreements and the clarification of recruitment requirements, hiring as specialists, clarifying job descriptions, responsibilities and rules for salary increases and promotions, and raising the level of recognition of Indian personnel by Japanese companies. Highly qualified IT personnel in India are part of the global competition for talent, and the importance of acquiring Indian personnel through public-private partnerships with an awareness of such a competitive environment is emphasized. The survey report also points to the importance of convincing evaluation feedback, building trust, providing continuous growth opportunities, closing the information gap caused by language differences, explaining management policies regularly, and gaining their understanding of the company.

(2) Implications from the research conducted by the APIR Cooperating with Asian Human Resources Study Group

The Asia Pacific Institute of Research commissioned SUNWELL Corporation, which dispatches foreign engineers, to design, conduct and collect the questionnaire. Additional interviews were conducted with four Indian engineers and two Vietnamese engineers who responded to the survey.

The questionnaire was conducted in October 2021. The number of respondents was 105 Indian engineers and 55 Vietnamese engineers, and for the survey tool, Google Forms were used for the web-based questionnaire. Additional interviews were conducted with four Indian and two Vietnamese engineers in October and November 2021. Both interviews asked the respondents about their evaluations of the Japanese companies which they work for and about Japan in which they are residing.

The questionnaire and interviews showed that both Indian and Vietnamese engineers have a good impression of safety and security in Japan, whereas they have issues and problems that need to be improved for Japanese companies. Nonetheless, they also want Japan to improve issues concerning education for children and employment for spouses in full-time employment in the case of families.

Comparisons between Indian and Vietnamese engineers showed differences in working difficulties due to differences in the language environment. Given that Indian engineers have English and Japanese language options, and that English is the common language in India, a working environment in a Japanese company where English is available is easier than a workplace where only Japanese is used. In contrast, Vietnamese engineers only work in Japanese, indicating the linguistic severity of the working environment. In particular, Indian engineers tend to have a more English-speaking working environment and satisfactory salary payments in IT engineering. Only 7.7% of the Vietnamese engineers surveyed were IT engineers, while the Vietnamese engineers employed were other mechanical and electrical engineers. IT engineers accounted for 50% of Indian engineers.

Many Indian engineers have a favorable impression of Japan, as shown in Figure 1-6-2. It is significant that the survey revealed that, compared to India, people are attracted to Japan for its high standard of medical care, friendly schools, and safe and equal society, and that they tend to stay in Japan with their families for longer periods of time.

In the future, Japanese companies will need to improve the aspects that Indian and Vietnamese engineers are commonly dissatisfied with. Specifically, the areas for improvement were the speed of company decision-making, clarification, and prior explanation of criteria for treatment and promotion, clarification of the company's vision, and strict hierarchical relationships. Other critical issues included improving the work-life balance, transparent decision-making processes and information disclosure, global management, improving education and training systems, approving extended leave for a temporary return to one's home country, improving education and training systems, education for Japanese employees to realize 'cooperation' with foreign employees, subsidies for children's education, and improving education and training systems.

In order to develop human resources in Japan who can act as bridges between the two countries to promote economic cooperation between Asia (in particular, Japan and India) and Japan, it is important to make good use of their

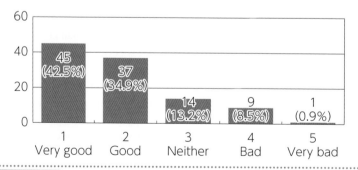

Figure 1-6-2 Indian engineers' impressions of Japan

Source: Compiled based on the results of the APIR questionnaire survey

positive impressions of Japan as a safe and secure country to attract competent Asian human resources to Japan and to develop them into human resources who can act as bridges between the two countries.

References

Fujii, T. (2003), Caste in History: 'Self-Portrait' in Modern India, (Japanese title: *Rekishi no Naka no Kasuto: Kindai Indo no Jigazo*), Iwanami Shoten

Fujita, M. (2020), Vol. 9: What is the approach to institution building in the digital age? (Vietnam), IDE Square Column: Innovation from Emerging Countries, (Japanese title: *Daikyukai Dejitaru Jidai no Seido Kochiku no Apurochi toha (Betonamu)*), Institute of Developing Economies, Japan External Trade Organization (IDE-JETRO)

Gurcharan, D., Noji, T. Interview, and composition (2020), Japanese & Indian truths, (Japanese title: *Nihonjin to Indojin: Sekaishijo Saigo no Seicho Enjin no Shinjitsu*), President Inc.

Hayashi, Y. (ed.), Higuchi, T. and Nishikawa, Y. (2016), India's Science and Technology Situation—Can a Human Resources Superpower Take Off?, (Japanese title: *Indo no Kagaku Gijutsu Josei: Jinzai Taikoku wa Ririku dekiru noka*), Maruzen Publishing Co.

Hirose, H. (2019), India's Changing World Map—Modi's Impact—, (Japanese title: *Indo ga kaeru Sekai Chizu: Modei no Shogeki*), Bungei Shunju

Ito, A. (2020), Digitalizing Emerging Countries: Beyond Developed Countries or the Coming of the Surveillance Society, (Japanese title: *Dejitaruka suru Shinkokoku: Senshinkoku wo koeru ka, Kanshi Shakai no torai ka*), Chuokoron-sha, 108 pp

Izumi, T. (2019) Foreign Workers in Japan: Research Overview and Prospects, (Japanese title: *Nihon ni okeru Gaikokujin Rodosha ni kansuru Kenkyu no Doko to Tenkai*), Kaetsu University Research Review, Vol. 62, No. 1, pp. 23–37

Kuroda, Y. (2020) A study on the curriculum for STEM human resource development in higher education: focusing on the case of Singapore University of Technology and Design, (Japanese title: *Koto Kyoiku ni okeru STEM Jinzai Yosei no Karikyuramu ni kansuru Ichi Kosatsu—Shingaporu Koka Dezain Daigaku no Jirei ni Chakumoku shite—*), Collection of Papers of the 44th Annual Meeting of the Japanese Society for Science Education

Moriya, T. (2012), A Study on the Recruitment of Foreign Students by Japanese Companies, (Japanese title: *Nihon Kigyo no Ryugakusei no Gaikokujin Saiyo heno Ichikosatsu*), The Japanese Journal of Labour Studies, No. 623, pp. 29–37

Moriya, T. (2018), Foreign workers' employment problems and improvement measures, (Japanese title: *Gaikokujin Rodosha no Shuromondai to Kaizensaku*)

Moriya, T. (2020), Conditions for companies where highly skilled foreign personnel play an active role: required career advancement · clarification of salary increase standards, (Japanese title: *Kodo Gaikoku Jinzai ga Katsuyaku suru Kaisha no Joken: Motomerareru Kyaria appu · Shokyu Kijun no Meikakuka*), Resonare, September 2020.

Moriya, T. (2020), Nurturing and Talent Management of Japan's "Global Human Resources" in the Human Resources Crisis Era: A Prescription for Breaking Free from Abandoned "Japan and Japanese Companies," (Japanese title: *Jinzai Kiki Jidai no Nihon no "Gurobaru Jinzai" no Ikusei to Tarento Manejimento: "Misuterareru Nihon · Nihon Kigyo" kara no Dakkyaku no Shohosen*), Koyo Shobo

Nakagawa, G. (2021), The essence of Singaporean-style meritocracy—its ideals and reality, (Japanese title: *Shingaporu Gata Meritokurashi no Honshitsu—sono Riso to Genjitsu—*), Journal of political science and economics, Vol. 8

Nikkei BP Research Institute (ed.) (2017), Preparing the Next Generation to be an 'Innovation Powerhouse': Singapore's Future Strategy and Japan's Path Forward, (Japanese title: *Inobeshon Taikoku Jisedai eno Fuseki: Ijigen no Seicho wo togeta Shingaporu no Mirai Senryaku to Nihon no Katsuro*), Nikkei Business Publications, Inc.

Nomura, A. (2015), Reconstruction of Systems Required for the Utilization of Foreign Human Resources: Perspectives on Foreigner Policy from Overseas Cases, (Japanese title: *Gaikoku Jinzai no Katsuyo ni muke motomerareru Seido no Saikochiku: Kaigai Jirei ni miru Gaikokujin Seisaku no Shiten*), Japan Research Institute review, Vol. 6, No. 25

Okumura, M. (2021) Multicultural Education in Singapore: An Analysis of Secondary School Social Studies Textbooks, (Japanese title: *Shingaporu ni okeru Tabunka Kyoiku: Chuto Gakko Shakaika Kyokasho Bunseki wo Chushin ni*), The Bulletin of the Institute of Human Sciences, Toyo University, Vol. 23, pp. 109–129

Sato, T., Ueno, M. (eds.), Takaguchi, K. (2021), Illustrated Comprehensive Guide to the Indian Economy: From Politics, Society and Culture to Business entry practice: A Compilation of 11 Industrial Fields (73 Industries), (Japanese title: *Zukai Indo Keizai Taizen: Seiji · Shakai · Bunka kara Shinshutsu Jitsumu made: Zen 11 Sangyo Bunya (73 Gyokai) Shuroku ban*), Hakuto Shobo

Tadokoro, M. (ed.) (2015), Rising India and China: interactions and strategic significance, (Japanese title: *Taito suru Indo・Chugoku: Sogo Sayo to Sen-ryakuteki Igi*), Chikura Shobo

Tanaka, Y. (2019), Introduction to New India: An Approach from Life and Statistics, (Japanese title: *Shin Indo Nyumon: Seikatsu to Tokei karano Apurochi*), Hakusuisha

Umeda, K. (2021), New Allies Who Share a "Sense of Caution about China": Japan's Crisis as Seen by Knowing Vietnam, (Japanese title: *Betonamu wo shireba miete kuru Nihon no Kiki: Taichu Keikaikan wo kyoyu suru Shindomeikoku*), Shogakukan

Yamada, M. and Karikomi, S. (eds.) (2020), Asian Dynamism and the Economic Development of Vietnam, (Japanese title: *Ajia Dainamizumu to Betonamu no Keizai Hatten*), Bunshindo

Yasuda, S. (2009), Innovation and Foreign High-level Human Resources in Japanese Companies, (Japanese title: *Nihonkigyo no Inobeshon to Gaikokujin Kodojinzai*), Doi, N. (ed.), Business Innovation System: Competence, Organization and Competition, (Japanese title: *Bijinesu Inobeshon Shisutemu: Noryoku Soshiki Kyoso*), Nippon Hyoronsha

Part I

Part II

Part III

Part IV

Section 7
THE MIDDLE CLASS IN THE ASIA-PACIFIC

KARAVASILEV, Yani

1. The Asian century

The 21st century has famously been dubbed the Asian Century. This refers to the rising dominance of Asia in the world economy, which parallels that of the British Empire in the 19th century and that of the United States in the 20th. Asia's share of global GDP was less than 20% in the 1980s, but it is projected to reach 52% in 2050 in nominal terms. In purchasing parity terms, the share is ever higher. One of the most notable consequences of this unprecedented growth has been the rise of the Asian middle class, which is expected to drive economic growth and shape the future of consumption and politics in the region.

An increasing number of influential institutions have been publishing reports about Asia's emerging middle class. For instance, the Brookings Institution, a major think tank, estimates that two billion Asians were already members of the middle class in 2020. This represents 54% of the global middle class, and the share is projected to reach 65% by 2030 (Kharas, 2017). According to Credit Suisse (2015), a major bank, China has already overtaken the United States as the country with the largest middle class. The Asian Development Bank (2012) estimates that by 2050 three billion Asians are likely to enjoy living standards similar to those in Europe today (56.6% of the estimated 5.3 billion total inhabitants of Asia in 2050). McKinsey & Co., a major consulting firm, predicts that the consumer spending in Shanghai or Beijing will soon exceed that in economic hubs like New York, Tokyo, or London (Tonby, 2021).

The middle class is often dubbed the backbone of the economy. Numerous studies have empirically shown that a large middle class contributes to economic growth through several channels, including increased consumption, political and social stability, and human capital accumulation. For that reason, the rise of the Asian middle class spells great opportunities for businesses eager to expand into Asian markets. In consideration of this, the purpose of this article is to elucidate how large the Asian middle class is in reality, and to assess how far countries in the Asia-Pacific have moved toward becoming middle-class societies as seen from the perspective of developed countries. Below, the status quo of the Asian middle class is analyzed from three perspectives: (1) income and wealth, (2) education and occupational status, and (3) societal values and cultural capital.

2. The income perspective

Scholars working in different disciplines use different definitions of middle class. Economists largely rely on definitions related to wealth or income, sociologists typically emphasize occupational status and education, and philosophers and anthropologists tend to focus on culture and values. Below, we summarize these three major ways of defining the middle class and we use various data to estimate its size in the countries of the Asia-Pacific.

First, we estimate the size of the middle class using the method favored by economists. Economists rely on income measures partly for convenience, since data on income are widely available, and partly because income tends to be highly correlated with the other trappings of social class, such as economic security, education levels, and consumer preferences. Income-based definitions tend to rely on three basic approaches. Here we refer to them as the absolute income approach, the relative income approach, and the mixed approach.

(1) The absolute income approach

The absolute income approach is based on a fixed range of purchasing power. Many economists have defined the global middle class as households with incomes between $11 and $110 in 2011 purchasing power parity (PPP) dollars. The report by the Brookings Institution quoted above, which estimates that two billion Asians are members of the middle class as of 2020, relies on this approach.

Combining data on income distribution from the World Income Inequality Database (WIID) with the latest available GDP per person data by the IMF, we calculated the income of each percentile of the population in countries in the Asia-Pacific in the years 2000 and 2020. We then calculated what percentage of the population lived on less than $11, on an income between $11 and $110, and on more than $110 in 2011 PPP terms. The results are presented in Figure 1-7-1.

This approach paints a very optimistic picture of the status quo of middle classes in Asia. The results imply that the middle class represents around 90% of Thailand's and Mongolia's population, over 80% of China's, Indonesia's and Vietnam's population, and close to half of India's. Using this approach, one would conclude that over half of Asia's 4.5 billion strong population belongs to the middle class as of 2020, in line with the estimates published by the Brookings Institution.

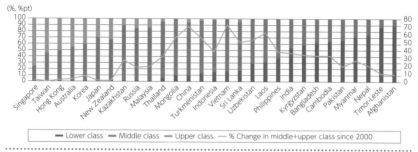

Figure 1-7-1   The size of the middle class in 2020 defined as people living on $11-110 per day in 2011 PPP dollars

Note: Author's calculation based on data by the IMF and World Income Inequality Database.

Curiously, even in fragile and conflict-ridden low-income countries, such as Myanmar, the middle class represents about 30% of the population. Many scholars would agree such a figure is unrealistically high. The likely reason for such inflated figures is that the $11 per person per day threshold is too low to be considered a lower limit of middle-class income. In fact, $11 a day is not far above the extreme poverty line used by the World Bank.[1] It is very similar to the ethical extreme poverty line of $7.40 per day proposed by Prof. Peter Edwards of the University of Newcastle, and it is less than the average poverty line of high-income countries. The practice of placing a person who is barely above the extreme poverty line into the global middle class category is a questionable technique.

Comparing 2000 and 2020, the largest increase in the share of non-poor people (middle class and rich) since 2000 is seen in Vietnam (72 percentage points) and China (70 percentage points). Unsurprisingly, middle-income countries boast the largest increases in middle-class populations, as high-income countries like Japan and Korea already have large middle classes and further growth is unlikely, whereas average incomes in low-income countries are still too far away from the middle-class lower income threshold. Although the income growth in those two countries is both undeniable and unprecedented, a growth of over 70 percentage points in 20 years seems a tad exaggerated. It is hard to imagine that a poor country could become a fully established middle-class society in less than a generation, let alone two decades. Indeed, the relative income

---

1) $1.90 in 2011 PPP dollars, or $2.15 per day in 2017 PPP dollars, which is derived as the median of the national poverty lines of 28 of the world's poorest countries. This poverty line, however, has been widely criticized as being too low, being closer to reflecting biological starvation rather than any reasonable level of poverty.

approach, discussed next, suggests that the size of the Asian middle class might in reality be much smaller.

(2) The relative income approach

In contrast to the absolute income approach, the relative income approach tries to estimate the income range of middle classes as a certain distance from a country's median income. In one of the most widely cited definitions, the Pew Research Center defines the middle class as all households with incomes between 75% and 200% of the national median.

It is noteworthy that under the median income approach, even if the total national income does not change, the size of the middle class can change if the income distribution within the country changes. For example, if the pace at which income inequality increases in a country exceeds the pace of economic growth in that country, the size of the middle class will shrink.

Although this approach is useful for tracking how the size of a country's middle class changes over time, it does not allow for country-to-country comparisons because median national income and poverty lines vary widely from country to country. In order to solve this problem, we calculate the size of the middle class in Asian countries based on the median national income in the U.S.

The median annual household income in the U.S. in 2020 was $67,521. Divided by the average household size (2.53 persons), we obtain an amount of $26,688 per person. The lower limit of middle-class income is 75% of this amount, or $20,016. In terms of 2011 PPP dollars, the amount is $16,737 or $45 per day, which is four times as much as the absolute income approach threshold of $11 and is intuitively more realistic. On the other hand, the upper limit of middle-class income per person per day is $122, which is higher but similar to the figure used by the Brookings Institution ($110). Based on the $45 and $122 thresholds, we calculated the size of the rich, middle class and poor in Asian countries. The results are shown in Figure 1-7-2.

A comparison of Figure 1-7-1 and Figure 1-7-2 reveals that the results of the relative approach are significantly different from those obtained by the absolute approach. For example, the absolute approach suggests that the size of the middle class is 84% of China's population, while the figure is only 30% under the relative approach by U.S. standards. In the case of India, the difference is even larger: the middle class is only 5% of the population by U.S. standards, while it is nearly 50% if the absolute income approach is used.

Based on the relative approach, the largest increase in the share of the non-poor over the past 20 years is not in China, as suggested by the absolute income approach, but rather in Russia and Kazakhstan (about 40 percentage

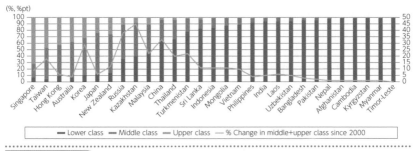

Figure 1-7-2   The size of the middle class defined as people living on 75%-200% of the U.S. median income in purchasing power parity

Note: Author's calculation based on data by the IMF and World Income Inequality Database.

points). Forty percentage points is a more realistic increase than the 70 percentage-point increase in China suggested by the absolute income approach. These considerations imply that the relative income approach might be a more realistic measure.

(3) The mixed approach

The absolute and relative income approaches can also be combined. For example, the U.S. federal poverty line is set as an absolute amount. Middle class income could then be defined in a relative way as a multiple of that amount. For instance, Haskins and Sawhill (2009) set the lower limit of middle-class income at 300% of the U.S. federal poverty line and the upper limit at 1000% of the poverty line.

According to the U.S. Department of Health and Human Services, the U.S. federal poverty line for an average family (2.53 persons) in 2020 was $19,614, or $7,753 per person. Three hundred percent of this amount is $23,258, or $19,445 in 2011 PPP dollars. This is equivalent to $53 per day, which is higher than the amount obtained using the relative approach ($45). The upper income limit for the middle class is $64,826 in 2011 PPP dollars. This is equivalent to $178 per person per day, which is considerably higher than the upper limit of the other two approaches. The lower and upper limits of middle class income based on the three approaches are summarized in Table 1-7-1.

Using the $53 and $178 thresholds, we calculated the size of the middle class in countries in the Asia-Pacific, as shown in Figure 1-7-3.

The results are very similar to the ones obtained using the relative income approach (Figure 1-7-2). Both approaches imply that more than half of the population in Taiwan, Australia, Singapore, Japan, Hong Kong, New Zealand, Korea, Russia, Kazakhstan and Malaysia are middle class or higher. Since the majority

Table 1-7-1	Lower and upper limits of middle-class income according to each approach	
	Lower threshhold of middle-class income	Upper threshold of middle-class income
Absolute income approach (Brookings Institution)	$11	$110
Relative income approach (U.S. median income)	$45	$122
Mixed approach (U.S. federal poverty line)	$53	$178

Note: Amounts are per person per day in 2011 PPP dollars

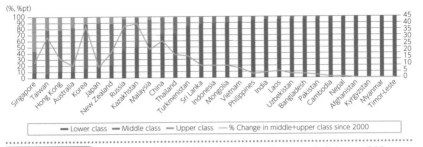

Figure 1-7-3   The size of the middle class defined as people living on 300-1000% of the U.S. federal poverty line in purchasing power parity

Note: Author's calculation based on data by the IMF and World Income Inequality Database.

of the people in those countries fall into the middle class even by U.S. standards, they can effectively be considered middle-class societies.

The rest of the countries, however, cannot yet be considered middle class societies by U.S. standards, including China and Thailand, which do have sizeable middle classes. Using the absolute income approach, middle-income countries like China, Thailand, Indonesia, Sri Lanka, Mongolia, Vietnam, the Philippines, and Laos would be categorized as middle-class societies, but the other two approaches largely refute that categorization.

In terms of the size of the middle class in the Asia-Pacific region as a whole, the absolute approach suggests a middle class of 2.8 billion people (2.6 billion if the former Soviet Union is excluded). In contrast, the relative approach based on the U.S. median national income suggests the figure is 850 million (750 million excluding the former Soviet Union), and the mixed approach based on the U.S. poverty line yields an even lower 800 million.

This result suggests that many existing reports may have overestimated both the size and the purchasing power of the Asian middle class. The findings of a recent study by Bonnet and Kolev (2021), who comprehensively analyzed the status quo of middle classes in Cambodia, China, Indonesia, Thailand, Pakistan, and Vietnam, confirm this finding. Bonnet and Kolev found that by measures such as number of children, level of education and incidence of informal employment, middle classes in all six countries are considerably closer to poor and near-poor households than to affluent ones.

(4) Other approaches

Some economists use wealth (assets) rather than income to define the middle class. For example, according to Credit Suisse, a major bank, a definition based on assets is more stable and less affected by sudden economic fluctuations than a definition based on income. Credit Suisse defines the middle class as adults with a net worth between $50,000 and $500,000 (in purchasing power parity). Based on this definition, Credit Suisse reported that in 2015 China surpassed the U.S. as the country with the largest middle class. China's middle class was estimated at 109 million people, and the U.S. middle class at 92 million. Although it is not clear whether this is the number of adults or the total population (i.e., adults and children), it is unrealistic that such a low percentage of the population of both countries are middle class (less than 15% of Chinese people and 30% of Americans). The relative income approach described above yields intuitively more realistic results—according to that approach the middle class represents more than 50% of the U.S. population (21% rich, 29% poor), and about 30% in China (5% rich, 65% poor).

It is possible that Credit Suisse's lower limit of net worth for the middle class is too high. However, even if that is not the case, a definition based on net worth is problematic for several reasons. First of all, data on assets are not readily available. Second, real estate is a large (if not the largest) portion of most people's assets, and its value is easily distorted by housing bubbles. For example, in cities like London and Hong Kong, where demand for housing is high and supply is short, many people are classified as wealthy simply by virtue of owning real estate that would be considered sub-middle-class by U.S. standards.

Another issue is the difference between total (gross) assets and net worth. Credit Suisse uses the latter. For example, a person with a relatively high income and a mortgage might not be considered middle-class under the asset-based approach because of their low net worth (assets minus liabilities). Such misclassification may also reflect cultural differences. Some studies have shown that U.S. citizens are much more likely to use credit and mortgages and significantly less likely to save than their Asian counterparts. Thus, a person with the same standard of living may be classified as middle class in Asia, but as poor in the

U.S. under the asset-based approach. In addition to real estate bubbles, crypto-currency bubbles cause similar distortions. For these reasons, this article uses an income-based approach rather than an asset-based approach.

3. The occupation-education perspective

Many sociologists see class as being about more than money. From a sociological perspective, status is defined not just by cash, but by particular credentials, especially in terms of occupation and education. Occupational definitions of middle class are especially popular among European scholars.

The intuition behind this kind of definition is that occupations and education are much more socially visible than income. Arguably, most people tend to assign a higher social rank to a museum curator with a PhD in fine art than a plumber with a certificate from a vocational school, even if the latter has a higher income. Whereas it is commonplace to open a conversation with "What do you do for a living?", asking "What is your salary?" is usually considered taboo. Similarly, nowadays, many résumés can be viewed online but few paychecks can be.

The problem with occupation-based definitions, however, is that occupation covers individuals, while social class generally covers families and households. For example, what if a husband and wife have occupations with different statuses? In sociology, it is often assumed that the "economically dominant" occupation determines the social class of the entire household. For example, if one spouse is a professor (i.e., middle-class) and the other is a firefighter (i.e., working-class), the household as a whole is defined as middle-class rather than working-class.

Since this might be problematic with regard to overestimating the size of the middle class, we prefer to look at education on an individual level as a proxy for occupation, since occupational and educational credentials tend to go hand in hand. Entry into occupations of a middle-class status depends on acquiring certain skills or qualifications. Most often, possession of a four-year college degree is used as a threshold for inclusion in the middle class.

Given the strong correlation between income and education, the size of the middle class defined on the basis of education should be similar to the size of the middle class as defined on the basis of income. Figure 1-7-4 shows the relationship between the ranking of the percentage of the population in the non-poor group (middle class and higher based on the mixed income approach) and the ranking of the percentage of the population who have attended an institution of higher education (the gross tertiary enrollment rate based on UNESCO data).

Part I

Part II

Part III

Part IV

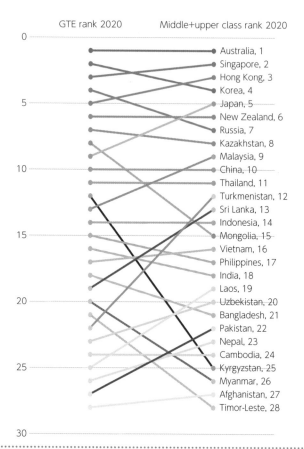

Note: Author's calculation based on data by the IMF, WIID and UNESCO.

Figure 1-7-4 Countries ranked by the Gross Tertiary Enrollment Rate (left) and by the size of the middle+upper class based on the mixed approach (right)

Juxtaposing the two rankings, it can be confirmed that they are quite similar—the difference between most countries' ranks in the two rankings is within three ranks. Some countries do show a difference of four or more ranks. In Japan, Malaysia, Turkmenistan, Sri Lanka, Laos, and Pakistan (blue-nuanced lines in Figure 1-7-4), the percentage of people who go on to university is low relative to the estimated size of the middle class using the income approach. In other words, in these countries, the size of the middle class as defined by education may be somewhat smaller than the size of the middle class as defined by income. On the other hand, in Mongolia, Kyrgyzstan, Myanmar, and Timor-Leste (red-nuanced lines in Figure 1-7-4), it is the opposite. In other words, in these countries, the size of the middle class as defined by education may be somewhat larger than the size of the middle class as defined by income.

4. The culture-values perspective

Finally, in philosophy and anthropology the middle class is seen as a cultural phenomenon. The middle class is defined through its values, cultural capital, lifestyle and aspirations. This opinion is also shared by many politicians. For example, according to a 2010 Commerce Department report prepared for then Vice President Biden's Middle Class Task Force, "middle class families are defined by their aspirations more than their income".

People's aspirations and lifestyles are often rooted in the values and culture of a society. Values and culture are very abstract and difficult to assess, but a large-scale project called "the World Values Survey" aims to do this. The World Values Survey is a comprehensive survey of attitudes toward democracy, tolerance of foreigners and minorities, gender equality, the role of religion and changing levels of religiosity, globalization, environment, work, family,politics and national identity. The first survey was conducted in 1981, and since then it has been conducted every few years in more than 100 countries. The survey data are frequently used not only by international organizations such as the World Bank and the United Nations, but also by politicians and scholars around the world.

Based on the responses to the World Values Survey items, the project leaders, Prof. Ingelhart and Prof. Welzel, have created a so-called "World Cultural Map" using factor analysis. This cultural map has two dimensions (horizontal and vertical axes) and it shows the prevalent values in each country. Figure 1-7-5 shows the location of Asian countries on the World Cultural Map.

Moving upward along the vertical axis indicates a shift from values emphasizing tradition and religion to values emphasizing secularity and rationality. Moving rightward along the horizontal axis shows a shift from survival and group-oriented values to self-expression and individual-oriented values. A somewhat simplified analysis is that following an increase in standards of living, and a transit via industrialization towards a middle-class post-industrial society, a country tends to move diagonally in the direction from the lower-left corner to the upper-right corner, indicating a transit in both dimensions.

Since the position of each country represents the average set of values of the whole nation, it can be thought to reflect the proportion of the middle class within that nation. However, middle classes in all countries do not necessarily have the same values. Middle-class values tend to be highly correlated with the philosophical, political, and religious ideas that are dominant in the country.

Part I

Part II

Part III

Part IV

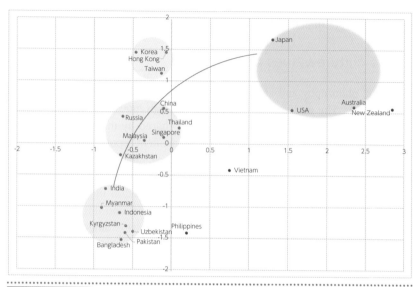

Figure 1-7-5   The location of countries in the Asia-Pacific on the Inglehart-Welzel World Cultural Map

Note: Based on the World Values Survey (2022).

For example, materialism, which represents values emphasizing secularity and rationality (upper part of the vertical axis), was formulated by philosophers and leftists of the French Revolution, and is often observed in countries with a long history of social democracy and socialist policies, as well as in countries with high rates of university attendance. On the other hand, survival and group-oriented values (left side of the horizontal axis) are characteristic of Asian countries, especially ones where Confucianism was prevalent, while self-expression and individual-oriented values (right side of the horizontal axis) are often observed in Western countries. This might mean that when the countries that were under the influence of Confucianism mature into middle-class societies, they move upward only, rather than diagonally from the bottom left to the top right.

Figure 1-7-5 shows that Asian countries are clearly concentrated in four clusters. Although interpretation is subjective, the upper right cluster consists of Japan, Australia, and New Zealand, which can be considered as established middle-class societies with values similar to those of Western developed countries. As symbolized by the expression "100 million middle class" that became popular in Japan in the 1960s, these countries are considered to be mature middle-class societies with the majority of the population having been middle-class for more than half a century. The lower left cluster consists of countries where the size of the middle class is small and middle-class values have not yet become an important socio-cultural factor.

In between these two clusters are two other clusters located relatively close to each other. They can be described as a middle-income cluster (China, Thailand, Malaysia, Kazakhstan, and Russia) and a high-income cluster (Korea, Taiwan, and Hong Kong). The former cluster consists of countries with sizable middle classes (one-fourth to one-half of the population using the strictest definition), and are transitioning toward becoming majority middle-class societies. On the other hand, the latter cluster (Korea, Taiwan, and Hong Kong) can be considered full-fledged middle-class societies as seen from the lens of education and income. However, since they have only recently become middle-class societies, the values typical of Western middle-class societies appear to have not yet taken deep roots there. These countries have experienced remarkable economic development since the late 1980s, and it seems that the general public does not yet take for granted the security of survival and the freedom of expression typical of Western democracies. Nevertheless, all three countries have been under the influence of Confucianism, which suggests that the process of these countries' maturing into middle-class societies may be reflected in moving upward only, rather than diagonally from the bottom left to the top right. Finally, the Philippines and Vietnam present an interesting case, as they seem to be strongly influenced by Western culture and have more self-expressive and individual-oriented values than other Asian countries in the same income bracket.

5. Conclusion

This article examined the size of middle classes in Asian countries from three perspectives: income, education-occupation, and culture and values. The analysis suggests that the size of the Asian middle class has increased significantly over the past two decades. Even by the strictest definition based on U.S. standards, its size is estimated to be at least 800 million people, which corresponds to one-fifth of the population of the Asia-Pacific region. Nevertheless, as a share of the entire population, Asia's middle class is still quite small and not as large as widely reported in the media. In particular, China, India, and other large emerging economies in Asia cannot be considered middle-class societies by developed country standards, and the emerging middle class has yet to become a major driver of socioeconomic trends in those countries. What the "Asian Century" will look like remains to be seen.

References

Assistant Secretary for Planning and Evaluation (2022) U.S. Federal Poverty Guidelines. U.S. Department of Health and Human Services.

Biden, J. (2010) "Annual report of the White House Task Force on the Middle Class". Vice President of the United States, Obama Administration, White House. https://obamawhitehouse.archives.gov/sites/default/files/micro-sites/100226-annual-report-middle-class.pdf.

Bonnet, A. and A. Kolev (2021), "The middle class in Emerging Asia: Champions for more inclusive societies?", OECD Development Centre Working Papers, No. 347, OECD Publishing, Paris, https://doi.org/10.1787/93af380b-en.

Credit Suisse (2015) "Global middle class net worth doubled since 2000 to USD 80.7 trillion, 32% of global wealth". Media Release. Zurich, Switzerland.

Haskins, R., & Sawhill, I. (2009). Creating an Opportunity Society. Brookings Institution Press.

International Monetary Fund (2022) World Economic Outlook, April 2022.

Kharas, H. (2017) "The unprecedented expansion of the global middle class". Global Economy & Development Working Paper 100, Brookings Institution, Washington, D.C., US.

Kochhar, R. (2021)"The Pandemic Stalls Growth in the Global Middle Class, Pushes Poverty Up Sharply", Pew Research Center.

Reeves, R. V., K. Guyot, & E. Krause (2018) "Defining the middle class: Cash, credentials, or culture?". Brookings Institution, Washington, D.C., US.

Tonby, O., R. Razdan, J. Woetzel, J. Seong, W. Choi, S. Smit, N. Yamakawa, & T. Devesa (2021) "Beyond income: Redrawing Asia's consumer map". McKinsey Global Institute Discussion Paper.

UNESCO Institute for Statistics (2021) School enrollment, tertiary (% gross). http://uis.unesco.org/.

UNU-WIDER, World Income Inequality Database (WIID). Version 31 May 2021. https://doi.org/10.35188/UNU-WIDER/WIID-310521.

World Values Survey Association (2022) The Inglehart-Welzel World Cultural Map - World Values Survey 7(2020) [Provisional version]. Source: http://www.worldvaluessurvey.org/

Part II

KANSAI'S ROLE AND FUTURE CHALLENGES UNDER THE COVID-19 PANDEMIC

INADA, Yoshihisa; NOMURA, Ryosuke

In Part II, we shift our focus from the world and the Asia-Pacific to the Kansai region. Our analysis is conducted from various angles, but its underlying theme can be summarized as "Kansai's role and future challenges seen through the lens of the COVID-19 Pandemic". Below is a summary of Chapters 2,3 and 4, which comprise Part II.

Chapter 2

Chapter 2 presents a macroeconomic analysis of the economies of Japan and Kansai, including both retrospective analyses and forecasts. The first half of the chapter presents a retrospective analysis of the economies of Japan and Kansai in FY2021 and the first half of FY2022. The second half presents the economic outlook for FY 2022 through FY 2024.

In Section 1, we analyze the Japanese economy, which has been alternating between negative and positive growth from the beginning of FY 2021 to the middle of FY 2022, and whose momentum of recovery has been weaker than that of other major economies. Our latest forecasts for the Japanese economy in FY 2022-24 presented here (+1.5% for FY 2022, +1.1% for FY 2023, and +1.4% for FY 2024) incorporate the second advance GDP estimate of GDP for 2022 Q3 as well as our new assumptions about exogenous variables. If no new constraints are imposed on economic activities during the forecast period, accumulated forced savings will be unleashed in the second half of FY 2022, and an ensuing recovery led by private final consumption expenditure, mainly through increased spending on services, can be expected in the second half of FY 2023. The contribution of private demand is expected to decelerate in FY 2023, and so will the overall growth rate. Real GDP is not expected to exceed the pre-pandemic peak until the 2024 Q1 or later.

In Section 2, we analyze the Kansai economy, which recovered somewhat from FY 2020 but continued to be lackluster in FY 2021 due to the increasing number of COVID-19 infections and new downward pressures, such as the shortage of semiconductors and the sharp rise in raw material prices. The current situation can be summarized by sector as follows. (1) The household sector recovered from the decline in the previous year, but growth was sluggish due to the resurgence of COVID-19 and the resulting two states of emergency. (2) The recovery in incomes and employment has also been sluggish. (3) Although the corporate sector has generally recovered from the sharp deterioration in the previous year, both the manufacturing and non-manufacturing sectors are under strong downward pressure due to various risk factors. (4) In the external sector, the exports of goods to China, Europe and the U.S. all recovered, and the exports of services finally began to show signs of recovery as economic activity normalized. Imports increased substantially, partly due to the sharp rise in energy prices. (5) The public sector (public works), has outperformed the nation as a whole. Reflecting the dynamics of each economic indicator, the real GRP growth rate for Kansai is forecast to be +1.5% in FY 2022, +1.2% in FY 2023 and +1.5% in FY 2024. Our analysis features a discussion of the impact of China's zero-COVID policy on the Kansai economy.

In Section 3, we analyze the income distribution in the Kansai region. In Kansai, the number of low-income groups was increasing and the middle-class was shrinking even before the pandemic. In view of this trend, the section analyzes the impact of the worsening economic conditions caused by the COVID-19 pandemic on incomes, focusing on the middle class.

Finally, in Column 2-A, we analyze the direct and indirect effects and risks facing the economies of Japan and Kansai from the perspective of international trade. The possibility of an economic slowdown in the EU is increasing due to economic sanctions against Russia as well as Russia's retaliation for energy-related goods. A deceleration in the EU economy will exert downward pressure on the economy of China through the channel of international trade. Since China and Japan have deep trade relations, with Kansai being particularly dependent on trade with China, there is a risk of economic slowdown in Kansai due to a slowdown in exports to China.

Chapter 3

In Chapter 3, we analyze the main issues of the Kansai economy in the wake of the COVID-19 pandemic.

Section 1 discusses the issue of population decline in the Kansai region. Specifically, we analyze the demographic and population movement dynamics using data from the 2020 National Population Census. It is predicted that the population of Kansai will decrease at a faster pace than that of the rest of Japan, and it will be an urgent task for each local government to take measures to cope with this situation.

Column 3-A summarizes the impact of the COVID-19 pandemic on local government finances. Although prefectures play a major role in the measures taken to deal with the pandemic, there are large disparities among regions arising from differences in the financial strength of local governments. There should be a debate on what kind of local fiscal infrastructure in order to achieve higher levels of decentralization and to improve the capability of taking timely economic measures in times of crisis.

Section 2 discusses the state of digital transformation (DX) in Kansai and Osaka. We analyze what kind of change is required in the "human process" associated with DX in order to (1) build long-term relationships with customers, and (2) build structures that can create new value. We conclude that in order to be able to use digital technology in line with the "human process," the "process of things" has to be innovated in a way such that these two processes can advance one another toward achieving the optimal combination of things and people.

In Section 3, we review the dynamics of tourism in the Kansai region in FY 2021, and we analyze the measures for attracting tourists taken by Destination Management/Marketing Organizations (DMOs) in the prefectures of Kyoto, Wakayama, and Nara. The DMOs in the three prefectures had steadily developed tourism promotion strategies and achieved certain results before the pandemic, but the spread of COVID-19 infections forced them to make major changes in their tourism strategies.

In Column 3-B, following the discussion in Section 3, we focus on brand power, which is important in the development of tourism regions. We pay particular attention to place branding efforts in Kansai.

Chapter 4

In Chapter 4, we analyze economic ripple effects of Expo 2025 Osaka-Kansai using a newly developed inter-regional inter-industry input-output table for the Kansai region.

Section 1 discusses the possibility to leverage Expo 2025 and integrated resorts (IR) in order to put the Kansai economy on a trajectory of positive growth. We show that the cause of the long-term stagnation of the Kansai economy is a lack of investment. We estimate that an additional investment of about 1 trillion yen would boost the economic growth rate of the Kansai region by about 0.54 percentage points. The key issue to be addressed in the future is how to attract sustained investment from both domestic and foreign sources.

Section 2 outlines the current state of infrastructure development in the lead-up to the Osaka-Kansai Expo 2025. We explain the economic effects of infrastructure development as an introduction to the analysis in Section 3. The infrastructure development in the Kansai region is lagging behind that of other regions in terms of efficiency. The future of the Kansai economy depends on the implementation of the "Osaka-Kansai Expo Infrastructure Development Plan".

In Section 3, we estimate the economic ripple effects of the Expo based on the new inter-regional inter-industry input-output table for the Kansai region developed by APIR, and on our new assumptions about final demand. In addition, we introduce the concept of a 'Greater Expo', which refers to expanding the Expo in terms of theme, time, space, and other aspects, in a way that the entire Kansai region can function as a pavilion. We estimate the economic impact of a potential 'Greater Expo' and we compare it with the impact of the conventional Expo.

Finally, Column 4-A discusses the methodology of how the Kansai region as a whole can make the most of the opportunities presented by the Expo. Using insights from the case of the Edinburgh International Festival, the concept of a 'Greater Expo' is discussed. We hope that the formulation of this concept will contribute to spreading the attractiveness of the Expo to other places throughout the Kansai region, thereby generating positive spillover effects.

INTRODUCTION

INADA, Yoshihisa

The COVID-19 pandemic alerted the world to the risks associated with the rapid advance of globalization and prompted various responses. These responses culminated when Russia invaded Ukraine on February 24, 2022. In response to the invasion, the NATO countries and Japan imposed economic sanctions on Russia. Russia retaliated, and as the situation in Ukraine deteriorated further, resource and grain prices soared, exerting upward pressure on inflation. It is feared that the impact of soaring oil prices on businesses and households might be comparable to that of previous oil shocks. The U.S. has shifted to a tight monetary policy to prevent the acceleration of inflation, while Japan has maintained an accommodative monetary policy. The divergence in these policies has resulted in a significant depreciation of the yen and an appreciation of the U.S. dollar. In consideration of these trends, the major risks to the Japanese economy are (1) China's zero-COVID policy, (2) the soaring natural resource prices, and (3) the yen's ongoing depreciation. These risks are discussed in more detail in Chapter 1 of Part I and Chapter 2 of Part II.

According to the IMF's World Economic Outlook (WEO) released in October 2022, global economic growth is projected to decelerate significantly from +6.0% in 2021 to +3.2% in 2022, and further to +2.7% in 2023. In addition to the impact of Russia's invasion of Ukraine, the significant slowdown in the global economy in 2022 was caused by the negative growth of the U.S. economy in the first half of 2022, the negative growth forecast for the EU economy in the second half of the year, and the impact of the lockdowns in China as part of the country's zero-COVID policy. The IMF predicts that the Russian economy will shrink by -3.4% in 2022 (+2.6 percentage points up from the previous forecast). The economies of China and EU are both projected to expand by +3.2%, the U.S. economy by +1.6%, and Japan's economy by +1.7%.

The impact of Russia's invasion of Ukraine manifested itself in the form of inflation, trade stagnation, and higher interest rates through the channels of commodity markets, trade, and financial markets. We pay particular attention to trade relations. Table 2-0-1 shows the economic size and trade dependence (import/export ratios) of the countries and regions involved, in descending order of nominal GDP (share of world GDP) for each country in 2021: US (23.9%), China (18.1%), EU (17.8%), Japan (5.1%), Russia (1.8%). The table also shows each country/region's trade dependence, i.e. exports and imports as a share of each country/region's GDP.

In the U.S., the export ratio is low and the import ratio is high, while in

98

Table 2-0-1 Economic Scale and Trade Dependence of Countries and Regions: 2021 (Unit: billion dollars, %)

Country	NominalGDP	Share:%	Export share	Import share
US	22,997.5	23.9	7.6	12.8
China	17,458.0	18.1	19.3	15.3
EU	17,094.2	17.8	15.1	14.6
Japan	4,937.4	5.1	15.3	15.6
Russia	1,775.5	1.8	22.9	12.7
World	96,292.6	100.0		

Source: Nominal GDP data by IMF. Trade data by UN Comtrade.

China and Russia, the export ratio is much higher than the import ratio. China's exports of many manufacturing products and Russia's exports of energy-related products exceed their respective imports, indicating that they generate trade surpluses. On the other hand, Japan and the EU have well-balanced export and import ratios.

Next, Table 2-0-2 is a trade matrix showing the exports and imports of each country/region by trading partner. Looking at the share of imports from Russia, it can be seen that the United States (1.0%) and Japan (1.8%) depend little on Russia for imports. On the other hand, China (2.9%) and the EU (6.8%) depend on Russian imports more.

The share of imports from the EU is as follows: Russia (39.8%), the U.S. (17.1%), China (11.5%), and Japan (11.1%). This suggests that Russia and the EU are highly dependent on each other, and once a crisis occurs, this high dependence can turn into a risk.

Looking at the share of imports from China, Russia (29.9%), Japan (24.0%), the EU (22.3%), and the US (18.5%) are all highly dependent on Chinese imports.

Finally, the share of imports from the U.S. is as follows: EU (10.9%), Japan (10.7%), China (6.7%), and Russia (2.8%).

To visualize the direct and indirect impact of Russia's invasion of Ukraine, Table 2-0-1 and Table 2-0-2 were used to create Figure 2-0-1. Below is a sample interpretation of the trade relations visualized in Figure 2-0-1.

Russia's economy is about one-tenth the size of the EU's. 4.1% of total EU exports ($2,575.6 billion) go to Russia while 6.8% of total EU imports ($2,494.2 billion) come from Russia.

The economies of the EU and China are about the same size. China's exports to the EU account for 15.1% of its total exports ($3,299.1 billion), and its imports from the EU account for 11.5% of its total imports ($2,684.4 billion), both high shares.

Japan's economy is about 30% the size of China's. Japan's exports to China

Table 2-0-2	Trade Share by Country/Region: 2021 (Unit: %)

■Import Share

	US	China	EU	Japan	Russia	Other regions	World
US		18.5	17.1	4.8	1.0	58.6	100.0
China	6.7		11.5	7.7	2.9	71.1	100.0
EU	10.9	22.3		2.9	6.8	57.0	100.0
Japan	10.7	24.0	11.1		1.8	52.3	100.0
Russia	2.8	29.9	39.8	3.5		23.9	100.0

■Export Share

	US	China	EU	Japan	Russia	Other regions	World
US		8.6	15.5	4.3	0.4	71.2	100.0
China	17.4		15.1	5.0	2.0	60.5	100.0
EU	18.0	10.1		2.8	4.1	65.0	100.0
Japan	18.0	21.6	9.2		1.0	50.1	100.0
Russia	7.5	19.4	38.9	3.5		30.7	100.0

Source: Authors' calculations based on data by UN Comtrade and the Ministry of Finance of Japan.

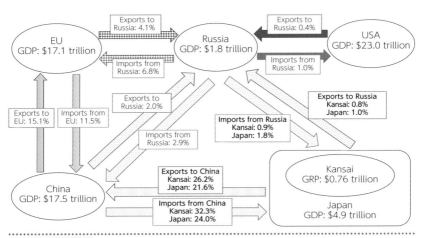

Figure 2-0-1	Economic Scale and Trade Dependency of Russia and Countries/Regions

account for 21.6% of its total exports ($757.1 billion), and its imports from China account for 24.0% of its total imports ($772.3 billion).

Kansai's exports to China comprise 26.2% of its total exports, while Kansai's imports from China account for 32.3% of its total imports, both shares being higher than those of Japan as a whole, indicating that the Kansai economy is highly dependent on the Chinese economy.

The economic sanctions against Russia by the NATO countries and Japan, and Russia's economic weaponization of energy-related goods have increased the possibility of an economic slowdown in the EU. As shown in Table 2-0-2 and Figure 2-0-1, trade relations between the EU and China are strong, and a slowdown in the EU economy will exert downward pressure on the Chinese economy through a slowdown in Chinese exports to the EU. Trade relations between China and Japan are even stronger, and the Kansai economy is particularly dependent on trade with China. Therefore, if the Chinese economy decelerates, a slowdown in exports to China will exert downward pressure on the Kansai economy. The recent decrease in exports to China due to China's zero-COVID policy is a further burden on the Kansai economy.

Japan's direct dependence on trade with Russia is low, so the direct impact of the escalation of the situation in Ukraine (through Japan-Russia trade) will be small, but the indirect impact of the high trade dependency between Russia, the EU, China, and Japan (Kansai) cannot be ignored. The indirect impact of Russia's invasion of Ukraine via the EU and China's economy is discussed in detail in Chapter 2 and Column 2A of Part II.

References

International Monetary Fund (2022 World Economic Outlook Countering the Cost-of-Living Crisis, October 2022, https://www.imf.org/en/ Publications/WEO/Issues/2022/10/11/worldeconomic-outlook-october-2022, last viewed on December 6, 2022)

Chapter 2

THE ECONOMIES OF JAPAN AND KANSAI: A RETROSPECTIVE AND OUTLOOK

Section 1
THE JAPANESE ECONOMY: RECENT DEVELOPMENTS AND SHORT-TERM FORECASTS

INADA, Yoshihisa; SHIMIDA, Mitsuru

Chapter 2 is structured as follows. In Sections 1 and 2, the first half provides a retrospective look at the economies of Japan and Kansai in FY 2021 and the first half of FY 2022, and the second half presents our forecasts for FY 2022-24. In Section 2, we also present our estimates GRPs for the six prefectures of the Kansai region in FY 2019-21, and compare their recoveries from the COVID-19 pandemic. In addition, we analyze the impact of China's zero-COVID policy on the Kansai economy. Section 3 sheds light on the decline of the middle class, which was exacerbated by the pandemic. Finally, in Column 2-A, we analyze the various risks to the Japanese and Kansai economies that have emerged from the Russian invasion of Ukraine from the perspective of trade relations.

1. Retrospective of the Japanese economy in FY 2021

(1) Stagnation of world trade in the second half of 2022 is inevitable

According to the CPB World Trade Monitor, world trade (in volume terms, 2010=100) increased slightly by +0.1% MoM in September 2022, marking the third consecutive monthly increase. As a result, Q3 saw a +1.2% QoQ increase, marking the third consecutive quarter of positive growth. Advanced economies accelerated their growth to +1.4% QoQ, while emerging economies barely grew at +0.9% QoQ (Figure 2-1-1). China's zero-COVID policy and rapid monetary tightening in China caused real GDP growth in China and the U.S. to fall into negative territory in Q2. In Q3 in major countries saw a recovery, but there is a strong possibility that the global economy will slow down from 2022 Q4 to the first half of 2023. This is because the U.S. and European economies have

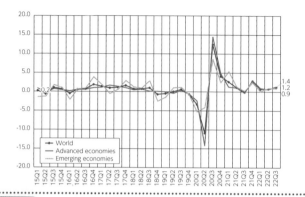

Figure 2-1-1   Change in World Trade Volume: 2010=100: QoQ: %.

Source: CPB World Trade Monitor, 21 October 2022

entered recession and the Chinese economy is expected to decelerate further. Therefore, a slowdown in global trade is inevitable in the second half of FY 2022.

Next, we discuss the outlook for export markets using a different statistic. According to the Cabinet Office, Japan's Q3 machinery orders (foreign demand) fell for the first time in two quarters, falling -16.5% QoQ. According to a survey conducted at the end of September, Q4 is expected to see a recovery for the first time in two quarters, +16.5% QoQ. However, if Q3 and Q4 are averaged out, the trend is flat. The global economy is expected to enter a recession in the second half of 2022 and the first half of 2023, and the capital goods export market is expected to enter an adjustment phase in the second half of 2022. According to the Global Semiconductor Market Statistics, global semiconductor sales (3-month moving average) in September were down for the second consecutive month, -3.0% YoY. By region, sales in Asia shrank -11.5% YoY, down for the second consecutive month (Figure 2-1-2). Considering this, demand for semiconductors is unlikely to pick up in the second half of 2022 or 2023.

(2) Current state of the Japanese economy
Second Advance Estimate of Q3 GDP

According to the second preliminary GDP report for July-September 2022 released on December 8, real GDP growth was -0.2% QoQ and -0.8% QoQ, somewhat upwardly revised from the first preliminary report (-0.3% QoQ and -1.2% QoQ). Due to the large downward revision in 2022 Q1, the clog in the 2022 growth rate fell 0.2 %pt (from +0.4% to +0.2%) from the first preliminary estimate. Thus, Q3 was the first time in two quarters that the economy has posted a negative growth rate, after four quarters of negative growth. The Japanese

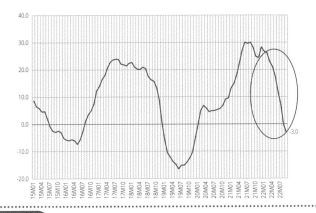

Figure 2-1-2   Global Semiconductor Sales: YoY Change: % (%)

Source: World Semiconductor Trade Statistics, September 2022

economy's real growth rate has alternated between positive and negative in FY 2021 and the first half of FY 2022, and the momentum of recovery has been weak compared to other major economies.

Looking at the contribution to real GDP growth (-0.2% QoQ) in Q3, domestic demand increased for the fourth consecutive quarter, +0.4%pt QoQ. Therein, private demand increased for the fourth consecutive quarter (+0.4%pt), and public demand increased for the second consecutive quarter (+0.0%pt). On the other hand, net exports declined for the first time in two quarters (-0.6%pt). The large negative contribution from net exports was due to a large increase in imports, which was in turn caused by a temporary spike in services imports.

The growth rate of gross domestic income (GDI), which reflects gains/losses from changes in the terms of trade (export price index/import price index) to GDP, was -0.9% for the seventh consecutive quarter, below the growth rate of real GDP. In FY 2021-22, the rapid deterioration in terms of trade caused income outflows for both households and firms (Table 2-1-1).

Trends in GDP components in Q3

Private final consumption expenditure increased for the second consecutive quarter, +0.1% QoQ. Despite a sharp increase in the number of COVID-19 infections in July-August, private consumption did not decline, partly because no restrictions on economic activities were imposed.

Within fixed capital formation, real private residential investment fell for the fifth consecutive quarter, -0.5% QoQ. Real private capital investment increased for the second consecutive quarter, +1.5% QoQ. Investment demand seems to

Part I

Part II

Part III

Part IV

Table 2-1-1   Real GDP and each demand item: QoQ: %, % points

	Annu-alized GDP	GDP	Domestic demand	Private demand	Private final consumption expenditure	Private residential investment	Private non-residential investment	Private inventory changes	Public demand	Government final consumption expenditure	Public investment	Public inventory changes	Net exports	Exports	Imports	GDI
			*	*				*	*				*	*		
19Q2	1.2	0.3	0.5	0.3	0.1	0.1	-0.1	0.2	0.2	0.1	0.1	0.0	-0.2	0.1	-0.3	0.1
19Q3	0.9	0.2	0.5	0.4	0.5	0.0	0.4	-0.5	0.2	0.2	0.0	0.0	-0.3	0.1	-0.4	0.3
19Q4	-10.4	-2.7	-2.9	-2.9	-1.8	-0.1	-1.2	0.2	0.1	0.1	0.0	0.0	0.1	-0.2	0.4	-2.7
20Q1	1.8	0.4	0.5	0.5	0.4	-0.2	0.7	-0.4	0.0	0.0	0.0	0.0	-0.1	-0.8	0.7	0.6
20Q2	-28.2	-8.0	-5.2	-5.4	-4.6	0.0	-1.2	0.4	0.2	0.0	0.2	0.0	-2.8	-2.9	0.1	-6.9
20Q3	24.2	5.6	2.8	2.2	2.9	-0.2	0.0	-0.5	0.5	0.5	0.0	0.0	2.8	1.5	1.3	5.4
20Q4	7.9	1.9	1.4	1.2	1.1	0.0	0.3	-0.2	0.2	0.2	0.1	0.0	0.5	1.5	-1.0	1.9
21Q1	-0.6	-0.1	-0.2	-0.2	-0.9	0.1	0.2	0.4	0.0	0.0	0.0	0.0	0.1	0.4	-0.3	-0.8
21Q2	1.3	0.3	0.5	0.2	0.1	0.1	0.2	-0.1	0.3	0.4	-0.1	0.0	-0.2	0.5	-0.7	-0.1
21Q3	-1.8	-0.5	-0.6	-0.7	-0.7	-0.1	-0.3	0.3	0.1	0.3	-0.2	0.0	0.1	-0.1	0.2	-1.2
21Q4	4.9	1.2	1.2	1.6	1.7	0.0	0.1	-0.2	-0.4	-0.2	-0.2	0.0	0.0	0.1	-0.1	0.5
22Q1	-1.8	-0.5	0.0	0.1	-0.6	-0.1	-0.1	0.8	-0.1	0.1	-0.2	0.0	-0.5	0.2	-0.7	-0.8
22Q2	4.5	1.1	1.0	0.8	0.9	-0.1	0.3	-0.3	0.2	0.2	0.0	0.0	0.1	0.3	-0.2	0.3
22Q3	-0.8	-0.2	0.4	0.4	0.1	0.0	0.2	0.1	0.0	0.0	0.0	0.0	-0.6	0.4	-1.0	-0.9

Note: Domestic demand, private demand, private inventory change, public demand and net exports are contributions. Others are year-on-year changes. * means contribution.
Source: National Accounts, Economic and Social Research Institute, Cabinet Office, Government of Japan, "Preliminary Quarterly GDP Report for July-September 2022 (2nd Preliminary Figures)

have reappeared. The contribution of changes in real private inventories to real GDP growth was +0.1 %pt QoQ, the first increase in two quarters.

Within public demand, real government final consumption expenditure increased for the third consecutive quarter, +0.1% QoQ. Real public fixed capital formation increased for the second consecutive quarter, up +0.9% QoQ.

Real exports of goods and services increased for the fourth consecutive quarter, up +2.1% QoQ. Therein, goods exports increased for the fourth consecutive quarter (+1.6% QoQ), while services exports increased for the second consecutive quarter (+4.6% QoQ). On the other hand, real imports of goods and services increased for the fourth consecutive quarter, +5.2% QoQ. Therein, goods imports increased for the fourth consecutive quarter, up +1.8% QoQ, while services imports increased for the first time in two quarters, up +18.6% QoQ.

Looking at deflators, the domestic demand deflator rose for the seventh consecutive quarter, +0.6% QoQ. In terms of external demand deflators, the export deflator for goods and services was +3.3% QoQ (up for the seventh consecutive quarter), while the import deflator was +6.5% QoQ (up for the seventh

Table 2-1-2	Adjustment process from the COVID-19 pandemic: Real GDP and each demand item: Peak=100

	GDP	Goods imports	Services imports	Private final consumption expenditure	Private invest-ment	Government spending	Goods exports	Services exports
19Q2	99.8	98.6	95.6	99.1	100.5	99.4	98.8	102.2
19Q3	100.0	100.0	100.0	100.0	100.0	100.0	100.0	100.0
19Q4	97.3	98.6	96.1	96.7	94.7	100.3	98.4	100.2
20Q1	97.7	93.9	94.8	97.4	95.3	100.3	95.7	88.3
20Q2	89.9	94.8	88.8	89.1	91.5	101.2	78.1	76.6
20Q3	95.0	87.2	84.9	94.0	88.5	103.1	88.8	73.2
20Q4	96.8	94.1	84.4	95.8	88.8	104.0	98.9	75.0
21Q1	96.6	96.1	85.5	94.2	92.3	103.8	100.9	78.3
21Q2	97.0	99.1	93.2	94.4	92.9	105.1	104.3	79.6
21Q3	96.5	98.4	90.5	93.2	92.9	105.5	103.8	80.1
21Q4	97.7	99.1	89.8	96.2	92.3	103.9	104.6	79.5
22Q1	97.2	103.0	92.1	95.2	95.3	103.7	106.8	77.2
22Q2	98.3	105.2	89.4	96.7	95.2	104.5	107.6	81.1
22Q3	98.1	107.1	106.0	96.8	96.7	104.6	109.3	84.9

Source: Authors' calculations based on National Accounts, Economic and Social Research Institute, Cabinet Office, Government of Japan, and "Preliminary Report on Quarterly GDP for July-September 2022 (2nd Preliminary Report)

consecutive quarter). As the latter exceeded the former, the terms of trade deteriorated for the seventh consecutive quarter. As a result, the GDP deflator fell for the second consecutive quarter to -0.5% QoQ. Thus, nominal GDP growth in Q3 was -0.7% QoQ (or an annualized -2.9%), marking the first decline in four quarters.

Real GDP peaked in 2019 Q3, just before the outbreak COVID-19 pandemic. 2022 Q3 GDP remains -1.9% below that peak. Recovery has been particularly slow in private final consumption expenditure (-3.2% lower than its peak), private capital formation (private residential investment + private capital investment + private inventory changes, -3.3% lower than its peak) and service exports (-15.1% lower than its peak, Table 2-1-2).

2. Japan Economic Forecast: FY 2022-24

(1) Assumptions about exogenous variables

Real public fixed capital formation in 2022 Q3 grew +0.9% QoQ, marking the second consecutive quarterly increase. According to the Ministry of Land, Infrastructure, Transport and Tourism, public works (volume basis) in September 2022 (seasonally adjusted, APIR estimate) decreased for the first time in seven months, -0.0% MoM. As a result, the 2022 Q3 period saw a +3.2%

Part I

Part II

Part III

Part IV

QoQ increase, the second consecutive quarterly increase. As a result, we assume that real public fixed capital formation growth will be -2.8% in FY 2022, +2.1% in FY 2023, and +1.5% in FY 2024.

Real government final consumption expenditure in 2022 Q3 increased for the third consecutive quarter, by +0.1% QoQ. On November 8, 2022, the Cabinet approved the FY 2022 supplementary budget. Of the 28.9 trillion-yen budget, 7.8 trillion yen is allocated for measures to cope with soaring prices and wage hikes. These measures will somewhat ease the burden of higher prices on households. Reflecting these factors, we assume that real government consumption expenditures will grow by +1.2% in FY 2022, +0.8% in FY 2023, and +0.5% in FY 2024. No major changes in monetary policy are assumed.

An important assumption for the overseas environment is the price of crude oil. The crude oil price (average price of WTI, Dubai, and North Sea Brent) has been above $100 for five consecutive months until July 2022, as Russia's invasion of Ukraine further accelerated the rise in the crude oil price. In August, the price fell below $100 as the global economy slowed down. In the current forecast, we assume that crude oil prices peaked in the 2022 Q2 (at $109.41 per barrel) and will decline but remain high from 2023 onward, reaching $83.33 per barrel in the 2024 Q1 and around $85.52 per barrel in the 2025 Q1. Therefore, we assume $94.8 for FY 2022, $82.5 for FY 2023, and $83.3 for FY 2024.

Our assumptions concerning world trade is based on S&P Global's Global Economic Outlook, November 2022. We assume that real world exports of goods and services will slow sharply from +9.7% YoY in 2021 to +5.7% YoY in 2022 and +2.0% YoY in 2023, but will recover to +3.5% YoY in 2024.

Regarding exchange rate assumptions, we assume that the U.S. Fed will take a tighter monetary policy stance from March 2022, raising its policy rate to 4.75-5.00% in March 2023 and stopping thereafter. On the other hand, we assume that Japan will maintain an accommodative monetary policy, and as a result, the exchange rate will be influenced by the U.S. monetary policy. We assume exchange rates of 137.3 yen in FY 2022, 133.9 yen in FY 2023, and 128.3 yen in FY 2024 (Table 2-1-3).

(2) Projected real GDP growth rate: +1.5% in FY 2022, +1.1% in FY 2023, +1.4% in FY 2024

We have revised our outlook for the Japanese economy for FY 2022-24, reflecting the second advance estimate of GDP for Q3 2022 and incorporating our new assumptions about exogenous variables (fiscal and monetary policy and variables related to overseas economies). We now forecast real GDP growth of +1.5% in FY 2022, +1.1% in FY 2023, and +1.4% in FY 2024 (Table 2-1-3), and

Table 2-1-3	Summary of Forecast Results

	2021	2022	2023	2024
Real GDP (%)	2.5	1.5	1.1	1.4
Private demand (contribution)	1.4	2.0	0.9	1.2
Private final consumption expenditure (%)	1.5	2.5	1.4	1.3
Private residential investment (%)	▲ 1.1	▲ 4.2	0.9	0.8
Private non-residential investment (%)	2.1	3.3	2.9	2.7
Private inventory changes (contribution)	0.1	0.3	▲ 0.4	0.0
Public demand (contirbution)	0.4	0.1	0.3	0.2
Government final consumption expenditure (%)	3.4	1.2	0.8	0.4
Public investment expenditure (%)	▲ 6.4	▲ 2.8	2.1	1.5
Public inventory changes (contribution)	0.0	▲ 0.0	0.0	▲ 0.0
External demand (contribution)	0.8	▲ 0.6	▲ 0.0	0.1
Exports of goods and services (%)	12.3	4.6	0.3	3.4
Imports of goods and services (%)	7.1	7.9	0.5	2.9
Nominal GDP (%)	2.4	1.6	2.8	2.6
GDP deflator (%)	▲ 0.1	0.1	1.6	1.1
Domestic corporate price index (%)	7.1	8.9	1.6	0.1
Core consumer price index (%)	0.0	3.0	1.9	1.2
Industrial production index (%)	5.8	1.4	2.1	2.0
New housing starts (%)	6.6	▲ 0.5	1.4	0.4
Unemployment rate (%)	2.8	2.5	2.4	2.3
Current account balance (JPY trillion)	20.3	6.3	6.8	6.1
% of nominal GDP	3.7	1.1	1.2	1.0
Crude oil price (USD/barrel)	78.3	94.8	82.5	83.3
USD/JPY exchange rate	112.4	137.3	133.9	128.3
USA real GDP (%, calendar year)	5.9	1.9	0.5	1.8

Note: YoY %, others are notes.

Part I

Part II

Part III

Part IV

+1.2% in 2022, +1.2% in 2023, and +1.4% in 2024 on a calendar-year basis.

Looking at the contribution to real GDP growth by major item in FY 2022, the contribution of private demand and public demand will boost the economy by +2.0%pt and +0.1%pt, respectively, while net exports will suppress growth by -0.6%pt. In FY 2023, the contribution of public demand will increase slightly to +0.3 %pt, while that of private demand will decrease to 0.9%pt. In FY 2024, private demand will contribute +1.2 %pt, public demand +0.2 %pt, and net exports +0.1 %pt (Figure 2-1-3).

Looking at the components of private demand, in FY 2022 all components are expected to make positive contributions to growth, except private residential investment. Real private final consumption expenditures are expected to boost growth by +1.3 %pt, real private residential investment are expected to suppress

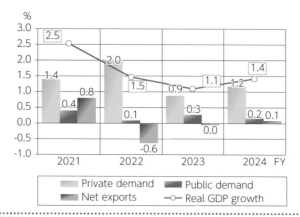

Figure 2-1-3   Real GDP Growth Rate and Itemized Contribution: %.

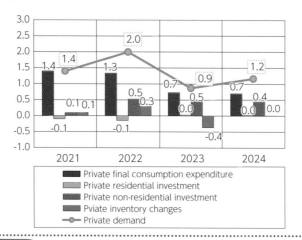

Figure 2-1-4   Contribution of private sector demand by item: %.

growth by -0.1 %pt, real private capital investment are expected to contribute +0.5 %pt, and real private inventory changes are expected to contribute +0.3 %pt.

In FY 2024, the contributions to growth are projected to be + 0.7%pt by real private final consumption expenditure, +0.0%pt by real private residential investment, +0.5%pt by real private capital investment by, and +0.4 %pt by real private inventory changes by. (Figure 2-1-4).

Looking at real GDP (actual and forecast) on a quarterly basis, 2022 Q3 real GDP remains -1.9% below the pre-COVID-19 pandemic peak. If no new restrictions of economic activities are imposed during the forecast period, households'

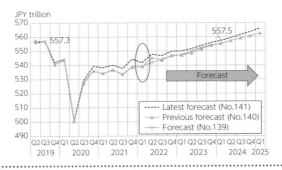

Figure 2-1-5   Quarterly GDP: Actual and Forecast: trillion yen

Note: Actual through Q3 2022; forecast thereafter.

accumulated forced savings will be unleashed in the second half of FY 2022, and a recovery led by private final consumption expenditures, especially service expenditures, can be expected. Since the contribution of private demand will decelerate in FY 2023, the overall growth rate will decline. Therefore, real GDP is not expected to exceed the pre-COVID-19 pandemic peak until 2024 Q1 or later. Since the second advance GDP estimate revised the historical data upward, real GDP is now expected to exceed the pre-COVID-19 pandemic peak two quarters earlier than in our previous forecast (Figure 2-1-5).

(3) Household sector: Wage hikes and recovery in consumption propensity essential for a recovery in private consumption

The trends in private final consumption expenditure in terms of disposable income and propensity to consume (Q1 1994 to April-June 2022). Real disposable income in the April-June period remained slightly higher (0.4%) than its peak (April-June 2019). Meanwhile, the propensity to consume is 3%pt below its peak (from 97.6% to 94.6%). For private final consumption expenditure to recover, a steady increase in disposable income and a recovery in the propensity to consume are necessary (Figure 2-1-6).

The household savings rate, which is the mirror image of consumption propensity, declined to an average of 5.2% from 1994 Q1 to Jan-Mar 2014 Q1 and 0.8% from 2014 Q2 to 2019 Q3, but since then the average savings rate has remained high at 9.7%. Households accumulated forced savings during the COVID-19 disaster and have not been able to withdraw them even after the infection situation subsided. The figure shows that a portion of the fixed benefit payments has gone into savings (Figure 2-1-7, "Other Benefits"). The high savings rate (sluggish propensity to consume) seems to be influenced by the worsening expectations of lifetime income. In addition, consumer price inflation,

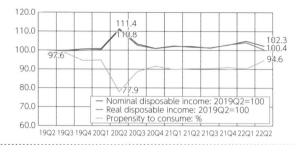

Figure 2-1-6 Disposable income and propensity to consume: seasonally adjusted, trillions of yen, %.

Source: Cabinet Office, "Advance Quarterly Report on Household Disposable Income and Household Saving Ratio."

Figure 2-1-7 Household Savings Rate: GDP basis: %.

Source: Calculations based on "Advance Quarterly Report on Household Disposable Income and Household Savings Ratio," Cabinet Office, Government of Japan

which has become more pronounced in recent years, has increased uncertainty about the future and has further suppressed the propensity to consume. In this sense, the government's efforts to address price inflation should not be short-term (subsidies), but rather medium- to long-term (policies that contribute to higher wages, centered on base wage increases).

If no restrictions are imposed on economic activities during the forecast period, expansion is expected mainly in face-to-face services. In FY 2022, households' forced savings are expected to be unleashed, leading to a recovery in private final consumption expenditures, mainly service expenditures. As a result, real private final consumption expenditure is expected to grow by +2.5% YoY in FY 2022, but this will be followed by a slowdown to +1.4% YoY in FY 2023 and +1.3% YoY in FY 2024.

According to the Ministry of Land, Infrastructure, Transport and Tourism, new residential investment starts in September increased for the second consecutive month, up 1.0% YoY. The seasonally adjusted figure was -5.1% MoM, the first decline in two months, while the Q3 figure was +1.0% QoQ, the first increase in two quarters. By type of use (seasonally adjusted), owner-occupied houses increased for the second consecutive month in September, up 1.9% from the previous month. Rental residential investment declined for the first time in two months, falling 1.3%. Houses for sale decreased for the first time in two months, -13.7% MoM. Compared to the previous quarter, in Q3, owner-occupied residential investment declined -1.0% (fourth consecutive quarterly decline), while rental residential investment increased +1.8% (first increase in two quarters) and for-sale residential investment increased +1.7% (first increase in two quarters).

Planned construction spending (residential +0.7* combined residential-industrial), which often explains GDP-based private residential investment, increased for the third consecutive month, +2.8% YoY in September. Seasonally adjusted (APIR estimate) was -2.9% MoM, the first decline in three months. As a result, the Q3 period saw a +2.5% QoQ increase, the first positive growth in two quarters. Meanwhile, the August residential investment construction cost deflator (2015 average=100) rose +6.5% YoY for the 19th consecutive month, with the July-August average rising +5.9% over the Q3 average. Building construction costs (residential) in real terms remain sluggish.

Reflecting the current increase in the residential investment construction cost deflator, real private residential investment in FY 2022 is projected to decline by -4.2% YoY, and then increase slightly by +0.9% YoY in FY 2023 and +0.8% YoY in FY 2024.

(4) Corporate Sector: Investment plans expected to remain at high levels; risks include supply constraints and growing uncertainty

According to the Ministry of Economy, Trade and Industry's Industrial Production Index (quarterly data: 2015=100), the industrial production index (quarterly data: 2015=100) declined in September for the first time in four months, falling -1.7% MoM. Due in part to easing supply constraints, the index rose +5.8% QoQ in Q3, the first increase in two quarters (Figure 2-1-8). METI kept its assessment of production ("gradually recovering") unchanged from the previous month. According to the Survey of Industrial Production Forecasts, industrial production in October declined -0.4% MoM (revised estimate: -3.7% MoM), but it is expected to inch up +0.8% MoM in November.

As a result, the industrial production index for FY 2022 is projected to increase +1.4% YoY in FY 2022, +2.1% in FY 2023, and +2.0% in FY 2024. Considering the current situation, our forecast for FY 2022 has been revised

Part I

Part II

Part III

Part IV

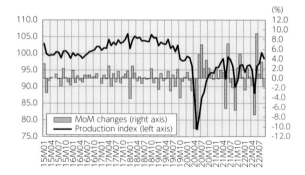

Figure 2-1-8   Industrial Production Index: seasonally adjusted: 2015=100

Source: Ministry of Economy, Trade and Industry, "Index of Mining and Manufacturing"

upward somewhat from the previous forecast, while the forecast for FY 2023 has been revised downward.

The tertiary industrial activity index (seasonally adjusted; 2015 average = 100) for September decreased -0.4% MoM, marking the first decline in two months. METI maintained its assessment from the previous month. As a result, the Q3 quarter saw a slight decline of -0.1% QoQ, the first decline in two quarters (Figure 2-1-9).

Of these, the September face-to-face service index (2015 average = 100) fell -1.2% MoM, the first decline in two months. As a whole, Q3 saw a +1.1% QoQ increase, the second consecutive quarter of positive growth, but a slowdown from the previous quarter (+6.2% QoQ) due in part to the impact of the surge in infections. The index for the face-to-face service sector is expected to recover in Q4, partly due to the impact of the national travel support program.

According to the Corporate Statistics Survey, 2022 Q2 corporate profits (seasonally adjusted, excluding financial and insurance industries) for all industries increased by +5.5% QoQ, marking the third consecutive quarterly improvement (Q1: +0.6% QoQ). Therein, profits in the manufacturing sector increased by +1.6% QoQ, the third consecutive quarterly increase, and profits in the non-manufacturing sector increased by +8.1% QoQ, the first increase in two quarters. Growth in labor costs has been weak, so corporate cash flows are at their highest levels. (Figure 2-1-10). Conditions are ripe for increased investment. Certainly, the worsening terms of trade are unfavorable for corporate earnings, but the weak yen continues to be a tailwind for export-oriented manufacturing firms. Corporate investment plans (BOJ's Tankan September survey)

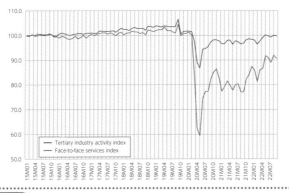

Figure 2-1-9   Face-to-face Services vs. Tertiary Industry Activity Index: 2015=100

Note: The face-to-face services index is a weighted average of the transportation, accommodation, restaurants, food services, other lifestyle-related services, and entertainment industry indexes; the tourism-related index is a weighted average of the tourism-related index among face-to-face services. 2015 average = 100.
Source: "Tertiary Industry Activity Index," Ministry of Economy, Trade and Industry

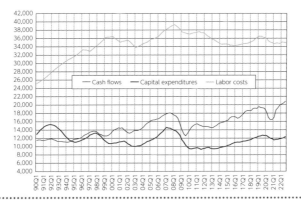

Figure 2-1-10   Cash flow, capital expenditures, and labor costs: billion yen (quarterly average)

Source: "Quarterly Survey of Corporate Business Enterprises (April-June 2022)," Ministry of Finance

have been revised upward, and the potential for investment expansion is strong. Downside risks include supply constraints and growing uncertainty about the economic outlook due to the slowdown in overseas economies.

Looking at investment-related indicators, the September capital goods shipments index decreased -4.0% MoM, the first decline in four months. As a result, Q3 saw a significant increase of -11.5% QoQ, the first increase in three quarters.

Core machinery orders (private-sector demand excluding ships and electric power: seasonally adjusted), a leading indicator of private capital investment, fell -4.6% MoM in September, the second consecutive monthly decline. As a result, the Q3 period saw a -1.6% QoQ decline, the first decline in two quarters. The Cabinet Office downgraded its assessment of the underlying tone of machinery orders from the previous month. According to the survey as of the end of September, core machinery orders for Q4 are expected to increase for the first time in two quarters, +3.6% QoQ. The outlook for external demand is also up for the first time in two quarters at +16.5% QoQ. Investment demand, which stagnated due to the COVID-19 pandemic, appears to remain strong, but there are concerns about a global economic slowdown.

Real private capital investment is projected to expand +3.3% YoY in FY 2022, +2.9% in FY 2023, and +2.7% in FY 2024. Our forecast for FY 2022 has been revised upward to reflect upward revisions in corporate investment plans.

(5) External Sector: Downward revision in FY 2023 trade due to slowdown in global economy

According to advance trade statistics released by the Ministry of Finance, the trade balance for October was -2,162.3 billion yen, the 15th consecutive monthly deficit. The deficit expanded by +2,283.5% YoY. This was the largest single-month deficit on record since 1979, when statistics were first available. It was also the third consecutive month that the trade deficit exceeded 2 trillion yen. On a seasonally adjusted basis, the deficit expanded for the 17th consecutive month, up +12.9% MoM, the first increase in two months. As a result, the trade deficit in October expanded +5.3% relative to the Q3 average (Q3: +20.9% QoQ).

Exports increased for the second consecutive month, up +2.2% from the previous month, and imports increased for the first time in two months, up +4.2%. Compared to the Q3 average, exports and imports increased by +4.2% and +4.5%, respectively.

On a volume basis, the October export volume index fell for the first time in two months to -4.5%MoM, while the import volume index declined for the second consecutive month, by-0.6%. Compared to the Q3 average, the export volume index fell -4.5% and the import volume index fell -3.0%.

Looking at October trends by region (seasonally adjusted data: APIR estimates), exports to Asia were down -7.2% from the previous month, exports to China were down -14.1%, exports to the U.S. were down -5.4%, and exports to the EU were down -1.7%. Exports to major regions were down across the board (Figure 2-1-11). Meanwhile, imports from Asia were -1.2%MoM, from China +1.8% MoM, from the US -12.8% MoM, and from the EU +4.9% MoM. Comparing October to the Q3 average, imports from Asia were down -3.5%, from China -2.8%, from the US -11.7%, and from the EU, up +16.3%. The impact of China's zero-COVID-19 policy and the economic slowdown in the U.S. and Europe is

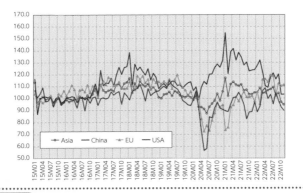

| Figure 2-1-11 | Export Volume Index by Region: 2015=100 |

Source: Trade Statistics, Ministry of Finance; seasonally adjusted values are APIR estimates.

clearly visible in exports (Figure 2-1-11).

Considering these factors, real exports of goods and services are projected to increase +4.6% YoY in FY 2022, +0.3% in FY 2023, and +3.4% in FY 2024. In contrast, real imports of goods and services are projected to increase +7.9% in FY 2022, +0.5% in FY 2023, and +2.9% in FY 2024. Our forecast for the exports of goods and services for FY 2023 has been revised downward from the previous forecast.

The terms of trade will worsen, resulting in a deficit trend in the trade balance. Since the recovery of inbound tourism will be only moderate, the services balance deficit will not escape the expansionary trend. On the other hand, although the primary income balance will remain high due to the weak yen, the current account balance is projected to be +6.3 trillion yen in FY 2022, +6.8 trillion yen in FY 2023, and+ 6.1 trillion yen in FY 2024.

(6) Price Trends: Wage hikes centered on base increases are necessary for consumer price inflation to become sustainable.

According to the Bank of Japan, the domestic corporate goods price index (2020 average = 100) rose for the 20th consecutive month in October to +9.1% YoY (Figure 2-1-12). The impact of Russia's invasion of Ukraine has kept resource prices high. In addition, the accelerating depreciation of the yen has led to widespread price pass-through, particularly in the case of electricity and gas.

The yen-based export price index (2020 average = 100) rose 18.8% YoY in October for the 20th consecutive month of increase. The yen-based import price index (2020 average=100) was +42.6% YoY in October, rising for the 20th consecutive month. As a result, the **terms of trade index** (export price index/import

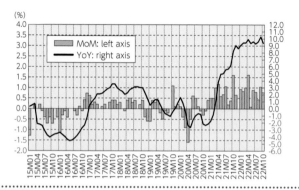

Figure 2-1-12   Domestic Corporate Goods Price Index: 2020=100: Growth Rate

Source: Bank of Japan, Domestic Corporate Goods Price Index

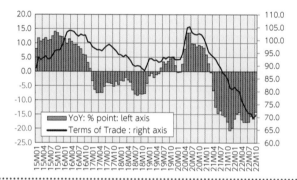

Figure 2-1-13   Terms of Trade: 2020=100

Source: Authors' calculations based on Bank of Japan, Domestic Corporate Goods Price Index.

price index*100) fell sharply by -14.2 points YoY in October, deteriorating for the 20th consecutive month. It was also the 18th consecutive month of double-digit deterioration (Figure 2-1-13).

According to the Ministry of Internal Affairs and Communications, the national consumer price index (CPI, 2020 average = 100) rose for the 14th consecutive month in October to +3.7% YoY. The **core CPI index**, which excludes fresh food, rose **+3.6% YoY for the 14th consecutive month** and for the first time since February 1982 (+3.6% YoY). The core-core CPI index which excludes both fresh food and energy rose for the seventh consecutive month by +2.5% YoY (Figure 2-1-14).

Looking at the October Composite Index by category, **energy prices rose for the 19th consecutive month,** +15.2% YoY. The contribution of energy

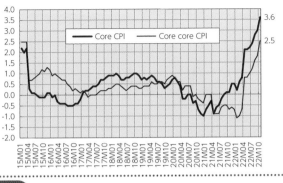

Figure 2-1-14 National Consumer Price Index: 2020=100: y/y: %.

Source: Authors' calculations based on "National Consumer Price Index," Ministry of Internal Affairs and Communications

prices to the index was +1.18%. Of these, gasoline prices rose for the 20th consecutive month, up +2.9% YoY, due in part to subsidies aimed at curbing inflation. The contribution of energy prices to CPI inflation was +0.06%. **Non-energy prices** rose for the seventh consecutive month to +2.8%. Their contribution to CPI inflation was +2.52%. Therein, food prices, excluding fresh food, rose for the 16th consecutive month, by +5.9%. Growth accelerated, reaching the highest rate of increase since March 1981 (+6.1%). Their contribution to CPI inflation was +1.33%.

Comparing the prices goods and services, **goods prices** in October increased for the 18th consecutive month, up 6.5% YoY. Their contribution to CPI inflation was 3.35%. **Service prices** rose a modest +0.8% YoY, the third consecutive monthly increase. Their contribution to CPI inflation was +0.40%. In the services expenditure category, rents fell for the first time in 17 months, -10.0% YoY, with a contribution of -0.09%. Their contribution to CPI inflation was -0.09%. Mobile phone charges rose for the first time in 19 months, +1.8% YoY. Their contribution to CPI inflation was +0.02%.

Looking at past trends in the prices of goods and services, the prices of services fluctuated in line with the prices of goods prices since the early 1990s. Recently, however, service prices have remained almost flat compared to the sharp increase in goods prices (Figure 2-1-15). Since service prices are determined almost entirely by wage trends, consumer price increases are not sustainable unless they are accompanied by wage increases, especially increases in base salaries.

With regard to the outlook for the CPI, in the second half of 2022, the CPI core index is likely to remain above the upper 3% level year-on-year due to the

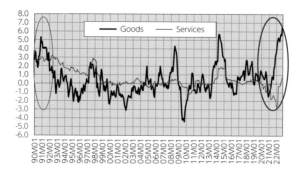

Figure 2-1-15   National Consumer Price Index by Item: % change from the same month last year

Source: Authors' calculations based on "National Consumer Price Index," Ministry of Internal Affairs and Communications

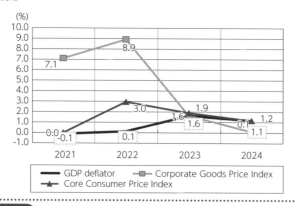

Figure 2-1-16   Trends in prices: % change from previous year

impact of surging energy and food prices. In FY 2023, the impact of surging energy prices will fade away, and the underlying tone of the CPI will be determined by trends in service prices. In this sense, wage increases in FY 2023 will be important.

Our latest forecast concerning inflation is as follows. The **national corporate goods price index** is projected to increase +8.9% in FY 2022, +1.6% in FY 2023, and +0.1% in FY 2024. The **national consumer price core index** is projected to rise +3.0% in FY 2022, +1.9% in FY 2023, and +1.2% in FY 2024. The **GDP deflator** is projected to be +0.1% in FY 2022, +1.6% in FY 2023, and +1.1% in FY 2024 (Figure 2-1-16).

Section 2
THE KANSAI ECONOMY: RECENT DEVELOPMENTS AND SHORT-TERM FORECASTS

IRIE, Hiroaki; INADA, Yoshihisa

1. Retrospective of the Kansai Economy in FY 2021

In FY 2021, the Kansai economy recovered somewhat from the previous year, but was still at the mercy of the COVID-19 outbreak and continued to be weak due to new downward pressures such as the shortage of semiconductors and soaring raw material prices. The number of new COVID-19 infections reached its fourth and fifth waves in April and August 2021, and a state of emergency was declared both times. New infections subsided in early fall, but at the beginning of 2022 they started increasing at an unprecedented pace. The resulting sixth wave was due to the emergence of the highly infectious Omicron strain. In mid-February the number of daily infections increased to nearly 25,000, almost five times the peak of the fifth wave. In the summer of 2022, there was a seventh wave of infections, but no restrictions were imposed. Entry restrictions into Japan were relaxed, and tourism resumed. Economic activity normalized on the premise of life "With Corona".

If we divide the Kansai economy into four major sectors (the household, corporate, external and public sectors), trends in FY 2021 can be summarized as follows. The household sector recovered from the previous year's decline, but remained weak due to the spread of COVID-19 and the two emergency states. Recovery in the income and employment environment was slow. The corporate sector generally recovered compared to the sharp deterioration in the previous year, but both the manufacturing and non-manufacturing industries remained stagnant due to significant downward pressure from a variety of risk factors. In the external sector, both exports and imports expanded. Goods exports to China, Europe and the U.S. all recovered. Service exports, such as inbound tourism, finally began to show signs of recovery as economic activity normalized. Imports rose sharply, partly due to soaring energy prices. Finally, Kansai's public sector performed well, in contrast to the nation as a whole. Below, we proceed to discuss these trends by sector in more detail.

(1) Household sector
In FY 2021, the household sector in the Kansai region recovered from the decline in the previous year, but did not reach a full-fledged recovery, partly

Part I

Part II

Part III

Part IV

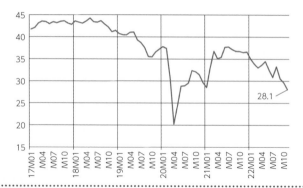

Figure 2-2-1   Consumer Confidence Index

Source: Cabinet Office, "Survey of Consumption Trends"

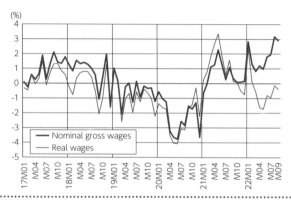

Figure 2-2-2   Gross Nominal Wages and Real Wages (% change from the same month of the previous year)

Source: Ministry of Health, Labour and Welfare, "Monthly Labor Survey," etc.

due to the two states of emergency. In particular, the income and employment environment recovered more slowly than in the rest of the country.

Consumer Sentiment

Consumer sentiment improved in FY 2021 compared to FY 2020, when it deteriorated sharply, but the pace of recovery was slow (Figure 2-2-1). The sentiment continued to deteriorate in FY 2022 due to growing uncertainty over the future, including the spread of COVID-19, Russia's invasion of Ukraine, and the accompanying high resource prices.

Income environment

Although the income environment improved compared to the previous year, it did not recover to its pre-pandemic level (Figure 2-2-2). Gross salaries in

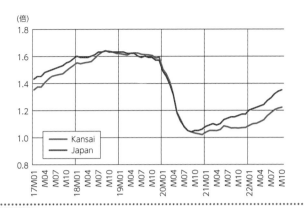

Figure 2-2-3   Effective Job Openings to Applicants Ratio (Seasonally Adjusted)

Source: Ministry of Health, Labour and Welfare, "General Employment Placement Situation"

Kansai (APIR estimate) averaged 312,654 yen per month in FY 2021. This was a decrease of -2.2% from the previous year, and the first YoY decrease in three years. The figure was slightly lower than the national average (320,256 yen), and -1.3% lower than the pre-pandemic FY 2019.

Real wages (i.e. excluding the effect of price fluctuations based on the consumer price index) were up +0.9% from the previous year, the first YoY increase in four years. However, they were -0.9% lower relative to the pre-pandemic FY 2019. In FY 2022, real wages keep decreasing as wage hikes are failing to keep pace with the pace of price hikes.

Employment environment

Compared to the nation as a whole, Kansai's recovery has been slow (Figure 2-2-3), with the ratio of job offers to job applicants in FY 2021 being 1.07. This was a decrease of 0.01 points from the previous year and the third consecutive year of deterioration. The national average was 1.16, exceeding the previous year's level for the first time in two years. The nation as a whole has been on a gradual but steady recovery trend, widening the gap with the Kansai region, where the recovery has lagged.

Large retailers' sales

The overall sales of large retailers in the Kansai region in FY 2021 was 3,494.5 billion yen, up 1.7% from the previous year, the first year-on-year increase in four years (Figure 2-2-4).

Therein, department store sales totaled 1,187.1 billion yen, up +6.9% from the previous year, marking the first increase in four years. The number of customers recovered too — although there were several states of emergency in FY 2021, the restrictions were less severe compared to FY 2020. However,

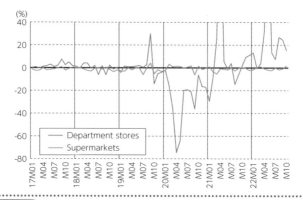

Figure 2-2-4   Department store and supermarket sales (y/y: %)

Note: Based on all stores; 150.4% in April 2021.
Source: "Department Store and Supermarket Sales", Kinki Bureau of Economy, Trade and Industry

department store sales remained -20.3% lower relative to the pre-pandemic FY 2019.

On the other hand, supermarket sales in FY 2021 totaled 2,307.4 billion yen, down -0.8% from the previous year.

(2) Corporate sector

In FY 2021, the corporate sector in the Kansai region recovered from the significant deterioration in the previous year, but failed to achieve a robust recovery. The manufacturing sector experienced ups and downs due to supply-constraining factors such as the global shortage of semiconductors and soaring raw material prices. In the non-manufacturing sector, growth was sluggish, especially in face-to-face services.

Business confidence

According to the Bank of Japan's Tankan survey, the Diffusion Index (DI) for business conditions in Kansai (firms of all sizes in all industries) continued to recover in FY 2021, turning positive for the first time in eight quarters at +5 in the December 2021 survey (Figure 2-2-5). Since then, it has remained in positive territory for five consecutive quarters, reaching +5 again in the December 2022 survey. There is no significant difference from the national average.

By industry, improvement in FY 2021 was led by the manufacturing sector. In FY 2022, the pace of recovery in the non-manufacturing sector was slow due to measures aimed at curbing the spread of COVID-19. In FY 2022, growth in the manufacturing sector has been sluggish due to high resource prices and lockdowns in China. According to the December 2022 survey, the DI for the

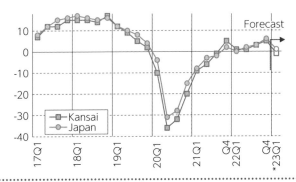

| Figure 2-2-5 | DI for business conditions according to the Bank of Japan's Tankan survey (all sizes, all industries) |

Note: * denotes that it is a forecast.
Source: Bank of Japan, Osaka Branch, "Short-term Economic Survey of Enterprises"

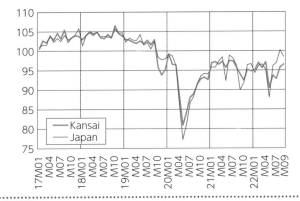

| Figure 2-2-6 | Industrial Production Index (seasonally adjusted, 2015=100) |

Source: "Kinki Region Industrial Production Trends," Kinki Bureau of Economy, Trade and Industry

manufacturing sector was +1, while that for the non-manufacturing sector was +9.

Industrial production

Although production picked up in FY 2021, growth was sluggish due to the global shortage of semiconductors and soaring raw material prices (Figure 2-2-6) The production index for the full year of FY 2021 was 95.6 (2015=100, seasonally adjusted). This was an increase of +5.0% over the previous year, marking the first increase in production in three years. However, production has not recovered to its pre-pandemic level, remaining -3.6% lower relative to FY 2019.

On a monthly basis, from July to October 2021, production declined for four consecutive months due to the impact of production adjustments caused by supply constraints in the automotive industry. In addition, since the beginning

Table 2-2-1   BOJ Tankan: Planned Capital Investment

	Kansai		
	All industries	Manufacturing	Non-manufacturing
FY 2021	-8.9	-4.9	-11.5
FY 2022	15.9	24.0	10.6
	Japan		
	All industries	Manufacturing	Non-manufacturing
FY 2021	-0.8	1.1	-1.9
FY 2022	15.1	20.3	12.1

Source: Bank of Japan, Osaka Branch, "National Short-term Economic Survey of Enterprises in the Kinki Region"

of 2022, production has been at a standstill due to soaring energy prices.

Capital investment

The impact of COVID-19 resulted in subdued investment in FY 2021, down -8.9% from the previous year (Table 2-2-1). By industry, the manufacturing and non-manufacturing sectors showed declines of -4.9% and -11.5%, respectively. A significant rebound is expected in FY 2022, as planned investment is +15.9% higher. By industry, planned investment in the manufacturing and non-manufacturing sectors is +24.0% and +10.6% higher, respectively.

(3) External sector

In FY 2021, both exports and imports expanded in the external sector of the Kansai region. Goods exports to Europe and the U.S. recovered in addition to firm exports to China. Exports of services, such as inbound demand, finally began to show signs of recovery from a bottoming-out phase as economic activity normalized. Imports increased substantially, partly due to a sharp rise in energy prices.

Trade in goods

Both exports and imports expanded in FY2021 (Figure 2-2-7). Exports totaled 19,237.5 billion yen, a significant increase of 22.4% over the previous year. This was the first year-on-year increase in four years. Exports of semiconductors and other electronic components and construction and mining equipment increased significantly, reaching a yearly record high. On a monthly basis, the monthly growth has been near double-digit for 20 consecutive months from March 2021 to October 2022.

By region, exports to Europe and the U.S. recovered significantly, in addition to those to China, which had recovered earlier in the previous year (Figure 2-2-8). Since the beginning of 2022, exports to the U.S. and the EU have been robust, while those to China have grown only modestly compared to Europe and

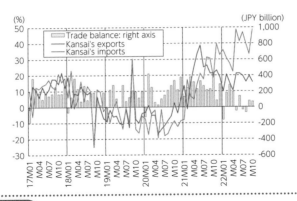

Figure 2-2-7   Exports, imports, and trade balance

Source: Osaka Customs, "Overview of Trade in the Kinki Region"

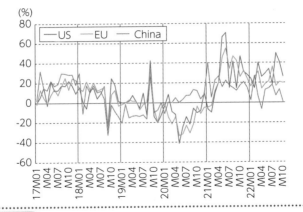

Figure 2-2-8   Exports by region (YoY)

Source: Osaka Customs, "Overview of Trade in the Kinki Region"

the U.S., partly due to the impact of the lockdown.

Imports totaled 16,597.0 billion yen, up 25.2% from the previous year, the first year-on-year increase in three years. Natural gas and manufactured gas increased due to soaring energy prices, and pharmaceuticals increased due to imports of new COVID-19 vaccines.

The trade balance, which is the value of exports minus the value of imports, showed a surplus of 2,640.5 billion yen, the seventh consecutive year of surplus. However, the recent remarkable growth in imports has led to a trade deficit in some months in 2022.

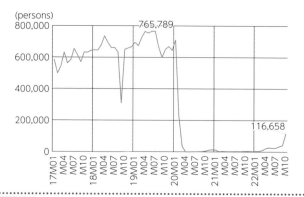

Figure 2-2-9   Number of international visitors to Japan (persons)

Source: Ministry of Justice, "Immigration Statistics"

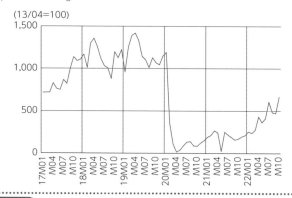

Figure 2-2-10   Department store duty-free sales (April 2013=100)

Source) Bank of Japan, Osaka Branch, "Department Store Duty Free Sales (Kansai Region)"

Inbound tourism

Inbound tourism (exports of services) continued to bottom out during FY 2021, and finally showed signs of recovery in FY 2022 as entry restrictions were eased sequentially. According to the Ministry of Justice, the number of international visitors to Japan in FY 2021 was 405,000, 42,000 of which arrived at Kansai International Airport (Figure 2-2-9). The number was +25.0% higher than FY 2020. The increase, which is attributable to the Tokyo Olympics, was the first year-on-year increase in three years. In October 2022, the number of visitors to Japan exceeded 100,000 for the first time since February 2020 due to the removal of the cap on the number of visitors and the lifting of the ban on the entry of individual travelers.

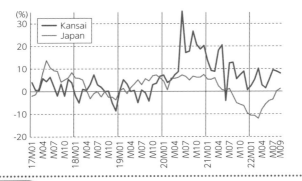

Figure 2-2-11   Public works output (YoY)

Source: Ministry of Land, Infrastructure, Transport and Tourism, "Comprehensive Construction Statistics"

Department store duty-free sales are recovering too (Figure 2-2-10). According to the Osaka branch of the Bank of Japan, duty-free sales at department stores in the Kansai region in FY 2021 increased +58.3% over the previous year. In FY 2022, the increase in the number of foreign tourists and the rapid depreciation of the yen acted as a tailwind for a recovery in spending by visitors.

(4) Public sector

The public sector (public works) in the Kansai region remained steady. In FY2021, the value of completed public works in the Kansai region totaled 2,757.5 billion yen, up +7.5% from the previous year (Figure 2-2-12). This is the third consecutive year of year-on-year increase. Large-scale public investment projects are in progress, including the development of land on Yumeshima in the Osaka Bay area, the new Nagoya-Kobe Expressway, and the Yodogawa Left Bank Route. In FY 2022, the public works are likely to grow YoY too.

On the other hand, nationwide, in contrast to Kansai, there was a slowdown: the value of completed public works in FY 2021 totaled 21,834.3 billion yen, down -8.0% from the previous year. This slowdown is thought to have been caused by the absence of demand for construction related to the Tokyo Olympics (the figure for the southern Kanto region was -10.4% YoY).

2. Kansai Economic Forecast: FY 2022-2024

Our forecasts for the Kansai economy presented below reflect the latest economic indicators within and outside the Kansai region, including the second preliminary GDP figures for 2022 Q3.

(1) Kansai GRP growth forecast: +1.5% in FY 2022, +1.2% in FY 2023, +1.5% in FY 2024

We forecast that Kansai's real GRP growth will be +1.5% in FY 2022, +1.2% in FY 2023, and +1.5% in FY 2024 (Table 2-2-2, Figure 2-2-12). After two consecutive years of negative growth in FY 2019 and FY 2020, positive growth in the 1% range means that the momentum of recovery is weak, and it will take until FY 2023 for Kansai's GRP to recover to its pre-pandemic level.

In terms of the contribution of demand categories to growth, private demand will drive growth by +1.7 percentage points in FY 2022, +0.9 percentage points in FY 2023, and +1.2% in FY 2024. Public demand will prop up growth modestly by +0.2 percentage points from FY 2022 to FY 2024. On the other hand, external demand will depress growth by -0.4 percentage point in FY 2022, and will contribute only +0.1 percentage point in FY 2023 and FY 2024.

Comparing the Kansai and Japan economic forecasts (Figure 2-2-13), there are no major differences.

| Table 2-2-2 | Economic Forecasts for Kansai |

FY	2020	2021	2022	2023	2024
Private final consumption expenditure	▲5.4	1.9	2.1	1.2	1.2
Private residential investment	▲3.0	▲4.0	▲3.4	1.8	1.7
Private non-residential capital investment	▲6.8	1.6	2.8	3.1	3.1
Government final consumption expenditure	2.8	3.0	1.0	1.0	0.7
Public fixed capital formation	8.0	▲1.5	0.9	2.6	2.2
Exports	▲2.1	6.9	2.2	0.6	2.8
Imports	▲2.4	5.6	3.7	0.1	2.7
Real GRP	**▲4.1**	**1.9**	**1.5**	**1.2**	**1.5**
Private demand (contribution)	▲4.9	0.8	1.7	0.9	1.2
Public demand (contribution)	0.7	0.4	0.2	0.2	0.2
Net exports (contribution)	0.1	0.7	▲0.4	0.1	0.1
Nominal GRP	▲3.3	1.9	1.5	2.6	2.8
GRP deflator	0.8	▲0.1	0.0	1.4	1.3
Consumer price index	▲0.3	0.0	3.1	2.0	1.5
Industrial Production Index	▲8.3	5.2	1.5	1.9	1.9
Unemployment rate	3.1	3.0	2.9	2.8	2.7

Note: Unit percentages are YoY growth rates except for the unemployment rate, which is the actual forecast for FY2020-21 and the forecast for FY2022-24.
Source: Prepared by the author

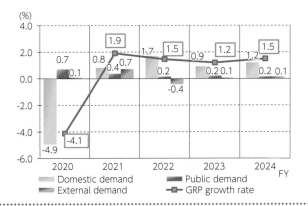

Figure 2-2-12   GRP Forecast Results and Contribution to Growth

Note: FY2020-FY2021 are actual forecasts; FY2022-FY24 are forecasts.
Source: Prepared by the author

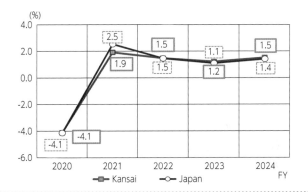

Figure 2-2-13   Economic Growth Rates in Kansai and Nationwide

Source: Prepared by the author

(2) Forecasts by sector
Private sector
The contribution of private demand to GRP growth is forecast to be +1.7 percentage points in FY 2022, +0.9 percentage points in FY 2023, and +1.2 percentage points in FY 2024. In FY 2021, the contribution of private demand to GRP growth turned positive for the first time in three years, and it is expected to keep underpinning economic growth in Kansai.

The household component of the private sector consists of real private final consumption expenditures and real private residential investment. The former is projected to grow by +2.1% in FY 2022, +1.2% in FY 2023, and +1.2% in FY 2024. The normalization of economic activity, including the easing of COVID-19 restrictions, will allow private consumption to recover and boost overall growth. On the other hand, real residential investment is projected to shrink by -3.4% in FY 2022 due to a sharp rise in construction material prices. However, it is expected to recover by +1.8% in FY 2023, and +1.7% in FY 2024.

Public sector

The contribution of public demand to real GRP growth is forecast to be +0.2 percentage points in FY 2022, +0.2 percentage points in FY 2023, and +0.2 percentage points in FY 2024. The public sector will provide solid underlying growth.

Therein, real government final consumption expenditure growth is expected to be +1.0% in FY 2022, +1.0% in FY 2023, and +0.7% in FY 2024. The growth rate will gradually contract as the boosting effect of COVID-related spending wears off. On the other hand, real public fixed capital formation is expected to grow by +0.9% in FY 2022, +2.6% in FY 2023, and +2.6% in FY 2024. The acceleration reflects expected progress in the development of infrastructure related to the World Expo 2025 which will be held in Osaka, Kansai. For that reason, the growth rate of public investment in Kansai is expected to be higher than that of the nation as a whole.

External sector

The external sector consists of international net exports (exports minus imports) and domestic extraterritorial net transactions (net economic transactions with other domestic regions). The contribution of external demand to real GRP growth is projected to be -0.4 percentage points in FY 2022, +0.1 percentage points in FY 2023, and +0.1 percentage points in FY 2024.

For overseas transactions, real export growth is projected to be +2.2% in FY 2022, +0.6% in FY 2023, and +2.8% in FY 2024. FY 2022 exports to Europe and the U.S., which are currently strong, and a recovery in inbound demand due to the relaxation of border control measures, will contribute to growth. In FY 2024, growth will be somewhat higher, but will not be strong enough to drive the economy. Real import growth is projected to be +3.7% in FY 2022, +0.1% in FY 2023, and +2.7% in FY2024. The contribution of net exports to real GRP growth will be -0.4 percentage points in FY 2022, +0.2 percentage points in FY 2023, and +0.1 percentage points in FY 2024.

The contribution of real domestic net exports, is projected to be -0.0 percentage points in FY 2022, -0.1 percentage points in FY 2023, and +0.0 percentage points in FY 2024. The contribution to growth is negligible.

Employment environment

The unemployment rate remained in the 2% range through FY 2019, but worsened to 3.1% and 3.0% in FY 2020 and FY 2021, respectively. Looking ahead, we forecast a gradual improvement to 2.9% in FY 2022, 2.8% in FY 2023, and 2.7% in FY 2024.

3. Advance Estimates of the GRPs of Kansai Prefectures (FY 2020-FY 2022)

In Japan, official prefectural GRP figures are released about two years later than the release of the national GDP figure. For that reason, APIR has been making its own early estimates of the actual GRPs for the six prefectures in the Kansai region for previous years that have not yet been published. In this section, we present the results of the early estimates up to FY 2022 as the latest version.

Table 2-2-3 shows our estimates. The total real GRP of the six Kansai prefectures is estimated at 84.7 trillion yen in FY 2020, 85.1 trillion yen in FY 2021, and 86.9 trillion yen in FY 2022. The real GRP growth rate is estimated at -3.8% in FY 2020, +0.4% in FY 2021, and +2.2% in FY 2022. FY 2020 marked be the first negative growth in five years. As a juxtaposition, the growth rate of the Kansai

| Table 2-2-3 | Summary of Early Estimates and Very Short-Term Forecast Results |

	Osaka	Hyogo	Kyoto	Shiga	Nara	Wakayama	Total (Kansai)	Japan
●Goodness of fit								
Adjusted R-square	0.83	0.96	0.87	0.79	0.77	0.73	-	-
MAPE of GRP (%)	0.94	0.41	0.92	1.98	0.57	1.08	-	-
MAPE of GRP growth(%)	1.42	0.70	1.67	2.42	0.74	1.67	-	-
Durbin-Watson statistic	2.17	2.75	2.77	1.59	1.45	2.71	-	-
●Real GRP (trillion yen)								
FY2019(confirmed)	40.7	22.1	10.7	7.0	3.9	3.7	88.0	549.9
FY2020(estimate)	39.2	21.2	10.3	6.7	3.7	3.5	84.7	524.9
FY2021(estimate)	39.6	21.4	10.3	6.6	3.7	3.5	85.1	536.9
FY2022(forecast)	40.3	21.7	10.6	7.0	3.7	3.6	86.9	
●Real growth rate (%)								
FY2019(confirmed)	-1.5	-0.2	0.2	0.2	-0.8	-0.3	-0.7	-0.9
FY2020(estimate)	-3.5	-4.0	-3.1	-3.7	-4.8	-6.5	-3.8	-4.6
FY2021(estimate)	0.8	0.8	0.0	-2.2	-0.1	0.4	0.4	2.3
FY2022(forecast)	2.0	1.6	2.2	5.7	0.9	3.5	2.2	-
●Contribution to the real growth rate								
FY2019(confirmed)	-0.7	0.0	0.0	0.0	0.0	0.0	-0.7	-
FY2020(estimate)	-1.6	-1.0	-0.4	-0.3	-0.2	-0.3	-3.8	-
FY2021(estimate)	0.4	0.2	0.0	-0.2	0.0	0.0	0.4	-
FY2022(forecast)	0.9	0.4	0.3	0.4	0.0	0.1	2.2	-

Note: MAPE stands for Mean Absolute Percentage Error.
Source: APIR "Kansai Economic Insight Quarterly" No. 61

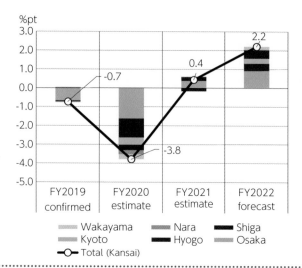

Figure 2-2-14   Kansai's contribution to real growth by prefecture

Source: APIR "Kansai Economic Insight Quarterly" No. 61

economy (calculated by summing the real GRPs of its prefectures) during the Global Financial Crisis was -3.1% in 2008 and -4.2% in 2009. Therefore, the impact of COVID-19 in FY 2020 is comparable to that of the Global Financial Crisis in a single year.

A glance at the contribution of each prefecture to the overall Kansai economy (Figure 2-2-14) shows that in FY 2020, all prefectures in the Kansai region suffered a significant setback due to the impact of COVID-19. In FY 2020, Osaka and Hyogo prefectures made a large negative contribution, while other prefectures experienced a deterioration comparable to the once seen during the Global Financial Crisis in 2008-2009. In FY 2022, all prefectures are expected to see positive growth and enter a phase of full-fledged recovery centered on Osaka Prefecture.

4. The risk of economic slowdown in China and its impact on the Kansai economy

(1) COVID-19 infection situation in China

The Chinese government has been implementing a policy to thoroughly suppress the spread of COVID-19, the so-called "zero-COVID policy," following the urban lockdown of Wuhan City in January 2020. As Figure 2-2-15 shows, the policy was initially successful, and the increase in the number of infections

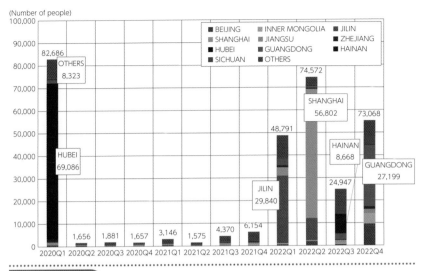

(Number of people)

Legend: BEIJING · INNER MONGOLIA · JILIN · SHANGHAI · JIANGSU · ZHEJIANG · HUBEI · GUANGDONG · HAINAN · SICHUAN · OTHERS

Figure 2-2-15   Number of new positives in China

Note: Jan-Mar 2020 to Oct-Dec 2022; Oct-Dec 2022 figures are as of Nov 24. Does not include asymptomatically infected patients.
Source: Prepared by the author from CEIC.

slowed sharply after April 2020 and remained low until 2021. However, with the emergence of the Omicron strain in 2022, the number of infections started increasing rapidly. A quarterly review of the number of infections by region shows a significant increase in the Jilin Province 2022 Q1 and in Shanghai and other cities in 2022 Q2. In response, lockdowns were imposed, and the curfews and factory shutdowns that resulted brought about a significant slowdown in China's real GDP growth rate, as discussed below.

(2) The Zero-COVID policy and growth slowdown

The aforementioned zero-COVID policy has had a significant impact on production and consumption in affected areas. In March 2022, lockdowns were imposed in Changchun City in the Jilin Province, which is home to automotive-related companies and high-tech industry clusters, as well as in Shenzhen City in the Guangdong Province. In April, a lockdown was imposed in Shanghai, resulting in the shutdown of factory operations, which had a major impact on supply chains both in China and globally.

Table 2-2-4 shows the nominal GRP of each province and directly controlled city in China as well as their real GRP growth rates (YoY) for the January-September period of 2022 in descending order of economic size.

Table 2-2-4   Economic Scale and Real Growth Rates of Chinese Regions

Rank	Provinces and Municipalities	2021 Nominal GRP(billion yuan)	share of GDP	2022(Jan-Sep) Real GRP growth rate (%)
1	GUANGDONG	12,437.0	10.9	2.3
2	JIANGSU	11,636.4	10.2	2.3
3	SHANDONG	8,309.6	7.3	4.0
4	ZHEJIANG	7,351.6	6.5	3.1
5	HENAN	5,888.7	5.2	3.7
6	SICHUAN	5,385.1	4.7	1.5
7	HUBEI	5,001.3	4.4	4.7
8	FUJIAN	4,881.0	4.3	5.2
9	HUNAN	4,606.3	4.0	4.8
10	SHANGHAI	4,321.5	3.8	-1.4
11	ANHUI	4,295.9	3.8	3.3
12	HEBEI	4,039.1	3.6	3.7
13	BEIJING	4,027.0	3.5	0.8
14	SHAANXI	2,980.1	2.6	4.8
15	JIANGXI	2,962.0	2.6	5.0
16	CHONGQING	2,789.4	2.5	3.1
17	LIAONING	2,758.4	2.4	2.1
18	YUNNAN	2,714.7	2.4	3.8
19	GUANGXI	2,474.1	2.2	3.1
20	SHANXI	2,259.0	2.0	5.3
21	INNER MONGOLIA	2,051.4	1.8	5.0
22	GUIZHOU	1,958.6	1.7	2.8
23	XINJIANG	1,598.4	1.4	3.9
24	TIANJIN	1,569.5	1.4	1.0
25	HEILONGJIANG	1,487.9	1.3	2.9
26	JILIN	1,323.6	1.2	-1.6
27	GANSU	1,024.3	0.9	4.1
28	HAINAN	647.5	0.6	-0.5
29	NINGXIA	452.2	0.4	4.9
30	QINGHAI	334.7	0.3	2.6
31	TIBET	208.0	0.2	2.0

Note: Real GRP growth rates are for January-September 2022 (YoY).
Source: Prepared by the author from CEIC.

Notably, Shanghai (-1.4%) and the Jilin Province (-1.6%), where lockdowns were particularly severe, experienced negative growth. In addition, in provinces with large economies, such as Guangdong (+2.3%) and Jiangsu (+2.3%), where lockdowns were imposed, the GDP growth rate was lower than that of China as a whole (+3.0%).

In 2022 Q4, the COVID-19 infection situation remained unsettled, with lockdowns in major cities such as Chengdu in the Sichuan Province, Chongqing, and Guangzhou in the Guangdong Province. As a result, there are concerns that China's GDP growth rate might deteriorate further.

(3) The impact of China's economic slowdown on the Kansai economy

To analyze the impact of the deterioration in the Chinese economy caused by China's zero-COVID policy on the Kansai economy, first we estimate an export function. This helps us assess the impact of the Chinese economy on the exports of the Kansai and Japan. The data used are Chinese real GDP and real export indices (on an annual basis) for Kansai and the nation as a whole. The functional form of the export function to be estimated is as follows:

$$\log(kan\_ex)=const+a\log(ch\_gdpr)$$

Note: kan_ex indicates Kansai real export index and ch_gdpr indicates Chinese real GDP.

According to our estimates, the income elasticity of Chinese real GDP with respect to Kansai and national exports is 0.462 for Kansai and 0.304 for Japan. This means that a 1% change in China's GDP would result in a 0.462% and 0.304% change in Kansai and Japan's exports, respectively. The results suggest that the impact of changes in the Chinese economy is greater in the Kansai region than in the nation as a whole.

Next, based on these estimates, we conducted a simulation using the APIR-developed Kansai Economic Forecasting Model to see how the slowdown in the Chinese economy would affect the entire Kansai economy through exports. Assuming that China's real GDP declines by -1%, real exports from Kansai would decline by -0.462%. This -0.462% decrease in Kansai's real exports would reduce Kansai's real GRP by -0.12% in FY 2022, -0.13% in FY 2023, and -0.13% in FY 2024. In monetary terms, the decrease is between 94.3 billion yen and 108.2 billion yen. The impact on private-sector facilities is particularly large, ranging from -0.33% to -0.36%. Simulation results are shown in Table 2-2-5.

Table 2-2-5   Simulation results

FY		2022	2023	2024
Private final consumption expenditure (JPY billion)				
A. base		47,424	47,951	48,470
B. simulation		47,420	47,945	48,463
	divergence(B-A)	-4	-7	-8
	deviation ratio(%)	-0.01	-0.01	-0.02
Private non-residential capital investment(JPY billion)				
A. base		14,240	14,533	15,006
B. simulation		14,189	14,480	14,956
	divergence(B-A)	-51	-53	-50
	deviation ratio(%)	-0.36	-0.36	-0.33
Exports(JPY billion)				
A. base		30,018	30,069	31,063
B. simulation		29,880	29,930	30,919
	divergence(B-A)	-139	-139	-143
	deviation ratio(%)	-0.46	-0.46	-0.46
Imports(JPY billion)				
A. base		27,238	27,151	28,074
B. simulation		27,130	27,027	27,944
	divergence(B-A)	-109	-124	-130
	deviation ratio(%)	-0.40	-0.46	-0.46
Real GRP(JPY billion)				
A. base		87,446	88,430	89,694
B. simulation		87,344	88,316	89,579
	divergence(B-A)	-102.4	-113.6	-115.4
	deviation ratio(%)	-0.12	-0.13	-0.13
Real GRP growth rate(%)				
A. base		1.8	1.1	1.4
B. simulation		1.7	1.1	1.4
	deviation ratio(%)	-0.12	-0.01	0.00

Source: APIR "Kansai Economic Insight Quarterly" No. 61

Section 3
INCOME DISTRIBUTION: A MAJOR CHALLENGE FOR KANSAI'S ECONOMY

KINOSHITA, Yusuke; INADA, Yoshihisa; NOMURA, Ryosuke; YOSHIDA, Shigekazu

1. Introduction: Zooming in on Income Distribution

In last year's *Economic Outlook*, we examined the adjustment process of households and firms after the COVID-19 pandemic and focused on firms' deteriorating earnings and their employment adjustment. From around 2014 until before the pandemic, demand by inbound tourism was robust and employment was growing, especially in the face-to-face service industry. However, after the onset of the pandemic, sales declined significantly in the non-manufacturing sector, especially in the lodging and restaurant industries, due to infection prevention measures such as requests to close or shorten business hours. The result was a significant adjustment in employment, which mainly affected women working part-time.

Prime Minister Fumio Kishida, who was elected in September 2021, emphasized at his inaugural press conference that the so-called 'new capitalism' has two pillars: a growth strategy and a distribution strategy. The latter is supposed to "increase working people's share of national income," "expand the middle class and thereby address the problem with low-birth rate problem," and "boost income distribution by the government in order to expand the income of the middle class". Subsequently, a major report by the Cabinet Office (2022), which analyzed the current state of and the outlook for the Japanese economy, identified income distribution as a key challenge.

How has the distribution of labor and capital income changed during the recovery from the COVID-19 pandemic? In this section, we analyze the income distribution in the Kansai region based on the discussion developed by the Cabinet Office (2022). We discuss the importance of boosting labor productivity through higher wages and investing in human capital in the distributional policies of the Kishida administration in order to regain a thick middle class.

2. Income Distribution before the COVID-19 pandemic

(1) Distribution of lab or income

First, we look at the distribution of labor income since the 2000s. Specifically, annual labor income of individuals is divided into several classes, and the income

[Japan]

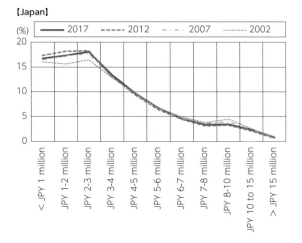

[Kansai]

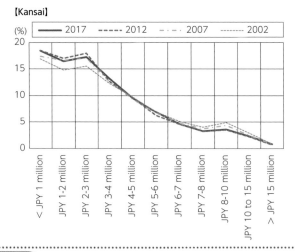

Figure 2-3-1   Changes in the Distribution of Annual Labor Income: Kansai vs. Japan

Note: Annual income from main job. The share for Kansai is calculated by summing the number of persons in each income bracket in Shiga, Kyoto, Osaka, Hyogo, Nara, and Wakayama prefectures.
Source: Compiled by the authors based on the Basic Survey of Employment Structure by the Ministry of Internal Affairs and Communications.

distribution showing the percentage of individuals who fall into each class is compared over time, and the median value is confirmed.

Figure 2-3-1 shows the distribution of annual labor income (annual income from main jobs) in Japan since 2002. It shows that the percentage of individuals earning less than 3 million yen has been increasing in recent years, except in 2012, the year after the Great East Japan Earthquake. On the other hand, there has been almost no change in the middle-income group earning 3-8 million yen, and the percentage of the high-income earners (8-15 million yen) has been decreasing.

A comparison of Japan and Kansai (the lower part of Figure 2-3-1) shows that the trend is the same. However, the share of low-income earners is higher in Kansai - in 2017, 18.4% of the respondents in Kansai had incomes of less than 1 million yen, compared with 16.7% in Japan as a whole. The average income in Kansai is lower than the national average.

Next, we look at trends in the median annual labor income. Figure 2-3-2 shows that median income has been declining both in Japan as a whole and in Kansai. The median labor income in 2017 was 2.76 million yen in Japan, and 2.71 million in Kansai. Compared to 2002, the median labor income decreased by 170,000 yen nationwide (from 2.92 million yen to 2.76 million yen), and by a staggering 270,000 yen in Kansai (2.98 million yen to 2.71 million yen).

Next, we compare the shares of households in the low-income bracket (less than 3 million yen), the middle-income bracket (3 to 8 million yen), and the high-income bracket (10 million yen or more) in 2014 and 2019. Figure 2-3-3 shows that the percentage of households in the low-income bracket remained almost unchanged nationwide (15.5% in 2014 → 15.3% in 2019), while the percentage in Kansai increased by 2.9 percentage points (14.4% in 2014 → 17.3% in 2019). In the middle-income bracket, while both Japan as a whole and Kansai have seen a decline, the decline has been larger in Kansai: -4.9 percentage points as compared to -1.9 percentage points in Japan as a whole. On the other hand, the percentage increase in the high-income group was smaller in Kansai (+1.5 percentage points) than nationwide (+2.0 percentage points). The shrinkage of the middle-income bracket is an indication of the polarization of income both in Japan and in Kansai. However, in contrast to Japan as a whole, Kansai is also characterized by an increase in the share of the low-income bracket.

Next, we calculated the median annual income per household for working households. The median income per household increased from 5.46 million yen in 2014 to 5.56 million yen in 2019 in Japan, while it decreased from 5.47 million yen to 5.33 million yen in Kansai. On a per capita basis, however, labor income declined both in Japan and in Kansai in that period. The increase in household income and the decline in per capita income suggest that on the national level there has been an increase in labor income earned by members other than the head of the household. In Kansai, however, incomes declined on both household and per capita basis.

In order to analyze the reasons for the decline in Kansai, we focus on the

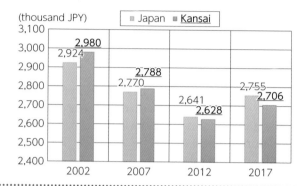

Figure 2-3-2   Changes in median annual labor income: Kansai vs. Japan

Note: Annual income from main job.
Source: Compiled by the authors based on the Basic Survey of Employment Structure by the Ministry of Internal Affairs and Communications.

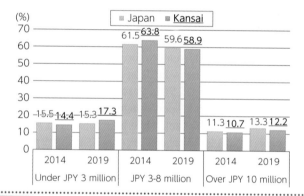

Figure 2-3-3   Changes in annual household income: Kansai vs. Japan

Note: Working households only. The figures for Japan are calculated based on Table 6-54 of the National Household Survey. The figures for Kansai are aggregates of data for Shiga, Kyoto, Osaka, Hyogo, Nara, and Wakayama prefectures based on Table 9-0 of the National Household Survey.
Source: Compiled by the authors based on Table 30-0 of the National Household Survey by the Ministry of Internal Affairs and Communications.

employment status. The reason is that, in general, non-regular workers work shorter hours and earn lower wages per hour, so an increase in the number of non-regular workers is likely to have an impact on the widening gap in labor income among workers.

Figure 2-3-4 shows the distribution of annual earnings by gender and employment status in Japan using the Ministry of Internal Affairs and Communications' Labor Force Survey.

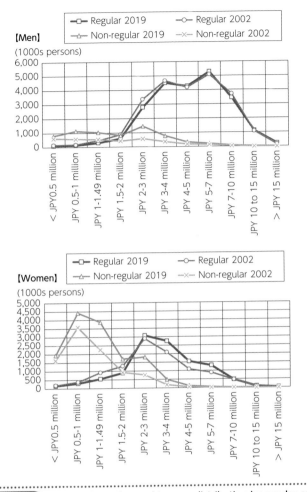

[Men]

(1000s persons)

-□- Regular 2019   -○- Regular 2002
-△- Non-regular 2019   -×- Non-regular 2002

[Women]

(1000s persons)

-□- Regular 2019   -○- Regular 2002
-△- Non-regular 2019   -×- Non-regular 2002

Figure 2-3-4 Comparison of annual income distribution by gender and employment type: Kansai vs. Japan

Note: Income from work (annual); non-regular employees in 2002 are the total of part-time employees, dispatched workers, and contract and temporary workers.
Source: Compiled by the authors based on the Labor Force Survey (Table II-12) by the Ministry of Internal Affairs and Communications.

For males, the majority of full-time employees in 2019 were in the income bracket of 2-10 million yen per year. On the other hand, the majority of non-regular employees were in the 1–2-million-yen income bracket. Comparing the shape of the distribution between 2002 and 2007, there is almost no change in the number of regular employees, while the number of non-regular employees in the income bracket of less than 4 million yen per year has increased.

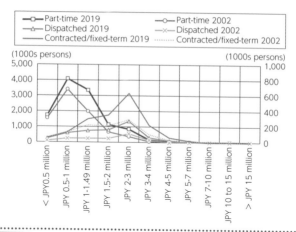

Figure 2-3-5   Comparison of annual income distribution among female part-time employees: 2002 vs 2019

Note: Left axis for part-time employees, right axis for others
Source: Compiled by the authors based on the Labor Force Survey by the Ministry of Internal Affairs and Communications.

For female, compared to 2002, the number of persons in the 1–2-million-yen income bracket decreased, while the number of persons in the 3–7-million-yen income bracket increased. Compared to 2002, the number of non-regular employees in the income bracket of 0.5-1.5 million yen has increased significantly. Figure 2-3-5 shows that this increase has mainly been driven by women.

The above suggests that the increase in the number of part-time and non-regular employees has been one of the determining factors of the polarization of income distribution.

What about the Kansai region? Since the "Labor Force Survey" used in Figures 2-3-4 and 2-3-5 does not provide data by region, the authors estimated the share of part-time workers in Kansai based on the "Monthly Labor Survey" published by each prefecture. Figure 2-3-6 shows that the share of part-time workers in Kansai is about 3 to 4 percentage points higher than the nationwide share, and this share has been increasing. Therefore, it is possible that the number of part-time workers is increasing in Kansai, as in the rest of Japan, and that the distribution of annual income is becoming more polarized.

As shown in Figure 2-3-3, even before the COVID-19 pandemic, the number of low-income households in Kansai was rising, and the number of middle-income households was shrinking. The boom of inbound tourism in Kansai between the mid-2010s and 2019 led to an increase in the number of people employed in tourism-related industries. Many of the employees in these industries were part-time or non-regular employees with relatively low incomes,

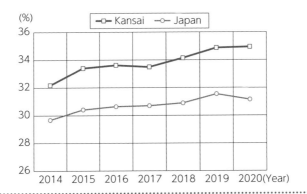

Part I
Part II
Part III
Part IV

Figure 2-3-6   Comparison of the shares of part-time employees: Kansai vs. Japan

Note : Businesses with 5 or more workers
Source : Compiled by the authors based on the Monthly Labor Survey by the Ministry of Health, Labor and Welfare and official data from local governments of Kansai prefectures.

which may have contributed to the decline in household incomes.

(2) Trends in Capital Income

The Cabinet Office (2022) examined the distribution of financial asset balances by decile of total household assets (the sum of net financial assets and housing and residential land assets) in 2014 and 2019 for the entire nation. In particular, the share of the decile holding 40% of total financial assets, or about 50 million yen per household on average, is said to have increased.

Figure 2-3-7 shows the total amount of financial assets held by households in Kansai as well as in Japan by asset class using the National Household Survey. As shown in the figure, the total amount of household assets per household position increased in Kansai as well for households holding more than 50 million yen. On the other hand, it shows a decrease for households with less than 6 million yen.

Figure 2-3-8 shows the breakdown of household asset balances in Kansai in 2019 by asset category. The figure shows that the larger the financial asset balance is, the larger is the share of securities holdings, including stocks. Although it has been declining, the return on financial assets held by the decile with the largest share of securities holdings in Japan is still quite high. In addition, the distribution of interest and dividend income also shows an increase in the share of the richest decile, indicating that the capital-income gap is widening. The fact that households owning securities are more likely to own high-value assets in Kansai and Japan alike, may be a factor in widening capital-income disparities.

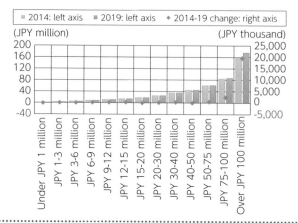

Figure 2-3-7   Change in financial assets held by asset category in Kansai: 2014/2019

Note : Working households only. Figures for Kansai are averages for each income group in Shiga, Kyoto, Osaka, Hyogo, Nara, and Wakayama prefectures. Total household assets are the sum of "net financial assets (financial assets minus financial liabilities)" and "housing and residential land assets."
Source : Compiled by the authors based on Table 30-0 of the National Household Survey by the Ministry of Internal Affairs and Communications.

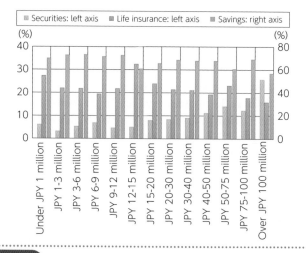

Figure 2-3-8   Breakdown of financial assets in Kansai: 2019

Note : Working households only. Figures for Kansai are averages for each income bracket in Shiga, Kyoto, Osaka, Hyogo, Nara, and Wakayama prefectures.
Source : Compiled by the authors based on Table 30-0 of the National Household Survey by the Ministry of Internal Affairs and Communications.

3. Income Distribution and the Middle Class during the COVID-19 pandemic

(1) Income distribution before and after the COVID-19 pandemic

In the previous section, we saw that the income environment of households in the Kansai region was severe even before the impact of COVID-19 crystalized. We proceed to discuss how the COVID-19 pandemic affected income distribution.

Table 2-3-1 shows the annual income by income decile for working households with two or more members in 2019-21, based on the "Family Income and Expenditure Survey" by the Ministry of Internal Affairs and Communications. It shows that the average annual income has increased slightly from 7.29 million yen in 2019, to 7.33 million yen in 2020, and then further to 7.37 million yen in 2021.

However, here is a decrease in annual income in the first (poorest) and third deciles from 2019 to 20, and in the first quintile from 19 to 21. On the other hand, annual income increased in the rest of the working households. Thus, the increase in average annual income was mainly due to the increase in annual income in the higher-income deciles.

Table 2-3-1   Annual Income by Income Decile: Nationwide

Units: JPY thousand

	Average	I	II	III	IV	V	VI	VII	VIII	IX	X
2019	7,290	2,920	4,230	5,010	5,690	6,360	7,090	7,910	8,860	10,370	14,490
2020	7,330	2,900	4,240	4,990	5,700	6,420	7,140	7,950	9,000	10,430	14,580
2021	7,370	2,900	4,250	5,030	5,720	6,380	7,090	7,930	8,960	10,490	15,000
2019-20 change	40	-20	10	-20	10	60	50	40	140	60	90
2019-21 change	80	-20	20	20	30	20	0	20	100	120	510

Note : Working households with two or more members.
Source : Compiled by the authors based on Table 2-5 of the Household Income and Expenditure Survey by the Ministry of Internal Affairs and Communications.

(2) A Shrinking Middle Class

As discussed above, due to the worsening economic situation caused by the COVID-19 pandemic, the incomes of low-income households have been shrinking, while those of high-income households have been increasing. However, what about middle-income households (hereafter referred to as the "middle class")? To investigate this matter, we use data from the Household Income and Expenditure Survey by the Ministry of Internal Affairs and Communications (Figure 2-3-9). The figure shows the shares of households in each of the three

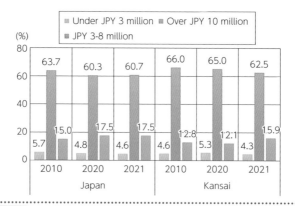

Figure 2-3-9 Comparison of the percentage of households in each income bracket: Japan vs. Kansai

Source : Compiled by the authors based on the Household Income and Expenditure Survey by the Ministry of Internal Affairs and Communications.

income brackets (less than 3 million yen, 3-8 million yen, and 10 million yen or more) both in Japan and in Kansai.

Comparing 2010 and 2021, the percentage of households in the low-income bracket has declined in both nationwide (from 5.7% in 2010 to 4.6% in 2021) and in Kansai (from 4.6% to 4.3%). The decline in Kansai is smaller than that in Japan. The percentage of middle-class households declined both in Japan (from 63.7% in 2010 to 60.7% in 2021) and in Kansai (from 66.0% to 62.5%). However, the extent of the decline was greater in Kansai. Finally, the percentage of households in the high-income bracket with annual incomes of 10 million yen or more has increased both in Japan (from 15.0% in 2010 to 17.5% in 2021) and in Kansai (from 12.8% to 15.9%). However, the increase in Kansai was lower than that in Japan.

A comparison of 2010 and 2020, the year the COVID-19 pandemic started, reveals a different picture from the comparison of 2010 and 2021 above. Whereas the percentage of low-income households declined nationwide (from 5.7% in 2010 to 4.8% in 2020), in Kansai it increased (from 4.6% to 5.3%). The percentage of high-income households rose nationwide (from 15.0% in 2010 to 17.5% in 2020), while it declined in Kansai (from 12.8% in 2010 to 12.1% in 2020). Thus, focusing on the Kansai region, the proportion of low-income households increased and that of high-income households decreased in 2020 due to the significant impact of the COVID-19 pandemic.

From the data presented above, it can be concluded that the already unfavorable income environment of middle-income households in Kansai was further exacerbated by the COVID-19 pandemic.

As mentioned above, in recent years, employment in the Kansai region, especially among non-regular workers in the food service and lodging industries, has been increasing due to the increased demand generated by inbound tourism. However, since 2020, in addition to the evaporation of inbound tourism due to the COVID-19 pandemic, several emergency declarations were issued, and restrictions aimed at curbing the spread of infections were imposed. This has exerted significant employment adjustment pressure, which affected workers employed in these industries.

The shrinkage of the middle class has led to a slump in consumption, which has put a damper on the momentum of the Kansai economy's recovery from the COVID-19 pandemic. Although the rise in inbound tourism was a major growth factor for Kansai's economy, it also thinned the middle class in terms of income distribution. This has created an economic structure that is vulnerable to economic shocks, as witnessed by the impact of the COVID-19 pandemic.

4. Conclusion: The Need to Invest in Human Capital

In this article, we compared the dynamics of labor and capital income in the Kansai region before and after the COVID-19 pandemic with the nationwide trends, using representative statistics.

We have seen that the polarization of income was an issue in Kansai even before the outbreak of the COVID-19 pandemic, as evidenced by the shrinkage of the middle-income group and an increase in the shares of the low-income and high-income groups (Figure 2-3-1 and Figure 2-3-3).

Due to the impact of the COVID-19 pandemic, middle-class incomes declined further, and the middle-income moved closer to the low-income group, leaving households in a difficult situation in terms of income (Table 2-3-1 and Figure 2-3-9).

With regard to these negative trends, we believe that wage increases and enhanced human capital investment are the key to regaining a thick middle class.

Prime Minister Kishida's administration has set forth three major pillars as part of the so-called "distribution strategy": (1) raising wages, (2) boosting investment in human capital, and (3) maintaining a middle class throughout the next generation. Among these policies, support for the middle class has already been proposed by economic organizations and think tanks, and it has become an important policy issue. However, there has been little progress with regard to raising wages.

The Survey of Corporate Statistics by the Kinki Regional Finance Bureau

Part I

Part II

Part III

Part IV

shows that the amount of funds allocated to labor costs (wages) by companies in Kansai has declined from 10.6 trillion yen in FY2001 to 8.1 trillion yen in FY 2019, a decrease of 23.3%. During the COVID-19 pandemic, it decreased further to 8.0 trillion yen in FY 2020 (dropped by -24.8%), and to 7.9 trillion yen in FY 2021 (dropped by -25.2%). The Monthly Labor Survey shows that wage growth has been lower in Kansai than in the rest of Japan, and this has led to a stagnation in private consumption.

As shown in Figure 2-3-9, the percentage of low-income households in Kansai has hardly declined compared to Japan as a whole. Therefore, in the short run, economic support measures targeting low-income groups are crucial. On the other hand, in the long run, the key challenge is to improve labor productivity by boosting investment in human capital. As the working population declines due to the aging population and the falling birthrate, increasing labor productivity is becoming increasingly relevant.

The Basic Policies for Economic and Fiscal Management and Reform (hereinafter Framework 2022), which were approved by the Cabinet on June 7, 2022, identified "investment in people" as a priority investment area. In addition to previously proposed policies, such as the promotion of side jobs and re-qualification, Framework 2022 policy promotes lifelong education (or "recurrent education") in order to facilitate labor mobility.

In line with Framework 2022, universities and technical colleges are also expected to accelerate their response to social changes by fostering innovative human resources who can respond to digitalization. This is considered a key element in achieving the so-called "new capitalism."

One of the challenges in terms of human resources in Kansai is the out-migration of many highly skilled workers to the Kanto region in response to the rise of high-value-added service industries there. In consideration of this, in the medium to long term, it will be important not only to ensure the availability of highly skilled human resources by boosting human capital investment, but also to transfer labor force from low-productivity sectors to growth sectors through special subsidies aimed at supporting long-term employment adjustments.

Section 1 of Chapter 6 of this Economic Outlook points out that one of the major reasons for the stagnation of Kansai's economy has been a lack of investment. This suggests that in addition to investing in human capital locally, it will be important to attract domestic and foreign investment, as well as highly skilled human resources.

A series of large-scale investments on the order of 1 trillion yen are scheduled to take place in Kansai in the near future, including the Osaka-Kansai Expo in 2025. We hope that the implementation of such projects will help the Kansai economy, which has been stagnant since the 1970 Osaka Expo, to turn around and achieve a virtuous cycle of growth and income distribution.

References

OECD (2019), "Under Pressure: The Squeezed Middle Class", https://www.oecd. org/publications/under-pressure-the-squeezed-middle-class-689afed1-en. htm (accessed on July 13, 2022)

21st Century Policy Institute (2022), Report on "A major shift in economic and fiscal management toward a middle class revival," June 2022, http:// www.21ppi.org/pdf/thesis/220602.pdf (accessed on July 13, 2022)

Ishii, Kayoko and Mio Higuchi (2015), "Increase in Non-regular Employment and Income Inequality: From the Perspective of Individuals and House-holds: Characteristics of Japan in an International Comparison", Mita Journal of Commerce, Vol. 58, No. 3, pp. 37-55

"Kansai, Annual Income Worse than Kanto: Urgent Need to Strengthen the Middle Class," Sankei Shimbun, December 6, 2021, Sankei West, https:// www.sankei.com/article/20211206-XGMTVEK3SVK6DDRFXZI6ESPIEA/ (accessed on July 13, 2022)

Kansai Economic Federation (2021), "Proposal for Medium- and Long-term Review of Tax and Fiscal Policy: Toward a Tax and Fiscal System that is Responsible for Realizing a Sustainable Economic Society and Pioneering the Future," https://www.kankeiren.or.jp/material/211206ikensho.pdf (accessed on July 13, 2022)

Yusuke Kinoshita and Kuo Chiu-Wei (2021), " Chapter3 Section5 COVID-19 pandemic and Corporate Responses", APIR Kansai and the Asia Pacific, Economic Outlook: 2021, Nikkei Printing Inc.

Ministry of Health, Labour and Welfare (2012), "Section 2: Challenges for the Revival of a Thick Middle Class," Labor Economy Analysis 2012, https:// www.mhlw.go.jp/wp/hakusyo/roudou/12/ (accessed on July 13, 2022)

Prime Minister's Office (2021), "Prime Minister Kishida Press Conference," October 4, 2021, https://www.kantei.go.jp/jp/100_kishida/statement/2021/1004kaiken.html (accessed on July 13, 2022)

—, Major Policies Top Page, — https://www.kantei.go.jp/jp/headline/seisaku_kishida/bunpaisenryaku.html (accessed on July 13, 2022)

—, Basic Policies for Economic and Fiscal Management and Reform 2022 Toward a New Capitalism: Turning Solutions to Challenges into Engines for Growth and Achieving a Sustainable Economy, https://www5.cao.go.jp/

Part I

Part II

Part III

Part IV

keizai-shimon/kaigi/cabinet/2022/2022_basicpolicies_en.pdf (accessed on July 13, 2022)

"Income Inequality Widens Among Young People, Spurring Fears of Declining Birthrate," Nihon Keizai Shimbun, February 7, 2022, https://www.nikkei.com/article/DGXZQOUA04A8T0U2A200C2000000/ (accessed on July 13, 2022).

Tanaka, Soichiro and Rito Shikata (2019), "Estimating the middle class in Japan: 1994-2009", Keio-IES Discussion Paper Series DP2019-001

Cabinet Office (2022), "Japan Economy 2021-2022 - Towards a Virtuous Circle of Growth and Distribution", February 2022, https://www5.cao.go.jp/keizai3/2021/0207nk/ keizai2021-2022pdf.html (accessed on July 13, 2022)

Shigekazu Yoshida, Yoshihisa Inada, Yoichi Matsubayashi, Ryosuke Nomura (2020), "Chapter3 Section4 Trade Structure with China and the Kansai Economy", APIR Kansai and the Asia Pacific, Economic Outlook: 2020, Nikkei Printing Inc.

Column A — The Economic Impact of Russia's Invasion of Ukraine on Japan and Kansai from a Trade Perspective

YOSHIDA, Shigekazu

1. Introduction

The economic impact of Russia's invasion of Ukraine is spreading around the world through various channels, including commodity markets, trade, and financial markets. This column analyzes the impact of Russia's invasion of Ukraine from a trade perspective.

Figure 2-CA-1 is a simple representation of the direct and indirect impacts of the conflict. It shows the economic size of major economies and the share of Russian exports and imports in their total international trade.

In the following paragraphs, we outline the state of trade between major countries/regions and Russia in 2021 by trade good categories. We then calculate the degree of dependence on Russia for major economies by trade good category, defined as Russia's share in each good's total exports and imports.

We define the trade share of country i and that of individual goods as follows:

$$\text{Trade share of country } i \text{ with country } j = \frac{X_{ij}}{\sum_j X_{ij}} \quad (1)$$

$$\text{Therein, the trade share of good } k = \frac{X_{ij}^k}{\sum_j X_{ij}^k} \quad (2)$$

(Note: i is the home country, j is the trading partner, X_{ij} is the trade value between country i and country j, and X_{ij}^k is the trade value between country i and country j for good k).

By comparing the trade share of the home country with respect to Russia (1) and the trade share of Russia for individual trade goods (2), we assess the amount of risk associated with each good for major economies. Even if Russia has a low share in a country's total trade as a whole, Russia's share might be very large for a specific trade good. For example, although Russia accounts for only 1.8% of Japan's total imports, with regard to lumber, Japan's dependence on Russia is up to 13.1%.

An analysis by trade good category is important, because if the supply of a particular good were to be disrupted due to a deterioration of the conflict, it might lead to supply problems in the importing country.

Part I

Part II

Part III

Part IV

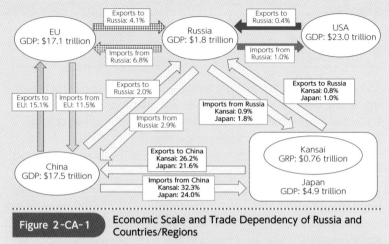

Source: Authors' calculations based on IMF DataMapper, UN Comtrade, and Ministry of Finance, Trade Statistics of Japan.

Figure 2-CA-1 Economic Scale and Trade Dependency of Russia and Countries/Regions

2. Major economies' trade with Russia and their trade dependence on Russia

Below, we outline the state of trade between Russia and the US, EU, and China by trade good category in 2021, and we focus on the goods whose exports and imports are heavily dependent on Russia.

(1) Trade between US and Russia

In 2021, the US exports to Russia totaled $6.4 billion and imports totaled $30.8 billion. The share of Russia-bound exports in total US exports is 0.4%, Russia's share in total US imports is about 1.0%. This suggests that the US is not highly dependent on trade with Russia.

Table 2-CA-1 shows the top 10 export/import good categories from/to the US, the dollar value of these exports/imports, the share of each good category in total exports/imports, and Russia's share in the exports/imports of each good category.

Among US exports to Russia, transportation machinery, including Automotive parts (6.7%), motor vehicles (4.7%), and aircraft (3.4%), account for a relatively high share. On the other hand, oil and oil products (42.9%) account for the majority of imports from Russia, followed

| Table 2-CA-1 | US trade with Russia and dependence on Russia | | | | | | |

US exports to Russia				US imports from Russia			
Trade good category	Billion yen	Share of total exports to Russia (%)	Dependence on Russia (%)	Trade good category	Billion yen	Share of total imports to Russia (%)	Dependence on Russia (%)
Auto motive Parts	42.6	6.7	1.2	Petroleum and rel. products	1,321.1	42.9	20.6
Auto mobiles	30.1	4.7	0.5	Crude oil	484.3	15.7	3.5
Aircraft	21.6	3.4	6.1	Platinum	245.0	8.0	13.4
Blood for medical use	20.5	3.2	0.5	Pig iron, etc.	119.8	3.9	35.0
Tractors	14.0	2.2	2.7	Crusta-ceans	110.8	3.6	10.1
Medical equip-ment	12.3	1.9	0.4	Iron	92.7	3.0	21.9
Engines	12.1	1.9	1.6	Nitrogen fertilizers	79.3	2.6	20.2
Food prepara-tions	10.0	1.6	1.4	Radioac-tive com-pounds	67.1	2.2	21.6
Data pro-cessing machinery	9.9	1.5	0.4	Aluminum	52.3	1.7	4.5
Tires	9.8	1.5	2.2	Ferro alloys	46.9	1.5	13.9
Total	638.8	100.0	0.4	Total	3,076.2	100.0	1.0

Source: Prepared by the author from UN Comtrade.

by crude oil (15.7%), platinum (8.0%), pig iron, etc. (3.9%), and shellfish (3.6%). Notably, energy-related products account for 60% of total imports from Russia.

Among the top 10 US exports to Russia, aircraft is the trade good category for which Russia has the largest share (6.1%) relative to its share in total US exports (0.4%).

On the other hand, relative to total US imports from Russia (1.0%), the US is much more dependent on Russia for pig iron, etc. (35.0%), iron (21.9%), radioactive compounds (21.6%), petroleum and its derivatives (20.6%), and nitrogen fertilizers (20.2%). However, despite the high

Part I

Part II

Part III

Part IV

Table 2-CA-2   EU's trade with Russia and dependence on Russia

EU's exports to Russia				EU's imports from Russia			
Trade good category	Billion yen	Share of total exports to Russia (%)	Dependence on Russia (%)	Trade good category	Billion yen	Share of total imports to Russia (%)	Dependence on Russia (%)
Medical supplies	679.0	6.5	4.8	Crude oil	5,739.0	34.0	24.9
Automotive parts	381.3	3.7	6.2	Petroleum and rel. products	2,662.3	15.8	39.4
Auto mobiles	365.3	3.5	2.4	Petroleum gas	2,232.2	13.2	30.5
Aircraft	264.6	2.5	6.1	Coal and briquettes	611.4	3.6	45.2
Blood for medical use	218.6	2.1	1.9	Miscellaneous	465.6	2.8	6.3
Data processing machinery	150.8	1.4	6.5	Coal tar distillates	324.5	1.9	39.3
Medical equipment	143.1	1.4	4.3	Iron	310.3	1.8	50.8
Centrifuges	127.6	1.2	7.1	Copper	271.1	1.6	35.8
Machinery	126.3	1.2	5.7	Platinum	248.6	1.5	22.0
Cocks, valves	123.0	1.2	5.9	Diamonds	213.0	1.3	17.3
Total	10,446.5	100.0	4.1	Total	16,875.4	100.0	6.8

Source: Prepared by the author from UN Comtrade.

dependence on petroleum and related products, in the case of a conflict deterioration, the US is able to supply its own crude oil production, meaning that there are no economic security concerns.

Table 2-CA-3				China's trade with Russia and dependence on Russia				
China's exports to Russia				China's imports from Russia				
Trade good category	Billion yen	Share of total exports to Russia (%)	Dependence on Russia (%)	Trade good category	Billion yen	Share of total imports to Russia (%)	Dependence on Russia (%)	
Tele-phones	538.7	8.0	2.1	Crude oil	4,054.1	51.3	15.7	
Data processing machines	330.2	4.9	1.6	Coal and bri-quettes	706.6	8.9	26.1	
Auto mobiles	151.8	2.3	6.2	Copper	390.5	4.9	10.8	
Auto-motive parts	142.3	2.1	3.1	Petro-leum gas	369.7	4.7	5.3	
Clothing and accesso-ries	137.6	2.1	54.8	Lumber	304.4	3.9	38.7	
Toys	128.0	1.9	2.8	Iron ore	148.8	1.9	0.8	
Foot-wear	108.6	1.6	4.8	Petro-leum and related products	132.2	1.7	7.9	
House-hold electrical applianc-es	100.0	1.5	3.1	Copper ore	121.9	1.5	2.1	
Lighting fixtures	94.2	1.4	1.9	Platinum	119.1	1.5	11.9	
Gas pumps	91.8	1.4	3.8	Frozen fish	103.9	1.3	29.6	
Total	6,694.6	100.0	2.0	Total	7,897.1	100.0	2.9	

Source: Prepared by the author from UN Comtrade.

(2) Trade between EU and Russia

EU's exports to Russia and imports from Russia in 2021 totaled $104.5 billion and $168.8 billion, respectively, accounting for 4.1% and 6.8% of the EU's total exports and imports. EU's dependence on trade with Russia is relatively high compared to that of the US (Table 2-CA-2).

Among the EU's top 10 exports to Russia, pharmaceuticals, auto parts, and automobiles collectively account for about 14% of EU' total

Part I

Part II

Part III

Part IV

exports to Russia. On the other hand, within EU imports from Russia, energy-related goods account for a very high 66.6%, including crude oil (34.0%), oil and oil products (15.8%), petroleum gas (13.2%), and coal and coal briquettes (3.6%).

Relative to Russia's share in EU's total exports to Russia (4.1%), among the EU's top 10 exports to Russia, the ones for which Russia has the largest share are centrifuges (7.1%), data processing machinery (6.5%), and automotive parts (6.2%). On the other hand, relative to EU's total imports from Russia (6.8%), the EU is much more dependent on Russia for imports of iron (50.8%), coal and coal briquettes (45.2%), petroleum and oil products (39.4%). In other words, the EU's dependence on Russia for raw materials and energy-related goods is very high. The escalation of the situation in Ukraine has led to a significant decrease in imports of these products, which is a major blow to the EU economy.

(3) Trade between China and Russia

China's exports to Russia in 2021 totaled $66.9 billion, which is around 2.0% of China's total exports. Imports from Russia totaled $79.0 billion, representing 2.9% of China's total imports. China's dependence on trade with Russia is low compared to the EU, but high compared to the US and Japan (Table 2-CA-3).

China's top exports to Russia are telephone equipment (8.0% of China's exports to Russia) and data processing machinery (4.9%). On the other hand, crude oil dominates imports (51.3%), followed by coal and briquettes (8.9%).

Relative to Russia's share in China's total exports (2.0%), among China's top 10 export categories to Russia, clothing and accessories (54.8%) is the category for which Russia has the largest share, followed by automobiles (6.2%) and footwear (4.8%). On the other hand, relative to China's total imports from Russia (2.9%), China is much more dependent on Russia for imports of lumber (38.7%), frozen fish (29.6%), coal and briquettes (26.1%), and crude oil (15.7%). In other words, as an import market, China is highly dependent on Russia for raw materials and energy.

Table 2-CA-4			Japan's trade with Russia and dependence on Russia				
Japan's exports to Russia				Japan's imports from Russia			
Trade good category	Billion yen	Share of total exports to Russia (%)	Depen- dence on Russia (%)	Trade good category	Billion yen	Share of total imports to Russia (%)	Depen- dence on Russia (%)
Auto mobiles	357.5	41.5	3.3	Natural and manu- factured gases	372.4	24.0	7.4
Auto- motive parts	100.1	11.6	2.8	Petro- leum and related products	296.5	19.1	3.3
Con- struction and mining equip- ment	57.9	6.7	4.4	Non- ferrous metals	292.4	18.9	10.3
Rubber products	46.6	5.4	5.3	Coal, coke and bri- quettes	283.1	18.3	9.8
Engines and motors	46.1	5.3	1.8	Seafood and related products	137.4	8.9	9.1
Re-ex- ported products	27.5	3.2	0.5	Lumber	53.4	3.4	13.1
Cargo handling machin- ery	20.8	2.4	3.5	Iron and steel	45.4	2.9	4.3
Pumps and cen- trifuges	16.6	1.9	1.2	Metal ores and scrap	15.1	1.0	0.3
Electri- cal car equip- ment, etc.	9.7	1.1	1.8	Organic com- pounds	9.2	0.6	0.5
Electrical mea- suring instru- ments	9.4	1.1	0.5	Pulp and paper	5.6	0.4	4.0
Total	862.4	100.0	1.0	Total	1,548.9	100.0	1.8

Source: Compiled by the author from Trade Statistics of Japan, Ministry of Finance, Japan.

Part I

Part II

Part III

Part IV

3. Trade between Japan/Kansai and Russia, and their trade dependence on Russia

Finally, we examine Japan's and Kansai's trade with Russia (imports and exports) by trade good category using data from the Ministry of Finance.

(1) Trade between Japan and Russia

Japan's exports to Russia in 2021 totaled 862.4 billion yen, and imports were 1,548.9 billion yen. Russia's share in Japan's total imports and exports is around 1.0% for exports and 1.8% for imports, indicating that Japan's dependence on trade with Russia is not high (Table 2-CA-4).

Among Japan's top 10 exports to Russia, automobile-related goods account for more than 50% of total exports. Automobiles (41.5%) accounts for high proportion of exports, followed by automotive parts (11.6%), construction and mining equipment (6.7%). On the other hand, imports are dominated by energy-related goods, raw materials: natural and manufactured gas (24.0%), petroleum and its derivatives (19.1%), nonferrous metals (18.9%), coal, coke and briquettes (18.3%), seafood and its products (8.9%), and lumber (3.4%).

Although Japan's dependence on Russia with regard to exports is low, dependence on Russia for rubber products (5.3%) and construction and mining equipment (4.4%) is high compared to Japan's overall export dependence on Russia (1.0%). On the other hand, relative to Japan's total imports from Russia (1.8%), imports of lumber (13.1%), nonferrous metals (10.3%), coal, coke, and briquettes (9.8%), and seafood and fish products (9.1%) are high. The suspension of these imports is expected to have a significant impact on the construction, energy, and food and beverage industries.

(2) Trade between Kansai and Russia

Kansai's exports to Russia amounted to 143.1 billion yen, and imports from Russia were 141.4 billion yen in 2021. Compared to Japan as a whole, whose dependence on Russia is 1.0% for exports and 1.8% for imports, Russia's share in Kansai's trade is lower: 0.8% for exports and 0.9% for imports (Table 2-CA-5).

Among Kansai's top 10 exports to Russia, construction and mining

Table 2-CA-5 Kansai's trade with Russia and dependence on Russia

Kansai's exports to Russia				Kansai's imports from Russia			
Trade good category	Billion yen	Share of total exports to Russia (%)	Dependence on Russia (%)	Trade good category	Billion yen	Share of total imports to Russia (%)	Dependence on Russia (%)
Construction and mining equipment	42.4	29.6	6.5	Natural and manufactured gases	63.9	45.2	7.5
Auto mobiles	23.6	16.5	10.9	Coal, coke and briquettes	29.2	20.7	11.8
Engines and motors	9.4	6.6	1.8	Seafood and related products	12.4	8.7	5.4
Cargo handling machinery	8.1	5.6	5.0	Iron and steel	9.1	6.4	2.9
Automotive parts	6.2	4.3	2.7	Non-ferrous metals	5.3	3.8	1.8
Re-exported products	5.5	3.8	0.5	Petroleum and related products	2.7	1.9	0.4
Rubber products	3.9	2.7	3.2	Metal ores and scrap	2.1	1.5	0.5
Petroleum products	3.2	2.2	2.3	Organic compounds	2.1	1.5	0.4
Pumps and centrifuges	3.2	2.2	1.2	Tobacco	2.0	1.4	0.7
Organic Compounds	2.1	1.4	0.5	Inorganic compounds	1.2	0.9	0.5
Total	143.1	100.0	0.8	Total	141.4	100.0	0.9

Source: Compiled by the author from Trade Statistics of Japan, Ministry of Finance, Japan.

equipment (29.6%) tops the list, followed by automobiles (16.5%), prime movers (6.6%), cargo handling machinery (5.6%), and parts of automobiles (4.3%). Imports, on the other hand, are dominated by natural and manufactured gas (45.2%), coal, coke and briquettes (20.7%), fish and seafood (8.7%), and iron and steel (6.4%).

Relative to Russia's share in Kansai's total exports (0.8%), dependence on Russia is the highest for automobiles (10.9%), construction and mining equipment (6.5%), and cargo handling machinery (5.0%). On the other hand, Relative to Russia's share in Kansai's total imports (0.9%), dependence on Russia is the highest for coal, coke and briquettes (11.8%), natural gas and manufactured gas (7.5%), and fish and shellfish and fish products (5.4%). Kansai is clearly more dependent on Russia for coal, coke, and briquettes than Japan as a whole.

4. Conclusion

This analysis has shown that the direct impact of Russia's invasion of Ukraine on EU-Russia trade has been noticeable, especially with regard to energy-related goods. This is due to the fact that the EU's dependence on Russia for iron, coal and coal briquettes, and petroleum and its products is very high.

The economic sanctions against Russia by NATO countries and Russia's retaliation with regard to energy-related goods have increased the possibility of an economic slowdown in the EU economy. The escalating situation in Ukraine is forcing the EU to break away from its energy dependence on Russia, but the adjustment will take time and will exert downward pressure on the EU economy for some time.

On the other hand, Japan's overall dependence on Russian imports is low as a whole. However, dependence on lumber, nonferrous metals, coal, and fish and seafood products from Russia is relatively high. Kansai's economy is also highly dependent on Russian imports of coal, coke and briquettes, natural gas and manufactured gas, and fish and seafood products, with the level of dependence on coal, coke, and briquettes being higher than that of Japan as a whole. Therefore, the suspension of imports of these goods would have a significant impact on the construction, energy, and food services industries.

Finally, with regard to the indirect impact of the worsening situation in Ukraine on the economies of Japan and Kansai, the key factor to consider is the trade dependence between the EU and China. As shown earlier, the EU is highly dependent on Russia, especially for energy-related goods, and if imports of energy-related goods from Russia were to cease, the EU economy would be forced to slow down. A slowdown in the EU economy will exert downward pressure on the Chinese economy through a slowdown in China's exports to the EU.

Figure 2-CA-1 above also shows the dependence of trade ties between China and Japan and the Kansai region. Japan's exports to China account for 21.6% ($163.9 billion) of its total exports, and its imports from China account for 24.0% ($185.7 billion) of its total imports. The shares for Kansai are noticeably higher, respectively 26.2% and 32.3%, suggesting that Kansai's economy is characterized by a high degree of dependence on China. Therefore, a slowdown in the EU economy might indirectly exert downward pressure on Kansai's economy through its impact on the Chinese economy.

This is an example of the indirect effects of the escalating situation in Ukraine. When considering the economic impact of Russia's invasion of Ukraine, it is important to take both direct and indirect effects into account.

References

APIR Kansai and the Asia Pacific, Economic Outlook: 2020, Chapter 1, Section 1, pp. 159-160, Maruzen Publishing Corporation, September 2019.

Yoshihisa Inada, Ryosuke Nomura, Shigekazu Yoshida (2022), "Various Risks for the Kansai Economy as Seen from Russia's Invasion of Ukraine," APIR Trend Watch No. 80, (https://www.apir.or.jp/research/11056/, accessed on July 5, 2022)

Nihon Keizai Shimbun (2022), "Soaring Fertilizer Prices Hurt Agriculture," June 21, 2022 evening edition article (https://www.nikkei.com/article/DGKKZO61897980R20C22A6MM0000/, accessed on June 30, 2022)

Part I

Part II

Part III

Part IV

Chapter 3

CHALLENGES AND PROSPECTS FOR THE KANSAI ECONOMY

Section 1
CHALLENGES POSED BY THE POPULATION DECLINE IN THE KANSAI REGION

NOMURA, Ryosuke; KINOSHITA, Yusuke

Introduction

The long-term trend of Japan's population peaked at 128.06 million in 2010 and has been on trending downward since then, with a projected decline to 88.08 million by 2060 (Figure 3-1-1). According to the "2020 National (Population and housing) Census (hereinafter referred to as Population Census)" published by the Ministry of Internal Affairs and Communications (MIC) in 2021, Japan's total population (including foreigners) was 126,146,000 in 2020, down 948,646 from the previous census ("2015 Population Census"), and the population decline has

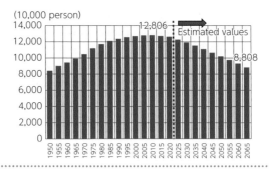

| Figure 3-1-1 | Total Population Trends in Japan: 1950 to 2060 |

Note: The future population projection is based on the median births (median deaths).
Source: Prepared based on Population Census, Ministry of Internal Affairs and Communications, until 2020; and National Institute of Population and Social Security Research (IPSS), "Population Projections for Japan" (released in 2017), after 2025.

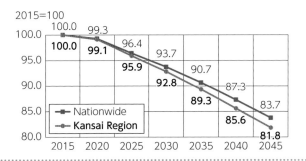

2015=100

Figure 3-1-2   Future Population Trends: Kansai vs. Nationwide

Note: The future population projection is based on the median births (median deaths).
Source: Prepared based on Population Census, Ministry of Internal Affairs and Communications, until 2020; and
    National Institute of Population and Social Security Research (IPSS), "Population Projections for Japan"
    (released in 2017), after 2025

not been halted. The population decline is also a pressing issue in Kansai, and it is important to note that Kansai's future population is expected to decline at a faster rate than that of the rest of Japan (Figure 3-1-2).

In this section, we will analyze the demographics and population movements in the Kansai region in 2015 and 2020 using the "2020 Population Census," which is the latest statistics. This section is organized as follows. The first section of this report will examine the demographic trends in each of the prefectures in the Kansai region in terms of total population and population by age group. In particular, the analysis by age group will focus on the dynamics of the working-age population, which is the core of the labor force. The numbers of workers by industry and by gender are also used to clarify the characteristics of the employment structure. In Subsection 2, we will analyze the population movements in the Kansai region by confirming the status of in-migrants and out-migrants by age group and region for the years 2015 and 2020. In Subsection 3, we will describe the measures taken by each municipality in the Kansai region to cope with the declining population based on the results of the above analyses and conclude with a discussion of future issues related to population decline in Kansai.

1. Demographic Characteristics: 2020/2015

In this section, the demographic characteristics of the prefectures in the Kansai region are clarified based on the latest Population Census. First, we will review the population trends in each prefecture and then look at them by age group. In particular, we will focus on the dynamics of the working-age population by age

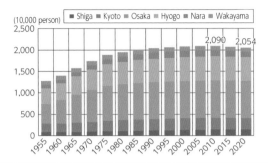

Figure 3-1-3   Total Population Trends in Kansai Prefectures: 1955 to 2020

Note: Figures for 2015 and 2020 are compiled by supplementing the figures for persons of unknown age.
Source: Compiled from Population Census, Ministry of Internal Affairs and Communications (1955 to 2020)

group. Finally, we will compare the number of workers in each prefecture by gender and by industry.

(1) Total Population of Each Prefecture

First, we will review the population trends in each of the prefectures in the Kansai region.

As shown in Figure 3-1-3, the total population of the Kansai region peaked at 20.9 million in 2010 and then began to decline, reaching 20.54 million in 2020, down 183,992 from the previous census ("2015 Population Census").

Table 3-1-1 shows that the total population in Shiga Prefecture increased slightly by 694 from 2015 to 2020, to 1,413,610, while the total population in the other prefectures decreased in all cases. Of these, Hyogo Prefecture had the largest decrease at 5,465,002, a decrease of 69,798 from 2015. Wakayama Prefecture followed at 922,584, a decrease of 40,995 from 2015. In Wakayama Prefecture in particular, the total population was 963,579 in 2015, falling below the one million mark, and since then the population has declined even further.

Looking at Tokyo, the total population is 14,047,594, an increase of 532,323 since 2015, accounting for 11.1% of the total population.

(2) Working-age population in each prefecture

Having examined the total population above, we will now examine the dynamics of the working-age population. The working-age population (15 to 64 years old) is the main age group in the labor force and is therefore important when considering the economic impact.

The change in the working-age population from 2015 to 2020 in each of the prefectures in the Kansai region shows that the working-age population is

| Table 3-1-1 | Comparison of Total Population of Kansai Prefectures, Nationwide, and Tokyo: 2020/2015 |

	Population : 2020	Population : 2015	Change rate: 2020/2015	Variation change: 2020/2015
Unit	Person	Person	%	Person
Shiga	1,413,610	1,412,916	0.05	694
Kyoto	2,578,087	2,610,353	-1.24	-32,266
Osaka	8,837,685	8,839,469	-0.02	-1,784
Hyogo	5,465,002	5,534,800	-1.26	-69,798
Nara	1,324,473	1,364,316	-2.92	-39,843
Wakayama	922,584	963,579	-4.25	-40,995
Kansai	20,541,441	20,725,433	-0.89	-183,992
Tokyo	14,047,594	13,515,271	3.94	532,323
Nationwide	126,146,099	127,094,745	-0.75	-948,646

Note: Figures for 2015 and 2020 are compiled by supplementing the figures for persons of unknown age.
Source: Compiled from Ministry of Internal Affairs and Communications, "2020 Population Census."

| Table 3-1-2 | Comparison of Working-age Population in Kansai Prefectures, Nationwide and Tokyo: 2020/2015 |

Working age population	2020	2015	Change rate: 2020/2015	Variation change: 2020/2015
Unit	Person	Person	%	Person
Shiga	849,686	868,481	-2.16	-18,795
Kyoto	1,527,284	1,578,536	-3.25	-51,252
Osaka	5,363,326	5,426,256	-1.16	-62,930
Hyogo	3,197,092	3,322,644	-3.78	-125,552
Nara	749,514	803,576	-6.73	-54,062
Wakayama	509,212	549,190	-7.28	-39,978
Kansai	12,196,114	12,548,683	-2.81	-352,569
Tokyo	9,284,428	8,927,428	4.00	357,000
Nationwide	75,087,865	77,354,097	-2.93	-2,266,232

Note: Figures for 2015 and 2020 are compiled by supplementing the figures for persons of unknown age.
Source: Compiled from Ministry of Internal Affairs and Communications, "2020 Population Census."

decreasing in all prefectures. Of these, Hyogo Prefecture saw a large drop of 125,552 compared to 2015. This was followed by a decrease of 62,930 in Osaka Prefecture, 54,062 in Nara Prefecture, and 51,252 in Kyoto Prefecture. Looking at Tokyo, the population is 8,927,428, an increase of 357,000 from the year 2015, accounting for 12.4% of the nation's working-age population (Table 3-1-2).

Next, we will examine the demographic characteristics in more detail by looking at the population by municipalities instead of by prefectures. Table 3-1-3 lists the 10 municipalities with the largest percentage increases and

Table 3-1-3	Ranking of Percentage Change in the Working-age Population by Municipalities: Kansai: 2020/2015, Unit: %		
Municipality name	Change rate	Municipality name	Change rate
Muko City	6.0	Soni Village	-27.6
Kizugawa City	4.5	Kasagi Town	-27.6
Oyamazaki Town	3.6	Mitsue Village	-27.5
Moriyama City	3.5	Yoshino Town	-25.9
Ritto City	3.5	Nosegawa Village	-23.7
Kusatsu City	3.0	Higashi-Yoshino Village	-23.4
Kyotanabe City	2.6	Yamazoe Village	-22.8
Osaka city	2.4	Wazuka Town	-21.7
Ibaraki city	2.0	Kurotaki Village	-21.6
Settsu City	1.9	Tenkawa Village	-21.1

Note: Figures for 2015 and 2020 are compiled by supplementing the figures for persons of unknown age.
Source: Compiled from Ministry of Internal Affairs and Communications, "2020 Population Census."

decreases in the working-age population by municipality from 2015. As shown in the table, the municipalities with the largest increases are Muko City (6.0%), Kizugawa City (4.5%), and Oyamazaki Town (3.6%), indicating an increase of 4 to 6% in the southern region of Kyoto Prefecture. On the other hand, municipalities with a large decrease rate are Soni Village, Kasagi Town (-27.6%), Mitsue Village (-27.5%) and Yoshino Town (-25.9%), with a decrease rate exceeding 20%, mainly in the eastern and southern regions of Nara Prefecture.

As shown in Table 3-1-2, the working-age population of Kyoto Prefecture as a whole has declined, whereas the population of municipalities with good access to Kyoto City and Osaka City has increased, which is a trend that differs from that on the unit of prefectures[1]. In addition, as Figure 3-1-8 below shows, the number of residents in the northern part of Osaka Prefecture (Ibaraki City, Settsu City, Suita City, etc.), from where transportation to Osaka City and Kyoto City is easy, is also increasing[2].

(3) Characteristics of the number of workers by industry
The following section examines the share of major industries in the Kansai region and the nation as a whole by dividing the number of male and female workers employed in those industries.

---

1) In particular, the opening of the AEON MALL Kyoto Katsuragawa in Muko City (Kyoto Prefecture) in October 2014 and the re-zoning of the surrounding area led to the construction of houses and large condominiums, which is thought to have attracted an influx of family households.
2) In an article published by Nihon Keizai Shimbun on July 16, 2021, the high accessibility of transportation and the livability of the northern Osaka area are also mentioned.

Figure 3-1-4 shows the share of male employment in each industry. The share in 2020 shows that the share of the manufacturing sector is high in each prefecture. Among them, Shiga Prefecture (34.6%) has a higher percentage than the other prefectures, while Hyogo (23.9%), Kyoto (20.5%), and Nara (20.3%) prefectures also have a higher percentage than the national average (20.0%).

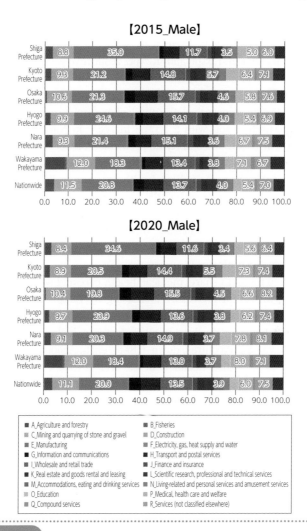

Figure 3-1-4   Workers' Share by Industry: Male: 2020/2015

Note: Figures for 2015 and 2020 are compiled by supplementing the figures for persons of unknown age.
Source: Compiled from Ministry of Internal Affairs and Communications, "2020 Population Census."

The high share of Shiga Prefecture is thought to be attributed to the prefecture having become one of the leading industrial clusters in Japan as a result of its efforts to establish itself as a suitable location for industrial facilities. Next, the share of wholesale and retail trade was higher in Osaka (15.5%), Nara (14.9%), Kyoto (14.4%) and Hyogo (13.6%) prefectures than in the nation as a whole (13.5%).

Compared to the share in 2015, the share of manufacturing declined in all prefectures except Wakayama Prefecture, with Osaka and Nara prefectures showing large declines of -1.5%pt. and -1.2%pt., respectively. Wholesale and retail trade declined in all prefectures, with a -0.5%pt. drop in Hyogo Prefecture, and a -0.4%pt. drop in Kyoto and Wakayama prefectures, respectively. Among the industries whose shares increased, the share of medical, health care and welfare increased in all prefectures, with a 1.1%pt. increase in Nara Prefecture and a 0.9%pt. increase in Wakayama and Kyoto prefectures, respectively.

Figure 3-1-5 shows the share of female workers by industry. The share in 2020 shows that the share of medical, health care and welfare is high in each prefecture. Wakayama Prefecture had the highest share at 25.8%, and except for Shiga Prefecture (22.3%), all prefectures exceeded the national share (22.6%). The share of wholesale and retail trade was next highest in Osaka (19.8%) and Nara (19.7%) prefectures and the shares exceeded the national share except for Shiga and Wakayama prefectures.

Compared to the 2015 share, medical, health care and welfare increased in all prefectures, with Nara Prefecture increasing by 1.3%pt., Hyogo Prefecture by 1.1%pt., and Shiga and Wakayama prefectures by 1.0%pt. On the other hand, wholesale and retail trade declined in all prefectures, including Kyoto, Hyogo, Nara, and Wakayama prefectures, down -0.8%pt. each. Accommodations, eating and drinking services also declined in all prefectures, especially in Kyoto Prefecture, where it declined by -0.6%pt., and in Shiga, Osaka, and Hyogo prefectures, where it declined by -0.5%pt.

As shown above, looking at the share of workers by industry and by gender, the share of both male and female workers in medical, health care and welfare has increased over the past five years alongside the aging of the population. On the other hand, in the wholesale and retail trade category, the share of both male and female workers decreased in 2020, partly because of reduced business hours and measures to close stores due to the COVID-19 pandemic. In particular, the decline in market share is generally larger for female workers.

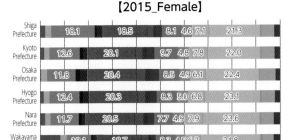

【2015_Female】

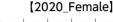

【2020_Female】

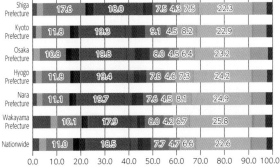

- A_Agriculture and forestry
- C_Mining and quarrying of stone and gravel
- E_Manufacturing
- G_Information and communications
- I_Wholesale and retail trade
- K_Real estate and goods rental and leasing
- M_Accommodations, eating and drinking services
- O_Education
- Q_Compound services
- B_Fisheries
- D_Construction
- F_Electricity, gas, heat supply and water
- H_Transport and postal services
- J_Finance and insurance
- L_Scientific research, professional and technical services
- N_Living-related and personal services and amusement services
- P_Medical, health care and welfare
- R_Services (not classified elsewhere)

Figure 3-1-5   Workers' Share by Industry: Female: 2020/2015

Note: Figures for 2015 and 2020 are compiled by supplementing the figures for persons of unknown age.
Source: Compiled from Ministry of Internal Affairs and Communications, "2020 Population Census."

2. Characteristics of Population Migration Dynamics: 2020/2015

(1) Status of In-migrants and Out-migrants by Age Group

In the previous subsection, we discussed the demographic characteristics of the Kansai region. In this section, we will analyze the characteristics of population migration by age group in each of the prefectures in the Kansai region.

Figure 3-1-6 shows the status of in-migrants and out-migrants by age group in the prefectures of the Kansai region in 2015 and 2020. As the figure shows, if we look at the number of excess in-migrants in the 20 to 24 age group, the number of excess in-migrants was +57,127 in 2015 for the entire Kansai region but expanded modestly to +58,323 in 2020. Within this total, the number of increases in Osaka Prefecture grew from +44,054 in 2015 to +58,270 in 2020, indicating that most of the expansion in the Kansai region has occurred in Osaka Prefecture.

Next, looking at the 25 to 29 age group, we see that the number of excess out-migrants shrank from -20,835 in 2015 to -11,818 in 2020. By prefecture, Osaka is the only prefecture with an excess of in-migrants, with the number of

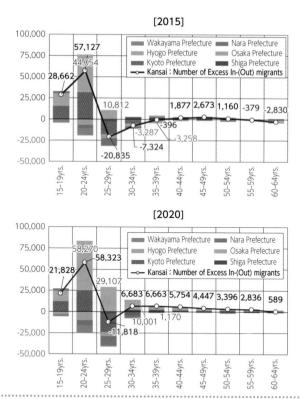

| Figure 3-1-6 | Number of Excess In-migrants and Out-migrants by Age Groups: 2020/2015 |

Note: Figures for 2015 and 2020 are compiled by supplementing the figures for persons of unknown age.
Source: Compiled from Ministry of Internal Affairs and Communications, "2020 Population Census."

excess in-migrants increasing from +10,812 in 2015 to +29,107 in 2020.

In the case of the 30 to 34 age group, the number of excess of out-migrants was -7,324 in 2015 for the Kansai region as a whole, whereas this figure changed direction and became an excess of in-migrants of +6,683 in 2020. Within this number, Osaka Prefecture is characterized by the fact that it has moved from an excess of out-migrants of -3,287 in 2015 to an excess of in-migrants of +10,000 in 2020.

In the 35 to 39 age group, the Kansai region as a whole shifted from an excess of out-migrants of -396 in 2015 to an excess of in-migrants of +6,663 in 2020, while by prefecture, Osaka Prefecture shifted from an excess of out-migrants of -3,258 in 2015 to an excess of in-migrants of +1,170 in 2020.

As shown above, the expansion of excess in-migrants in the Kansai region as a whole is thought to be largely due to the expansion of excess in-migrants in Osaka Prefecture for each age group.

(2) Status of In-migrants and Out-migrants by Age Group and Region

In this subsection, we will look at the above-mentioned status of in-migrants and out-migrants by age group broken down by region[3]. What are the appeals of Kansai from the viewpoints of other prefectures outside of Kansai? In the following sections, we will analyze migration dynamics by examining the status of in-migrants and out-migrants moving to the Kansai region only from other regions outside of Kansai, excluding migration dynamics within the Kansai region (see Table 3-1-5 below for details).

Figure 3-1-7 shows that in the 30 to 34 age group that turned into excess in-migrants from excess out-migrants in number, compared to in 2015, South Kanto (-14,122), Kyushu (-1,008) and Okinawa (-702) remained with excess out-migrants, while Hokuriku (+391), Tokai (+408), Chugoku (+6), and Shikoku (+99) regions turned into excess in-migrants from excess out-migrants. The Tokai region in particular is characterized by a shift from excess out-migrants of -2,195 in 2015 to excess in-migrants. In addition, the number of new residents from abroad increased (+9,296), contributing to the overall increase in the

---

3) The regional divisions are as follows. Hokkaido Region: Hokkaido Prefecture; Tohoku Region: Aomori, Iwate, Miyagi, Akita, Yamagata, Fukushima prefectures; South Kanto Region: Saitama, Chiba, Tokyo, Kanagawa prefectures; North Kanto/Koshin Region: Ibaraki, Tochigi, Gunma, Yamanashi, Nagano prefectures; Hokuriku Region: Niigata, Toyama, Ishikawa, Fukui prefectures; Tokai Region: Gifu, Shizuoka, Aichi, Mie prefectures; Chugoku Region: Tottori, Shimane, Okayama, Hiroshima, Yamaguchi prefectures; Shikoku Region: Tokushima, Kagawa, Ehime, Kochi prefectures; Kyushu Region: Fukuoka, Saga, Nagasaki, Kumamoto, Oita, Miyazaki, Kagoshima prefectures; Okinawa Region: Okinawa Prefecture

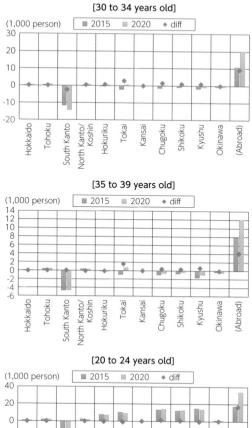

Figure 3-1-7   Comparison of the Number of Excess In-migrants and Excess Out-migrants by age Group and Region: 2020/2015

Note: Figures for 2015 and 2020 are compiled by supplementing the figures for persons of unknown age.
Source: Compiled from Ministry of Internal Affairs and Communications, "2020 Population Census."

number of excess in-migrants.

Similarly, among the 35 to 39 age group by prefecture, the number of excess out-migrants (-875) turned to excess of in-migrants (+739) in the Tokai region, while the excess of out-migrants shrank in the Tohoku, South Kanto,

Chugoku, Shikoku, and Kyushu regions. In addition, the number of in-migrants from outside of Japan increased (+4,124), which has turned an excess status of out-migrants into an excess status of in-migrants.

On the other hand, the number of excess out-migrants among the 20 to 24 age group expanded in the South Kanto region (-13,407), while the number of excess in-migrants shrank in all regions except Chugoku and Shikoku. However, the increase in the number of in-migrants from outside of Japan (+16,671) resulted in an overall increase in the excess of in-migrants.

The above findings clearly show that the increase in the number of in-migrants from abroad has a significant impact on the excess of in-migrants. This may be due to an increase in the number of foreigners living in Japan in recent years, as well as the return of Japanese people who had been living abroad due to the COVID-19 pandemic. In Japan, the declaration of a state of emergency[4] in 2020 that restricted inter-prefectural traffic might also have had an impact on the decrease in the number of out-migrants who would have otherwise moved out of the Kansai region to go to college or for work transfers.

3. Coping with the Population Decline in Kansai Municipalities

As we have seen, the demographic trends in the Kansai region show an increase in the working-age population in the municipalities around urban areas and a decrease in the rest of the municipalities. In addition, population movements in the Kansai region by age group show that young people in the 20 to 24 and 25 to 29 age groups are continuing to move out of the region, mainly to the South Kanto region. This section therefore introduces measures to cope with the population decline in the Kansai region (see Table 3-1-4). The target municipalities are Wakayama, Nara, and Hyogo prefectures, which have been experiencing significant population decline, as indicated in Subsection 1.

In Wakayama Prefecture, as described in (1) in Section 1, the total population dropped below one million in 2015, and since then the resident population has continued to decline. Therefore, we will examine the measures being taken in the prefecture to cope with the declining population. In 2015, Wakayama Prefecture formulated the "Wakayama Prefecture Comprehensive Strategy for Revitalizing Towns, People, and Jobs (Revised March 2020)," and it has been developing measures to cope with the declining permanent population based on one of the basic goals of the strategy that has "Create Local Communities"

---

4) In 2020, a state of emergency was declared for the period from April 7 to May 25.

Table 3-1-4	Measures to Cope with the Declining Population in Wakayama, Hyogo, and Nara Prefectures

Initiatives in Wakayama Prefecture

[Expansion of the related population]

Increase the number of people who know about and are interested in Wakayama byactively disseminating information on the attractions of Wakayama, such as its abundant nature, traditional history, and culture, favorable climate, and distinctive industries

Enhance opportunities for people to experience the attractiveness of Wakayama's products, services, agriculture, forestry and fisheries by promoting the expansion ofoverseas development of local companies in the prefecture and helping to widen their domestic and international sales channels for local produce

Create opportunities for the Kansai region to work together on the Expo 2025 Osaka, Kansai, to interact with people from all over the world and to communicate the attractions of Wakayama

Increase the number of "Wakayama fans" who are interested in and feel close to Wakayama and who have an attachment to Wakayama

[Expansion of the interacting population]

Create a Wakayama that attracts many visitors by actively promoting tourism through utilizing the prefecture's diverse resources, encouraging exchanges through sporting and cultural activities, and revitalizing industry and creating a lively atmosphere

Increase the number of visitors from home and abroad by improving highways and trunk roads and by working to improve the convenience of Kansai International Airport, Nanki-Shirahama Airport and other airports

Promote a living style of residing in two regions and increase the numbers of in-migrants and permanent residents by having many people visit Wakayama and directly experiencethe warm humanity and lifestyles of the local people

Initiatives in Hyogo Prefecture

[Creation and expansion of the permanent and related populations]

Promotion of a living style of residing in two regions and urban-rural exchanges
· Promotion of exchanges between urban and rural areas planned and implemented by NPOs and universities
· Support for the development of farms using idle farmland and the renovation of vacant housing into residences, agricultural experience guesthouses, etc.

Development of regional revitalization operations
· Promotion of local activities by regional revitalization cooperatives and prefectural versions of regional revitalization cooperatives
· Support for the development of commercial and social centers to maintain community functions in settlements, etc.

Effective use of vacant housing and other properties in accordance with local characteristics
· Promotion of effective use of vacant housing and land in urban areas
· Development of a model for uncovering and distributing vacant housing in new towns

[Expanding the interacting population by making use of local resources]

Promoting the attraction of visitors from within Japan and overseas
· Development of content utilizing Hyogo's regional resources, such as Japanese heritage, historical and cultural heritage, nature such as Mt. Rokko and San'in Kaigan Geopark, sports, food, and hot springs
· Review of existing tourist attractions in the region, such as natural and cultural resources and sports bases to refine them into tourism resources

Promoting international tourism
· Promotion of the formation of wide-area tourism tour routes through collaborations between Hyogo Tourism Headquarters and wide-area collaborative DMOs such as Setouchi DMO and Kansai Tourism Headquarters, and neighboring DMOs such as Toyooka and Awaji, etc.

Development of tourist reception infrastructure
· Promotion of multilingual tourist information centers, information boards, etc., installing western style public toilets, and support for Halal, vegetarian, etc.
· Development of accommodation facilities using traditional houses, etc.

Initiatives in Nara Prefecture

· Creating places to work
· Creating comfortable and livable communities
· Developing disaster resilient infrastructure
· Promoting in-migrants and permanent settlers
· Creating a related population
· Discovering and creating local resources for tourism
· Disseminating information to make the southern and eastern regions known to a largenumber of people
· Creating mechanisms and attractions to encourage people to actually visit the southernand eastern regions

Note: The portion relating to population decline is partly excerpted.
Source: Compiled from Nara Prefecture's "The Second Stage of Nara Prefecture's Comprehensive Strategy for Regional Revitalization," Hyogo Prefecture's "Hyogo Prefecture Regional Revitalization Strategy (2020 to 2024)," and Wakayama Prefecture's "Wakayama Prefecture Comprehensive Strategy for Revitalizing Towns, People, and Jobs (Revised March 2020)."

as its pillar. Specifically, in addition to disseminating information on Wakayama Prefecture's natural, historical, cultural, and other attractions both domestically and internationally, the prefecture is working on measures to increase the related population[5] and interacting population by developing highways and trunk roads to make it easier for people to visit the prefecture.

Next, Hyogo Prefecture experienced the largest decline in population in 2020, as shown in (1) in Section 1. According to the "Hyogo Prefecture Regional Revitalization Strategy 2020 to 2024" formulated by Hyogo Prefecture in 2020, the prefecture is working on measures based on one of its priority goals, which is "to create a vibrant Hyogo through interactions between the inside and outside worlds." Specifically, the prefecture is working to create and expand the permanent population by effectively utilizing vacant housing and vacant land in urban areas. In addition to the permanent population, the prefecture is also working to increase the interacting population by attracting both domestic and international visitors through utilizing its tourism resources, such as Japanese heritage and historical and cultural heritage sites in the prefecture.

Finally, as pointed out in (2) in Section 1, Nara Prefecture has experienced a large decline in the working-age population in the eastern and southern parts of the prefecture. The following is an overview of the measures that the prefecture has been taking to cope with the declining population. According to the "The Second Stage of Nara Prefecture's Comprehensive Strategy for Regional Revitalization" formulated by Nara Prefecture in 2020, the prefecture is working on measures based on one of its basic goals, which is "to create our proud 'Miyako' prefecture." Specifically, the prefectural government will disseminate positive information about the southern and eastern regions of Nara Prefecture to introduce these regions, where the population is declining and promote the creation of small-scale, multifunctional centers where entrepreneurs can "gather," "connect," and "grow," thereby creating new employment opportunities.

As shown above, the different strategies to cope with population decline notwithstanding, the three prefectures are basically promoting an increase in the permanent population by creating and expanding the number of related population and people to interact with, while disseminating information to outside the prefecture and utilizing the local resources in the prefecture.

---

5) According to the Ministry of Internal Affairs and Communications (MIC), the term "related population" is defined as "people who engage in a variety of ways with the local community" and that is neither the 'permanent population' that has moved to the area nor the 'interacting population' that has come for tourism.

Part I

Part II

Part III

Part IV

Conclusion

Regarding the medium- to long-term issue of population decline in the Kansai region, we have analyzed the demographic and migration dynamics of the Kansai region using the Population Census and confirmed the measures that each municipality is taking to cope with the decline in population. As the birth-rate further declines and the population ages in Kansai and Japan, the challenge will be how to solve labor shortages in the future. The Kansai region in particular is expected to experience population decline at a faster pace than the rest of Japan, making the implementation of countermeasures an urgent necessity. As discussed in the case studies of each prefecture, it is important to expand and create not only the permanent population but also the interacting population by making effective use of the local resources available in each municipality. In addition, the COVID-19 pandemic has changed people's lifestyles and mind-sets, so an increasing number of people are considering moving from urban areas to rural areas. It has become even more important for local governments to provide a hospitable environment for in-migrants and to create comfortable communities that are highly livable. In sum, it is necessary to further improve the brand power of the region.

References

Hyogo Prefecture (2020), Hyogo Prefecture Regional Revitalization Strategy (2020 to 2024), March 2020. (Japanese title: *Hyogoken Chiiki Sosei Senryaku 2020 to 2024*), (https://web.pref.hyogo.lg.jp/kk07/ documents/0603dai-2kisenryaku.pdf, last viewed July 5, 2022)

Nara Prefecture (2020), *The Second Stage of Nara Prefecture's Comprehensive Strategy for Regional Revitalization, March 25, 2020. (Japanese title: Dain-iki Naraken Chiho Sosei Sogo Senryaku*), (https://www.pref.nara.jp/40445. htm, last viewed July 5, 2022)

Nihon Keizai Shimbun (2021), Kansai's Population is Increasingly Concentrat-ed in Urban Centers and Bed towns, July 16, 2021. (Japanese title: *Kansai no Jinko, Toshi Shuchu Ichidanto Beddo Taun no Zoka Kencho*), (https:// www.nikkei.com/article/DGXZQOUF2942W0Z20C21A6000000/Last viewed July 7, 2022)

Wakayama Prefecture (2020), W*akayama Prefecture Comprehensive Strategy for Revitalizing Towns, People, and Jobs (Revised March 2020)*. (Japanese title: Wakayamaken Machi・Hito・Shigoto Sosei Sogo Senryaku 2020 (Reiwa 2) Nen 3 Gatsu Kaitei), (https://www.pref.wakayama.lg.jp/prefg/020100/tihousou-sei/tihousousei_d/fil/03senryaku_kaitei.pdf, last viewed on July 5, 2022)

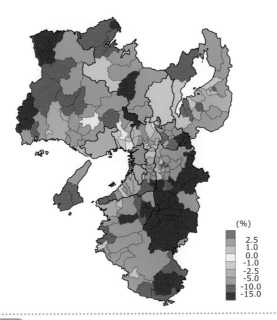

(%)

2.5
1.0
0.0
-1.0
-2.5
-5.0
-10.0
-15.0

Figure 3-1-8   Percentage Change in the Working-age Population

Note: Figures for 2015 and 2020 are compiled by supplementing the figures for persons of unknown age.
Source: Compiled from Ministry of Internal Affairs and Communications, "2020 Population Census."

Table 3-1-5   Comparison of the Number of Excess In-migrants and Out-migrants by Age Group and Region: 2020/2015

■2015	Total	15-19yrs.	20-24yrs.	25-29yrs.	30-34yrs.	35-39yrs.	40-44yrs.	45-49yrs.	50-54yrs.	55-59yrs.	60-64yrs.
Hokkaido	2,748	422	856	761	146	110	169	215	150	61	-120
Tohoku	5,298	959	2,006	588	472	431	304	123	-66	-283	-367
South Kanto	-82,967	-4,410	-25,249	-31,649	-11,630	-4,690	-2,288	-1,949	-1,087	625	1,984
North Kanto/Koshin	4,223	1,032	2,452	-684	51	403	199	257	231	132	15
Hokuriku	10,245	3,622	7,654	-109	-318	-86	-232	84	9	-160	-141
Tokai	7,214	5,871	10,277	-7,375	-2,195	-875	-469	417	381	103	166
Kansai	0	0	0	0	0	0	0	0	0	0	0
Chugoku	11,507	5,546	13,611	-117	-1,504	-958	-668	-300	-303	-716	-1,498
Shikoku	12,524	5,041	12,199	28	-796	-691	-348	42	-80	-413	-1,068
Kyushu	5,768	4,717	14,749	311	-1,796	-1,595	-988	-635	-558	-1,138	-2,680
Okinawa	-1,457	478	1,018	-575	-543	-324	-243	-160	-165	-157	-202
(Abroad)	86,738	5,384	17,554	17,986	10,789	7,879	6,441	4,579	2,648	1,567	1,081
Total	61,841	28,662	57,127	-20,835	-7,324	-396	1,877	2,673	1,160	-379	-2,830

Part I

Part II

Part III

Part IV

■2020	Total	15–19yrs.	20–24yrs.	25–29yrs.	30–34yrs.	35–39yrs.	40–44yrs.	45–49yrs.	50–54yrs.	55–59yrs.	60–64yrs.
Hokkaido	2,864	274	683	1,134	293	95	126	185	164	91	-35
Tohoku	6,231	456	1,833	1,231	702	479	284	353	217	188	34
South Kanto	-113,877	-3,481	-38,656	-47,113	-14,112	-4,629	-2,240	-2,619	-1,797	844	2,011
North Kanto/ Koshin	4,491	749	2,158	-589	521	335	309	235	403	261	4
Hokuriku	9,974	2,391	7,205	386	391	-149	-111	4	-48	-41	-87
Tokai	13,103	5,000	9,167	-7,335	408	739	686	557	903	548	401
Kansai	0	0	0	0	0	0	0	0	0	0	0
Chugoku	17,589	3,214	14,292	2,738	6	-524	-205	59	-46	-355	-849
Shikoku	15,886	3,898	12,695	1,912	99	-332	-275	-113	-70	-309	-640
Kyushu	10,335	3,204	14,013	1,548	-1,008	-923	-764	-250	-131	-681	-1,595
Okinawa	-2,361	446	708	-846	-702	-431	-309	-195	-223	-184	-160
(Abroad)	144,746	5,677	34,225	35,116	20,085	12,003	8,253	6,231	4,024	2,474	1,505

Difference 2020 to 2015	Total	15–19yrs.	20–24yrs.	25–29yrs.	30–34yrs.	35–39yrs.	40–44yrs.	45–49yrs.	50–54yrs.	55–59yrs.	60–64yrs.
Hokkaido	116	-148	-173	373	147	-15	-43	-30	14	30	85
Tohoku	933	-503	-173	643	230	48	-20	230	283	471	401
South Kanto	-30,910	929	-13,407	-15,464	-2,482	61	48	-670	-710	219	27
North Kanto/ Koshin	268	-283	-294	95	470	-68	110	-22	172	129	-11
Hokuriku	-271	-1,231	-449	495	709	-63	121	-80	-57	119	54
Tokai	5,889	-871	-1,110	40	2,603	1,614	1,155	140	522	445	235
Kansai	0	0	0	0	0	0	0	0	0	0	0
Chugoku	6,082	-2,332	681	2,855	1,510	434	463	359	257	361	649
Shikoku	3,362	-1,143	496	1,884	895	359	73	-155	10	104	428
Kyushu	4,567	-1,513	-736	1,237	788	672	224	385	427	457	1,085
Okinawa	-904	-32	-310	-271	-159	-107	-66	-35	-58	-27	42
(Abroad)	58,008	293	16,671	17,130	9,296	4,124	1,812	1,652	1,376	907	424

Note: Figures for 2015 and 2020 are compiled by supplementing the figures for persons of unknown age.
Source: Compiled from Ministry of Internal Affairs and Communications, "2020 Population Census."

Column A The Impact of the COVID-19 Pandemic on Local Government Finances

FUJIWARA, Yukinori

1. Stagnation of Local Economies due to the COVID-19 Crisis

The spread of COVID-19 infections has restricted the entry of overseas visitors, including foreign tourists, and reduced socio-economic activities in Japan through stay-at-home requests and business suspension orders, which has significantly slowed down local economies. As a result of the widespread stagnation of local economies, local companies and business operators, particularly in the railroad, bus, hotels, Japanese inns, food and beverage, and retail industries, have unavoidably experienced a significant sales decline and difficulties in surviving.

In response to the COVID-19 crisis, local governments have been responsible for field-level measures, such as preventing the spread of infections, developing medical care provision systems, and supporting local economies and residents' lives.

In November 2021, the FY 2020 financial results for the ordinary accounts of prefectures and municipalities were released. FY 2020 was the first full year impacted by COVID-19. Therefore, I will consider the impact of the COVID-19 crisis on local government finances based on the FY 2020 financial results.

2. Local Government Finances in the First Year of the COVID-19 Crisis

(1) Significant Decrease in Revenues from Two Corporate Taxes

Local taxes are major sources of finances for local governments. Tax revenues are greatly influenced by the income and earnings situation of individuals and corporations. In particular, shocks such as economic crises and natural disasters can lead to a significant decrease in local tax revenues.

In other words, if corporate earnings deteriorate, then within the local taxes paid by companies, corporate inhabitant tax and corporate enterprise tax that are levied on corporate income or profits will decrease.

If an employee's income decreases or employment is terminated, the individual inhabitant tax paid by that employee will also decrease. The deterioration in corporate earnings due to the COVID-19 crisis has an impact on the trends in tax revenues from two corporate taxes.

From this perspective, the many local governments that have tried to revitalize their local economies by attracting tourists from overseas to Japan in recent years will also see a decrease in local taxes due to the damage to the tourism industry.

As shown in Table 3-CA-1 and Table 3-CA-2, the financial results for FY 2020 saw significant decreases in two corporate taxes (corporate inhabitant tax and corporate enterprise tax), reflecting the worsening business conditions of business operators impacted by the COVID-19 crisis.

Although no decrease was seen in revenue from individual inhabitant tax, the impact of COVID-19 will become apparent in the FY 2021 financial results as individual inhabitant tax is imposed on that individual's income in the previous year.

Table 3-C A-1   Prefectural tax revenue payment amount by tax item

(Unit: JPY 100 million, %)

Category	FY 2020 revenue	Amount change from the previous year	Percentage change from the previous year
Prefectural inhabitant tax on individuals	49,545	1,146	2.4
Prefectural inhabitant tax on corporations	5,480	−2,732	−33.3
Enterprise tax on corporations	40,823	−3,028	−6.9
Enterprise tax on individuals	2,160	45	2.1
Local consumption tax	54,238	6,282	13.1
Real estate acquisition tax	3,743	−299	−7.4
Prefectural tobacco tax	1,335	−61	−4.4
Motor vehicle tax	16,234	353	2.2
Light oil delivery tax	9,101	−347	−3.7
Others	1,028	−1,109	−51.9
Total	183,687	250	0.1

Source: Based on Summary of Prefectural Settlement Accounts of Ordinary Accounts by the Ministry of Internal Affairs and Communications (MIC).

| Table 3-CA-2 | Municipal tax revenue payment amount by tax item |

(Unit: JPY 100 million, %)

Category	FY 2020 revenue	Amount change from the previous year	Percentage change from the previous year
Municipal inhabitant tax on individuals	84,267	1,015	1.2
Municipal inhabitant tax on corporations	18,126	−5,826	−24.3
Fixed property tax	93,801	940	1.0
Municipal tobacco tax	8,171	−368	−4.3
City planning tax	13,296	119	0.9
Others	6,909	11	0.2
Total	224,570	−4,108	−1.8

Source: Based on Summary of Municipal Settlement Accounts of Ordinary Accounts by the Ministry of Internal Affairs and Communications (MIC)."

(2) State Grants as Financial Resources for Spending

Local taxes are levied and collected in accordance with the rules stipulated in the Local Tax Act. Therefore, it is difficult to increase tax revenues by raising local tax rates in case of emergencies such as the COVID-19 crisis. Even while tax revenues decline from corporations in financial difficulty and economically distressed residents, such corporations and residents may benefits from a tax reduction, exemption, and even deferral.

On the other hand, local governments have been forced to increase expenditures to respond to COVID-19. The net settlement amounts in the ordinary accounts of local governments in FY 2020 increased significantly compared to in the previous year, with expenditures reaching a record high of JPY 125.5 trillion. According to the results of a survey of expenses related to the responses to COVID-19 in local governments' ordinary accounts in FY 2020 conducted by the Ministry of Internal Affairs and Communications (MIC), the relevant net expenses amounted to JPY 25.6 trillion, which is roughly equivalent to the year-on-year increase of JPY 26.4 trillion in the ordinary balance of the net amount of settlement amounts for expenditures in ordinary accounts.

For local governments with insufficient general financial resources[1],

---

1) Financial resources, such as local tax revenues, that can be freely used by local governments at their own discretion without restrictions.

Part I

Part II

Part III

Part IV

special grants from the national government are playing a major role in securing the financial resources for expenses related to the responses to COVID-19. Special grants are intended to enable local governments to implement necessary projects in accordance with the actual situation of each region in order to support local economies and the lives of residents affected by the spread of the infections. A total of JPY 6.9 trillion was budgeted for FY 2020 by the national government.

However, there was a gap in perception regarding special grants between the national government that determines the grant system and local governments that engage in field-level responses, and this has made it difficult to flexibly operate the system in line with the actual situations in the regions. As a notable example, the national government initially explained that special grants could not be used for compensation for the suspension of business operations, but later when faced with opposition from local governments, it approved the use of the grants as compensation for business suspension.

The bigger problem was that local governments with a high financial strength index[2] received very low grants, despite having large financial demands for COVID-19 measures. The amount of special grants allocated to each local government is calculated based on population, infection status, and financial strength. As a result, the grant per capita is calculated with a higher weight for municipalities with a smaller population and lower financial strength.

This is confirmed by the data in Figure 3-CA-1. This figure shows the relationships between the amount of special grants to each prefecture, the sum of special grants to each prefecture and municipalities in the prefecture, and the financial strength index (prefecture). Obviously, local governments with a high financial strength index received very small per capita grants, despite having a high number of cases and high financial demands for COVID-19 measures. The level of per capita grants received by Tokyo is the lowest among all the prefectures. The three neighboring prefectures of Tokyo, as well as Aichi, Kyoto, Osaka, and

---

2) The financial strength index is an indicator that reflects the financial strength of a local government, which is calculated by dividing the amount of revenue required to operate the local government by the amount of expenditure. An index of 1.0 indicates that the revenue and expenditure are balanced, and an index above 1.0 indicates that financial resources exceed demand.

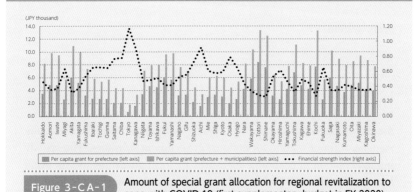

Figure 3-C A-1　Amount of special grant allocation for regional revitalization to cope with COVID-19 (first supplementary budget in FY 2020)

Note 1: Grant amount per capita by prefecture
Note 2: The financial strength index is a three-year average between 2018 and 2020 on a prefectural basis.
Source: Based on Local Public Finance Survey by the Ministry of Internal Affairs and Communications (MIC), materials prepared by the Secretariat for Promotion of Regional Revitalization, Cabinet Office, and results of the 2020 National Census.

Hyogo, which have high numbers of infected people, also received low levels of grants.

Prefectural governments play major roles in COVID-19 measures. They provide a wide range of COVID-19 control measures, including providing loans and cooperative grants to business operators and assistance to medical institutions in securing hospital beds to receive infected patients. Given these roles of prefectural governments, it would not be desirable for local governments with large cities, such as Tokyo and Osaka, to receive a lower amount of grants even though they are rated high in the financial strength index.

An important question is whether it is acceptable for local governments with large cities in which large numbers of infected people concentrate, such as Tokyo and Osaka, to receive lower grant amounts. Given the trend of the spread of infections due to the flow of people from large cities to rural areas, the appropriate allocation of grants to areas with large numbers of infected people and large financial demands may have been effective in suppressing the spread of infections nationwide. Going forward, it will be necessary to review the grant allocation criteria for anti-infection measures, including the removal of adjustments based on the financial strength index, while verifying the effects of the current

Part I

Part II

Part III

Part IV

grant system.

3. Challenges for Local Government Finances

In a crisis situation, such as the spread of COVID-19 infections, it is necessary for local governments to be able to take their own economic measures speedily and in accordance with their respective circumstances, without waiting for national government subsidies. The speedy implementation of economic measures by local governments will bring hope and motivation to local SMEs and individual business operators. Local governments' economic measures have a considerable effect on halting the collapse of local economies and in facilitating the resumption of local economic activities.

However, individual economic measures implemented by each local government can cause problems that may lead to regional disparities, depending on the financial strength of each local government. During the first state-of-emergency period in 2020, prefectural governments provided cooperation money to business operators that chose to follow the governors' requests to suspend operations, but there were large differences in the amounts of cooperation money paid as compensation for a business suspension even when considering the differences in prices and wages among the prefectures. It is not desirable that disparities in the financial strengths of local governments lead to policy differences, resulting in disparities in their economic recoveries.

There should be a discussion on the local financial base that is required for local governments to take swift economic measures when faced with a crisis, such as the spread of COVID-19 infections[3].

The measures that local governments should take are not limited to anti-infection measures, but they are also responsible for responding to various regional financial demands, including disaster countermeasures, education, welfare, medical care, nursing care, childcare support, measures for deteriorating social infrastructure, and the digitalization of public administration.

---

3) HIRAOKA, Kazuhisa and MORI, Hiroyuki (2020) is informative as it points out issues relating to COVID-19 measures and municipal financial management in detail based on surveys of local government financial departments.

Therefore, I believe that the financial base of local governments needs to be fundamentally enhanced. As a measure to achieve this, I propose the expansion of general financial resources of local governments and the establishment of a local tax system that provides stable revenues with an even distribution of tax sources.

Finally, most of the local financial resources to address the current COVID-19 crisis have to rely on the issuance of additional government bonds, which imposes a heavy fiscal burden on the government. I would like to point out that the national fiscal situation that has further deteriorated should not be overlooked.

References

FUJIWARA, Yukinori (2020), "Local Financial Strength Disparities Observed in COVID-19 Measures: Correcting the Uneven Distribution of Local Taxes and Stabilizing Tax Revenues through Tax Revenue Exchange" (Japanese title: Shingata Korona Uirusu Taisaku de Mieta Chiho no Zaisei-ryoku Kakusa – Zeigen Kokan ni Yoru Chihozei no Henzai Zesei, Zeishu Anteika o -), APIR Trend Watch No.64, August 2020

HIRAOKA, Kazuhisa and MORI, Hiroyuki (2020), "COVID-19 Countermeasures and Municipal Finance: Considerations from an Urgent Questionnaire" (Japanese title: Shingata Korona Taisaku to Jichitai Zaisei – Kinkyu Anketo kara Kangaeru-), Jichitai Kenkyusha, December 2020

Part I

Part II

Part III

Part IV

Section 2
THE UTILIZATION OF DX IN KANSAI AND OSAKA

OSHIMA, Hisanori; SHIMOJO, Shinji

1. The Transformation of Human Processes as the Essence of DX

While digital transformation (hereinafter referred to as "DX") is increasingly permeating our lives, there are still many misconceptions that DX is limited to the ICT domain. It is necessary to understand that the introduction of DX, or digital technologies, is one of the means of promoting transformation and that its essence is the transformation of governance as well as of corporate and organizational management.

The research project on IoT and DX by the Asia Pacific Institute of Research (APIR) has considered that, as a model for the sustainable evolution of urban services through digital technologies and in order to realize people's happiness, "the processes of things" will be optimized, leading to the optimization of "human processes," and vice-versa.

If the contents of the processes of things change due to digitalization, human processes, that is, organizations and operations, will also need to be transformed accordingly.

In this report, we would like to discuss what kind of transformation is required for the human processes associated with DX from the following two perspectives: "changes in business models" and "transformation of the organization, corporate culture, and climate." In doing so, we will refer to the contents of the research group project Comprehensive Digital Transformation in Kansai and Osaka conducted by APIR in FY2021 and the symposium Post-COVID-19 Sustainable Enterprise Design and DX held in March 2022[1].

2. Changes in Business Models: Building Long-term Relationships with Customers

Even without mentioning the COVID-19 pandemic, the business environment is becoming more complex and is changing rapidly. Also, as consumers'

---

1) For details of the research group project, refer to Asia Pacific Institute of Research (2022a), and for details of the symposium, refer to Asia Pacific Institute of Research (2022b).

preferences are changing "from things to experiences" or "from ownership to experiences," relying solely on a sell-out model will lead to strong fluctuations in business performance due to changes in product life cycles and the number of customers.

Therefore, in addition to acquiring new customers, maintaining and expanding relationships with existing customers, in particular, is one of the trends in business models.

Meanwhile, by accumulating customer service usage data and continuously-collected sensor data, and by using AI to learn and analyze this data, it is becoming easier to change services to achieve higher levels of customer satisfaction.

Thus, we will consider the measures required on the side of human processes to maintain and improve long-term relationships with customers using digital technologies from the two perspectives of the "continuous provision of new values" and the "social implementation of new technologies."

(1) Continuous Provision of New Values

Customer satisfaction can be continuously improved by continuously providing new values to service users. We will explain this point by giving "subscription" as an example.

Subscription is a business model that charges a fixed fee based on the period of use rather than the number of times the product or service is used[2]. Since it is a business model that assumes a long-term contract, if the service does not change for a long time, customers will get bored and stop using it, or they will switch to another company's service that seems better for them. Therefore, subscription providers need to increase the value they provide by reflecting the preferences of individual customers (personalization), providing products and services with higher-level functions (upselling), and expanding their services into other areas (cross-selling). If service usage records are accumulated and analyzed as data, it will be easier to make changes to services.

In addition, how the subscription should be in concrete terms will differ depending on whether the product handled is hardware or software and how

---

2) The definition of the term "subscription" has expanded from the original meaning of "subscription (to magazines, etc.)." The Ministry of Economy, Trade and Industry (METI) (2020a) defines subscription as a "business model that provides services by charging consumers a fixed usage fee on a regular basis" (p. 38). On the other hand, Tzuo (2018) argues that subscription is "to start with the wants and needs of a particular customer base, then create a service that delivers ongoing value to those customers," putting more emphasis on continuity and creativity (p. 1).

| Table 3-2-1 | Subscription types and examples |
| | |

Target services	Specific products	Examples
Use of contents	Movies, music, news	Netflix, Amazon, Apple, Nikkei, etc.
Use of software	Business apps, game software	Microsoft, Adobe, Sony, etc.
Use of services	Restaurant, beauty and healthcare	favy, Kirin (Tap Marché), Jocy, Sparty, etc.
	Analysis services for business operators	Neautech, Casio, KYB, Optex, etc.
Home delivery of consumer goods	Foods, flowers, sundries, toys	Oisix ra daichi, Hibiya Kadan, Trana, etc.
Use of durable consumer goods	Automobiles, furniture, home electric appliances, clothing, housing equipment	KINTO, subsclife, Panasonic, Laxus Technologies, airCloset, Daikin Industries, etc.
Use of real estate	Houses, mountains	HafH, XROSS HOUSE, unito, ADDress, MOKKI, etc.

Source: Prepared by the author based on various media reports.

the value is provided (Table 3-2-1). In particular, with respect to servitization in the manufacturing industry that deals with hardware, the following servitization trends are taking place through subscriptions.

One service model is that service providers own things including equipment and operate them on behalf of customers, and they provide the services obtained through it to customers. By operating the equipment and also continuously collecting and analyzing the equipment usage data, service providers can propose new value, including energy conservation and failure prevention. In the case of Daikin Industries, which was taken up in the research group meeting, business operators own air conditioning equipment and provide air conditioning services to customers on a subscription basis.

One more model for hardware-related services is a subscription to the rights to use things. The concept is similar to sharing, where one can use things only when necessary. Here again, the use of digital technologies is effective for analyzing and understanding what kind of hardware is in high demand based on customers' usage records. In the example of Daikin Industries mentioned above, cases were observed where it analyzed the usage status of shared offices and based on this analysis, made changes to the office layouts to increase the usage rate.

In these servitization models, the use of software is suitable for subscriptions as it makes it relatively easy to enhance the value of services by updating the software as needed even without changing the functions of hardware. However, if customer needs are not clearly understood, the creation of new values cannot be completed all at once. Instead of aiming for perfection from the beginning, it may be more effective to conduct trials of new products and services and to repeatedly modify them. Such a process is called prototyping" and is described later.

(2) Social Implementation of New Technologies

When new technologies are used to provide new services, it is often the case that legal regulations cannot keep up with the new technologies. Therefore, in the absence of laws, it is necessary for service providers themselves to define the rules for dealing with customers. This is discussed below from two perspectives.

1) Accountability for New Technologies

The true value of and risks associated with a service will not be known until the service is actually used. Speaking of digital technologies, such as camera images and AI, customers may have concerns about what kind of technologies they are using and whether there are any risks caused by using such technologies. Therefore, when providing new technologies and services, it is necessary to eliminate information asymmetry and remove these concerns by providing sufficient explanations. Eventually, the accumulation of these efforts will lead to these new technologies being highly evaluated in society.

2) Participation in the Formation of Rules for New Technologies

Even in the R&D phase where services have not been completely formed yet and there are no customers, ethics are necessary, albeit in a different form.

One of the examples discussed by the research group was R&D at Mercari. Mercari formulated and announced its ethical guidelines for R&D by itself to ensure that it conducts R&D activities in an ethically sound manner. This can be seen as an act of building trust with future service recipients from an early stage. Mercari also focuses on actively disseminating information on research results to quickly earn a good reputation in society. Various usages are derived from new technologies, so existing rules cannot cover all of these usages. Therefore, it is possible to make changes by working on existing laws and regulations and social norms from the company side.

For companies that want to be among the first to socially implement a new technology, it is advantageous for them to be able to participate in the rule-making process. In doing so, however, it is difficult to formulate rules without an

Part I

Part II

Part III

Part IV

image of how they can make the world better by spreading the new service[3]. If it is difficult for a company to fully examine a new technology on its own, it may be necessary to discuss it with other companies or universities that are considering the social implementation of a similar technology.

As a common basis for both the accountability and rule formation mentioned above, companies need to have ethical perspectives and imagination. This applies to in-house R&D as well as to the use of external technologies.

3. Transformation of the Organization, Corporate Culture, and Climate: Building Organizations that Continue to Create New Values

At the beginning of this report, we discussed that the essence of DX is the transformation of the management of companies and organizations. Organizational culture is important when conducting trials to create new values. In particular, if an organization has a shared culture, members of the organization naturally head in the same direction, while moving in an autonomous decentralized manner, and vice versa.

Next, we will discuss the culture of organizations that continue to create new values with a focus on the aforementioned prototyping and design thinking.

(1) Prototyping Environment

Prototyping, as described above, refers to the process of creating prototypes repeatedly, comparing them with actual needs, and finding points for modification. The challenge here is how to design an environment for this purpose.

1) Creating an environment where failures are accepted

One of the requirements for prototyping is to create an environment (a so-called sandbox) in which failures are accepted.

Failures are not limited to physical ones, but include social failures such as so-called "blowups" on social media.

In order to avoid major failures in trying out new measures, we need "safe places to blow up," so to speak. Since failures dealt with are not limited to physical ones, the necessary environments are not also limited to physical ones. It is

---

3) Ministry of Economy, Trade and Industry (METI) (2022), which outlines the concept of enhancing corporate value in Society 5.0, also states that a company must develop a management vision and design business models in consideration of "the effects on the company caused by changes in society and competitive environment due to digital technologies" (p. 3).

also necessary to secure human resources, including experts who support trials, people who are comfortable taking new risks like students, and those serving as hubs who can coordinate trials from a neutral standpoint and perspective.

However, it is difficult to prepare such places in a normal corporate setting. There are significant advantages to using external places including universities, and such places are now increasing in number. In addition to the open innovation sites[4] in Kansai introduced in last year's Kansai and the Asia Pacific Economic Outlook, QUINTBRIDGE, opened by NTT West in Kyobashi, Osaka in March 2022, and point0, a consortium operated by Daikin Industries and other companies since 2019, are also being used as sites for trials across corporate boundaries. Rather than covering everything with each company's own resources, these activities should be promoted premised on open collaboration.

2) Accumulation of both seeds and needs

When the needs for a new service are ascertained, if many seeds have already been identified, there are more options to combine them, which makes it easier to start prototyping. It is also important to have a sufficiently broad, even if shallow, knowledge about seeds.

Mr. Nobuaki Nagai of Kobe City Government, one of the panelists at the symposium, cited the importance of being knowledgeable about seeds. In other words, in addition to identifying measures required to achieve the desired result, research must be conducted on the means to achieve it. As an example of the response to the Covid-19 pandemic, when Kobe City supported restaurants to provide takeout services, restaurants that shifted to takeout were required to take stricter measures to prevent food poisoning than ever before, and they needed to seek support from experts at the City Government.

With respect to the collection of needs, the question is whose needs should be picked up. It is necessary to listen to the voices of as diverse a range of stakeholders as possible to respond to challenges, but what is also important is to have as many people as possible, both inside and outside the organization, who you can ask for their advice and opinions on a routine basis.

3) Turning feedback into improvements

According to Mr. Nagai, when Kobe City implemented countermeasures against COVID-19, they promptly delivered measures to the public with particular emphasis on speed, rather than taking time to develop complete measures, and then refined the measures while asking for opinions from the public. This is

---

4) Refer to Asia Pacific Institute of Research (2022c) p. 194.

exactly what prototyping is all about.

Regarding the first measures that emphasized speed, some problems were pointed out on Twitter and other social media, which provided tips for solutions, as well as lessons. Whether or not such negative comments on social media can be used as positive feedback information also depends on the culture of the organization.

(2) Organizational design

Above, we discussed the environment for prototyping, and next, we will discuss the organizational structure that makes prototyping possible.

Design thinking is a concept to practice prototyping[5]. In design thinking, the organization itself is subject to design. Here we will discuss the following two points.

1) Building communities to share challenges

According to Mr. Shunsuke Ishikawa of KESIKI Inc., another panelist at the aforementioned symposium, it is extremely important for those who are the first to explore and create new values to have followers who support them. For this reason, it is effective to build relationships with people who can share challenges and support value creation and to create communities in which people gather who are connected by a shared sense of what the issues are.

However, some people do not participate in measures such as communities, feeling that the hurdles to participation are too high, even if they share the same sense of what the issues are. According to Mr. Ishikawa, the following two points are necessary: how to lower the hurdles for community participation and how to set up easy-to-understand incentives.

2) Ensuring psychological safety

Another important point that Mr. Ishikawa pointed out is being able to handle the "ambiguity" that accompanies exploring new values with a sense of ease, or in other words, to secure "psychological safety." This is a prerequisite for the

---

5) Citing the words of Tom Kelley, a leading expert in design thinking, the Ministry of Economy, Trade and Industry (METI) (2020b) defines design thinking as "to apply the toolsets and mindsets that designers have developed through their work not only to design products, but also to design services and systems involving more complex problems" (p. 4). Nomura Research Institute (2014) states that "design should be incorporated into corporate activities, recognizing that design is relevant to all corporate activities, including marketing, planning, advertising, and branding in the development of products and services" (p. 3). Both discuss the application of design techniques to corporate management and solving social issues.

spread of prototyping.

For example, the point is whether we can present unfinished ideas to others without anxiety. We need to actively share our "hypotheses," even if they are incomplete and full of inaccuracies, with others to bring them closer to perfection while receiving feedback. We will be unsure whether the ideas meet the actual needs until they are shared. If we have a mindset of "I cannot share any idea unless it is perfect," we will not be able to proceed with anything.

Another point is whether we can "solve complex and ambiguous problems without forcibly simplifying or quantifying them, while allowing for some ambiguity." Simplifying a problem makes it easier to solve, but various aspects of the issue may be left out, making it impossible to reach a fulfilling solution. It is desirable to resolve problems through the participation of various experts, while intentionally leaving ambiguity.

Regarding ambiguity, Mr. Nagai also pointed out that it is important to have the right sense of discomfort, such as a sense that "Something is weird" or that "The theory is correct, but I feel something is wrong." It is difficult but important to break down and verbalize this sense of discomfort. It is important to stop whenever you feel any discomfort, rather than just turning a deaf ear to the calls of SOS from customers who are facing challenges.

We need a psychologically safe organization that allows us to feel, and even share, any of the anxieties, ambiguity, and discomfort mentioned above.

(3) The Understanding of Organizational Leaders

Since prototyping takes time until the final form takes shape and does not directly lead to immediate profits, the understanding of management is essential for the implementation of prototyping and design thinking[6]. Here I would like to provide some examples of points to keep in mind when prototyping.

1) Prototyping as branding

According to Mr. Ishikawa, who was mentioned earlier, whether a company has a culture of prototyping or not directly leads to employees' intention to stay in that company and their motivation, and a company with highly motivated employees

---

6) Improving companies' competitiveness by bringing design thinking into management is also promoted by government agencies, as seen in the case study of Osaka Prefecture (2021) and the Kansai Design Driven Management Project by the Kansai Bureau of Economy, Trade and Industry (METI Kansai).

Part I

Part II

Part III

Part IV

directly relates to corporate sales performance[7]. The ability to create the next market by gaining insights from customers through prototyping will make a difference in the medium to long term. If a company positions prototyping as a means to pursue its missions, prototyping itself may become its brand. Branding in this context is not mass marketing, but something that evokes empathy corresponding to individual customers' perspectives. The use of data will also make it possible to identify what responses can be expected from which recipients.

2) Media exposure of "stories"

There is a way to communicate a mission in the form of stories (storytelling) to make individuals empathize with the mission of the company. It is preferable to assume that the stories communicated will be taken up by the media. The aforementioned Mr. Nagai said that when launching a new measure in Kobe City, he considers the ripple effects of the media as well as how he wants the media to cover it.

3) Unity of will within the organization

The larger the organization and the more fragmented the roles of individuals and the more difficult it will be to spread a culture of prototyping. Especially when prototyping across departments, it is necessary to spend time interacting to share the intentions and goals of measures. In the case of JR West (West Japan Railway Company), which was discussed in the research group meeting, the department responsible for DX promotion and the railway management department had very different views on trials, so they promoted inter-departmental exchanges and mutual understanding when promoting DX.

In the case of local governments, while Kobe City was successful in rapid prototyping even amidst the COVID-19 pandemic, it would be difficult for Osaka City, for example, to conduct prototyping in the same way due to their different scales. How to proceed with these measures will be a very difficult challenge as governmental bodies become larger in scale, from cities, to prefectures, and to the national government.

4. Conclusion

In this paper, we discussed that the essence of DX is the transformation of

---

7) The Ministry of Economy, Trade and Industry (METI) and the Japan Patent Office (JPO) (2018) found that introducing design into management has a positive effect on sales, profits, stock prices, etc., according to the results of surveys in Europe and the U.S. (p. 5).

organizational governance. We also discussed innovation in "human processes" that accompanies innovation in "the processes of things" through digital technologies, citing as examples the subscription model from the perspective of "building long-term relationships with customers" and prototyping and design thinking from the perspective of "building organizations that continue to create new values." Building long-term relationships with customers and ensuring transparency for this purpose is now a global trend, which is now regarded as an ESG investment target.

Once these human processes have been transformed and made more efficient, the next step is to seek innovation in digital technologies as the processes of things. Even if the flow is not uniform as it depends on the industry and initiative, both things and humans will need to continue to evolve alongside each other in order to achieve the optimal combination of processes. The goal is "people's happiness," and transformation requires both ethics and imagination.

References

Asia Pacific Institute of Research (2022a), "Research Project: Comprehensive digital transformation in Kansai and Osaka" Research Group Report" (Japanese title: *Kenkyu Purojekuto: Kansai, Osaka ni Okeru Toshi Gurumi, Toshi Reberu no DX*) (FY2021) (https://www.apir.or.jp/wp/wp-content/uploads/2021_apir_research_report_DX.pdf, Last viewed on August 3, 2022)

Asia Pacific Institute of Research (2022b), "Post-Covid-19 Sustainable Enterprise Design and DX" (Japanese title: *Korona go no Jizoku Kano na Kigyo no Dezain to DX*), APIR NOW, No. 31, p. 12. (https://www.apir.or.jp/wp/wp-content/uploads/ apir_now_no31.pdf, Last viewed on August 3, 2022)

Asia Pacific Institute of Research (2022c), "Kansai and the Asia Pacific: Economic Outlook 2021–22"

Ministry of Economy, Trade and Industry (METI) and Japan Patent Office (2018) "Design Driven Management Declaration" (Japanese title: *Dezain Keiei Sengen*) (https://www.meti.go.jp/report/whitepaper/data/pdf/20180523001_01.pdf, Last viewed on August 3, 2022)

Ministry of Economy, Trade and Industry (METI) (2020a), "Results of the FY2020 Industrial Economic Research Commissioned Project (E-Commerce Market Survey)" (https://www.meti.go.jp/policy/it_policy/statistics/outlook/210730_new_hokokusho.pdf, Last viewed on August 3, 2022)

Ministry of Economy, Trade and Industry (METI) (2020b), "Handbook on

'Design-Driven Management' for Business Persons with Unclear Visions of Designs" (https://www.meti.go.jp/press/2019/03/20200323002/20200323002-1.pdf, Last viewed on August 3, 2022)

Ministry of Economy, Trade and Industry (METI) (2022) "Digital Governance Code" (https://www.meti.go.jp/shingikai/mono_info_service/dgs5/pdf/20201109_01.pdf, Last viewed on August 3, 2022)

Nomura Research Institute (2014) "Report on the Survey of Management Practices Using Design Thinking to Strengthen International Competitiveness" (Japanese title: *Kokusai Kyosoryoku Kyoka no Tame no Dezain Shiko o Katsuyo Sita Keiei Jittai Chosa Hokokusho*" Website of the National Diet Library (http://warp.da.ndl.go.jp/info:ndljp/pid/10217941/www.meti.go.jp/policy/mono_info_service/mono/creative/design_thinking_report.pdf, Last viewed on August 3, 2022)

Osaka Prefecture (2021) "Improving the Competitiveness of Small and Medium Enterprises from the Perspective of Design Driven Management" (Japanese title: *Dezain Keiei Shiten deno Chusho Kigyo no Kyosoryoku Kojo ni Tsuite*) Osaka Prefecture Material No. 186.

Tzuo, T. (2018), *Subscribed: Why the Subscription Model Will Be Your Company's Future – and What to Do About it*, Portfolio Penguin.

Website of the Kansai Bureau of Economy, Trade and Industry (METI Kansai), "Kansai Design Driven Management Project" (Japanese title: *Kansai Dezain Keiei Purojekuto*), (https://www.kansai.meti.go.jp/2tokkyo/ 10design_keiei/design_top.html, Last viewed on August 3)

Section 3
TOURISM IN KANSAI: MEASURES TO ATTRACT VISITORS IMPLEMENTED BY DMOS IN THE KANSAI REGION

INADA, Yoshihisa; NOMURA, Ryosuke; OSHIMA, Hisanori

As of 2021, the number of inbound and domestic tourism in Japan has not recovered to the level of before the novel coronavirus pandemic (hereafter COVID-19) due to its infections situation and the measures taken in response to it. Last year, in Kansai and the Asia Pacific Economic Outlook 2021, we focused on the role of Destination Management/Marketing Organization (hereafter DMO), a regional tourism development corporation involved in the management of various tourist destinations in Japan, and we pointed out that its further contribution is expected in the future. In this section, we will first use major statistics to check the impact of the long-lasting COVID-19 pandemic on the tourism industry. Also, we will analyze the effectiveness of the measures taken by the municipalities in the Kansai region to stimulate demand for travel based on the trend of the total number of overnight domestic visitors in Japan. Then, we will analyze the effectiveness of the DMOs in attracting visitors within their marketing and management areas by focusing on some of the unique DMOs in the Kansai region that were included in last year's Economic Outlook. Finally, we will present some implications from the obtained results of the analysis.

1. Tourism Dynamics in FY 2021 and Measures to Stimulate Demand in Each Prefecture

(1)Activity Dynamics in the Service Sector
COVID-19 has significantly impacted the production of goods and services, both of which have yet to recover to their pre-COVID-19 levels. Figure 3-3-1 shows that both the mining and manufacturing production index and the tertiary industrial activity index bottomed out in May 2020 (mining and manufacturing production: 77.2, tertiary industry: 86.7) and have continued to gradually recover since then.

Among the service industries, the index for the face-to-face service industry[1] has repeatedly risen and fallen following the issuance and lifting of the

---

[1] The face-to-face service industry refers to transportation, lodging, restaurants, catering services, other living-related services, and entertainment.

Part I

Part II

Part III

Part IV

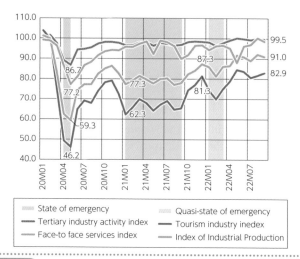

▨ State of emergency	▨ Quasi-state of emergency
— Tertiary industry activity index	— Tourism industry inedex
— Face-to face services index	— Index of Industrial Production

Figure 3-3-1 Trends in the mining and manufacturing production index, the tertiary industrial activity index, the face-to-face service industry index, and the tourist-related industry index: January 2020 to September 2022

Source: Prepared based on the mining and manufacturing production index and tertiary industry activity index by the Ministry of Economy, Trade and Industry

states of emergency and quasi-states of emergency[2]. In the face-to-face service industry, the recovery of the tourism-related industry[3], in particular, has been delayed. In the following sections, we will mainly examine the trends in the face-to-face service industry and the tourism-related industry.

In May 2020, the index for the face-to-face service industry was 59.3 and the index for the tourism-related industry was 46.2, showing a further decline compared to the aforementioned mining and manufacturing production index and tertiary industrial activity index. The indexes showed a recovery trend in the latter half of 2020, partly due to the lifting of the state of emergency and the start of the government's Go To Travel project.

However, due to the suspension of the Go To Travel project and the

---

2) The periods of issuing the states of emergency and the quasi-states of emergency are as follows.
The states of emergency (1st April 7–May 25, 2020, 2nd January 7–March 21, 2021, 3rd April 25–June 20, 2021, and 4th July 12–September 30, 2021)The quasi-states of emergency (April 5 to September 30, 2021, and January 9 to March 21, 2022)
3) The tourism-related industry index here refers to the weighted average of railroad passenger transport, road passenger transport, water passenger transport, air passenger transport, passenger transport, other rental, auto rental, lodging, restaurants, catering services, travel services, cinemas, theaters, and performing troupe, which correspond to the categories in the Japan Tourism Agency's Travel and Tourism Satellite Accounts in the tertiary industry activity index.

re-issuance of the state of emergency, in January 2021, the indexes for the face-to-face service industry and the tourism-related industry fell to 77.3 and 62.3, respectively, significant declines from the latter half of 2020 when they showed a recovery trend. Since then, there have been repeated issuances of a state of emergency and a quasi-state of emergency, and both indexes remained low until September. In addition to the improvement of the infections situation from October, the resumption of measures to stimulate travel demand by various municipalities helped the indexes of the face-to-face service industry and the tourism-related industry to rise to 87.3 and 81.4, respectively, in December.

The face-to-face service industry, which had been gradually recovering, deteriorated again in 2022 due to the spread of infections caused by a new variant (Omicron). From January, the quasi-state of emergency was sequentially issued in every prefecture, and both indexes for the face-to-face service industry and the tourism-related industry declined for two consecutive months. The overall lifting of the quasi-state on March 21 raised the indexes for March. However, comparing the January–March period with the level before COVID-19 (October–December 2019) (100.4 for the face-to-face service index and 102.4 for the tourism-related index), both indexes were low, down 16.0% points for the face-to-face service index and down 29.4% points for the tourism-related index.

(2) Measures to Stimulate Demand for Travel in Each Municipality during the COVID-19 Period

As mentioned above, infection-prevention measures, such as the issuances of a state of emergency, have had a significant impact on the tourism industry, which has not recovered to its pre-pandemic level. The domestic travel consumption[4] in the Kansai region in 2021 was 1,715.7 billion yen, down 58.4% from the 2019 level, a further decrease from the 2020 level (2,014.5 billion yen, down 51.2% from the 2019 level). In response, the government and local governments implemented their own measures to stimulate demand in order to recover depressed travel demand[5]. This section focuses mainly on the measures implemented by the prefectures in the Kansai region to stimulate demand after 2021 and analyzes the impact of these policies. Although the government implemented the Go To Travel project from July 2020, it suspended this project after 2021

---

4) The domestic travel consumption in Japan in 2021 was 9,183.5 billion yen, down 58.1% from the 2019 level (9,973.8 billion yen in 2020, down 54.5%).
5) According to Chapter 6, Section 4 of the Asia Pacific Institute of Research (2021), the demand creation impact of the Go To Travel project is assumed to have recovered 7.8% of the decrease in value added and 7.5% of the decrease in employment due to the COVID-19 pandemic in terms of its total ripple effects.

due to the worsening of the infections situation. While the project was halted, the various local governments started their own measures to stimulate travel demand, mainly targeting residents in their prefecture. Table 3-3-1 shows the measures taken independently by each prefecture in the Kansai region[6] in 2021 and 2022 to stimulate demand for travel. As shown in the table, although some prefectures including Fukui, Tottori, and Wakayama started their campaigns at

Table 3-3-1   Policies for promoting travel in the Kansai region: 2021/2022

	Campaign Name	Campaign Period (Lodging Discount)	Target Prefectures (Including Planned)
Fukui Pref.	Fukui discount campaign	February 17, 2021 to December 31, 2021 (Suspended from June 28, 2021 to July 21, 2021 and August 4, 2021 to September 30, 2021) January 1, 2022 to June 30, 2022 (except April 29 to May 8)	Niigata, Nagano, Toyama, Ishikawa, **Fukui**, Shiga, Shizuoka, Gifu, Aichi, Mie, and Kyoto
Mie Pref.	Mie special travel coupons	Phase 2: October 15, 2021 to December 1, 2021 Phase 3: December 1, 2021 to December 31, 2021	**Mie**
Shiga Pref.	Now is the time to travel Shiga!	Phase 4: July 9, 2021 to December 31, 2021 (sales of convenience store tickets was suspended from August 5, 2021, and new reservations were refrained from August 27, 2021) Phase 5: January 14, 2022 to March 6, 2022 (suspension of use from January 25, 2022)	Phase 4: **Shiga** Phase 5: **Shiga**
Kyoto Pref.	Travel Project to Rediscover the Charm of Kyoto	October 22, 2021 to March 31, 2022 (new reservations were suspended from January 25, 2022 to March 18, 2022).	Shiga, **Kyoto**, Osaka, Hyogo, Nara, Fukui, and Mie
Osaka Pref.	Welcome to Osaka Campaign 2021	November 24, 2021 to February 28, 2022 (new reservations were suspended from January 12, 2022)	**Osaka**, Hyogo, Kyoto, Nara, and Wakayama
Hyogo Pref.	Hometown support! Let's travel Hyogo campaign	October 14, 2021 to February 28, 2022 (Suspension of use from February 2, 2022)	Hyogo, Osaka, Kyoto, Wakayama, Nara, Shiga, Okayama, Tottori, Tokushima, and Kagawa
Nara Pref.	Now is the time to travel to Nara campaign 2021	December 1, 2021 to February 28, 2022	**Nara**
Wakayama Pref.	Plan to refresh yourself in Wakayama, the 2nd	June 22, 2021 to December 31, 2021	**Wakayama**
	Plan to refresh yourself in Wakayama, the 3rd	October 8, 2021 to December 31, 2021	**Wakayama**
Tottori Pref./ Shimane Pref.	#We Love Sanin Campaign	March 1, 2021 to July 11, 2022 (planned) (temporary suspension from July 26, 2021 to September 30, 2021)	**Tottori, Shimane** *Okayama, Yamaguchi, Tokushima, Kagawa, Ehime, and Kochi were included from May 25, 2022.
Tokushima Pref.	Tokushima support discount	October 1, 2021 (Discounts resumed) to March 10, 2022 (New reservations were suspended from January 20, 2022)	**Tokushima**, Hyogo, Wakayama, Kagawa, Ehime, and Kochi

Source: Prepared from publicly available data released by each local government

---

6) The Kansai region here refers to ten prefectures: Fukui, Mie, Shiga, Kyoto, Osaka, Hyogo, Nara, Wakayama, Tottori and Tokushima prefectures.

an early stage, many of them started them after October 2021 partly due to the impact of the issuance of the state of emergency and quasi-state of emergency. The initial coverage of the project implemented by each prefecture was mainly targeted at its residents. Still, some prefectures expanded the coverage to residents in neighboring prefectures while observing the trend of the infections situation.

In order to confirm the effectiveness of the measures taken by municipalities in the Kansai region to stimulate demand, we will look at the change in the growth rate (compared to the same month of 2019) of the total number of overnight stays by Japanese visitors in the Kansai region, breaking it down into those from within the prefecture and those from outside the prefecture.

As shown in Figure 3-2-2, the rate of decrease in the number of visitors from within the prefecture has contracted since May 2020 (down 73.9% compared to the same month in 2019) and exceeded the pre-pandemic level in October 2020 with an increase of 7.5% compared to the same month in 2019. However, on entering 2021, the trend remained weak due to the suspension of the Go To Travel project. Nonetheless, due to the impact of measures to stimulate travel demand implemented by each prefecture, the growth rate increased for three consecutive months, up 20.9% compared to the same month in 2019 in

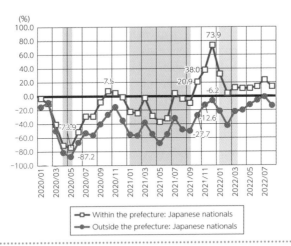

| Figure 3-3-2 | Trends in the growth rate of the number of overnight visitors from within and outside the prefecture: January 2020 to August 2022 in the Kansai region |

Note: The area shaded in gray indicates the period of the state of emergency and the area shaded in yellow indicates the period of the quasi-state of emergency. Preliminary figures for the period from January to August, 2022. The growth rate is the comparison with the same month in 2019.
Source: Prepared based on Overnight Travel Statistics Survey by the Japan Tourism Agency

Part I

Part II

Part III

Part IV

October, up 38.0% in November, and up 73.9% in December. In 2022, the growth rate showed a downward trend due to the reimplementation of infection-preventive measures, but it was still higher than the pre-pandemic level.

As for tourists from outside of the prefecture, the decline rate has contracted after bottoming out in May 2020 (down 87.2% compared to the same month in 2019), as was the case for tourists from within the prefecture, but the growth rate is still lower than the pre-pandemic level, contrary to the case for tourists from within the prefecture. In 2021 and thereafter, the rate of growth remained in the negative range, but the rate of decline decreased for three consecutive months in October (–27.7%), November (–12.6%), and December (–6.2%). However, in 2022, the decline rate increased again and the growth rate has yet to recover to the pre-pandemic level.

It is fair to conclude that the demand stimulation measures taken by each local government have had a certain level of impact on visitors from within the prefecture.

As discussed above, each local government implemented measures to stimulate demand for travel, which had declined due to the prolonged COVID-19 pandemic. Although the measures to stimulate demand had a certain degree of impact on tourists from within the prefecture, domestic tourism has yet to fully recover in both the Kansai region and the nation as a whole. Nonetheless, the government launched the national travel support program on October 11, 2022, and it has been steadily implementing measures to restore domestic tourism demand. Signs of a change also began to emerge in the situation for international tourists to Japan. Japan had been maintaining strict border control measures, but on October 11, 2022, the government implemented significant easing measures, such as lifting the entry limit, lifting the ban on individual travel for international tourists, and exempting them from obtaining short-term visas.

As described above, signs of a recovery have been emerging for domestic and inbound tourism in the latter half of 2022. As for inbound tourism in the future, in particular, it will be necessary to improve the environment to receive international tourists in a manner that responds to COVID-19, including comprehensive infection prevention, based on the idea of safety, trust, and peace of mind, as pointed out in the Asia Pacific Institute of Research (2020). In addition, it will be even more important for each local government to appeal to international visitors to Japan about the attractiveness of the region. In the following section, We will analyze the effectiveness of the tourism promotion measures implemented mainly in the pre-pandemic period by DMOs, which lead to the development of tourism regions, focusing on the examples in the Kansai region.

2. Tourism Promotion Measures Implemented by DMOs in the Kansai Region and Their Effectiveness: Case Studies of Kyoto, Wakayama, and Nara Prefectures

As mentioned earlier, the tourism industry was severely affected by COVID-19 and has yet to fully recover.

To address this, the prefectures in the Kansai region have begun to reconsider their tourism strategies. In other words, they are definitely aiming to enhance the value of the overall tourism industry, including not only inbound tourism but also domestic tourism. In this case, the role of DMOs, which are in a position to lead to the development of tourism regions together with local governments, is becoming more important.

We will therefore look back at the unique case studies of DMOs in the Kansai region that we covered in last year's White Paper and evaluate their effectiveness in attracting visitors to the areas that they market and manage. Finally, we will summarize the implications and future issues obtained from the analysis and point out the importance of refining tourism resources.

The analysis is based on the individual data from the Overnight Travel Statistics Survey, which provides information on the number of Japanese and international visitors staying overnight in each municipality[7].

(1) Case Study of DMOs in Kyoto Prefecture[8]

(i) Activities of DMOs in Kyoto Prefecture
First, we will look at the history of the establishment and activities of DMOs in Kyoko Prefecture. Table 3-3-2 shows the chronological order in which the DMOs were established in the prefecture. Kyoto Prefecture is promoting a wide-area tourism project called "Another Kyoto" and has divided its area into "Kyoto by the Sea," "Kyoto in Forests," "Kyoto Infused with Tea," and "Kyoto Otokuni Bamboo Groove," and it is working to promote tourism in cooperation

7) This analysis is the result of joint research with the Kinki District Transport Bureau of the Ministry of Land, Infrastructure, Transport and Tourism. We would like to express my gratitude for the cooperation.
8) For a detailed analysis of the DMOs in Kyoto Prefecture, please refer to Yoshihisa Inada, Kenta Koyama and Ryosuke Nomura (2022-a).

with Kyoto City[9].

A DMO in "Kyoto by the Sea" was established one year earlier than the DMOs in the other areas, and it is characterized by the fact that it has formulated

Table 3-3-2   History of the establishment of DMOs in Kyoto Prefecture

Year	Kyoto by the Sea	Kyoto in Forests	Kyoto Infused with Tea
2013	April: Based on the concept focusing on "Kyoto by the Sea," established Council for the Promotion of Tourism "Kyoto by the Sea"		
2014	June: Certified as a Tourism Region based on the Tourism Region Development Act		
2015		June: Formulated a concept focusing on "Kyoto in Forests"	June: Formulated a concept focusing on "Kyoto Infused with Tea"
2016	**June: Established a DMO to promote "Kyoto by the Sea"**		
2017	November: Registered as a Japanese version of DMO	**March: Established a DMO to promote "Kyoto in Forests"**	**March: Established a DMO to promote "Kyoto Infused with Tea"**
2018		March: Formulated **a strategy to develop a tourism region in "Kyoto in Forests"** July: Registered as a Japanese version of DMO	March: Formulated **a strategy to develop a tourism region through the DMO to promote the Yamashiro area of Kyoto** July: Registered as a Japanese version of DMO
2019	January: Formulated the plan for the development of the tourism region in "Kyoto by the Sea" February: Formulated **a strategic plan to promote inbound tourism to "Kyoto by the Sea" through the DMO** April: Employed one non-Japanese staff member		

Source: Prepared by the author based on the Kyoto Prefectural Government's website and the Plan for Formation and Establishment of Destination Management/Marketing Organization on the Japan Tourism Agency's website

9) The constituent cities, towns, and villages of each area are as follows.
Kyoto by the Sea:
Fukuchiyama City, Maizuru City, Ayabe City, Miyazu City, Kyotango City, Yosa-gun (Ine Town, Yosano Town)
Kyoto in Forests:
Fukuchiyama City, Ayabe City, Kameoka City, Nantan City, Funai-gun (Kyotanba Town)
Kyoto Infused with Tea:
Uji City, Joyo City, Yawata City, Kyotanabe City, Kizugawa City, Kuse-gun (Kumiyama Town), Tsuzuki-gun (Ide Town, Ujitawara Town), Soura-gun (Kasagi Town, Wazuka Town, Seika Town, Minami Yamashiro Village)
Kyoto Otokuni Bamboo Groove:
Muko City, Nagaokakyo City, Otokuni-gun (Ooyamazaki Town)

an inbound strategy plan and is actively engaged in overseas promotions and the development of an environment for accepting visitors.

Each DMO in Kyoto Prefecture has set its own target group of tourists and is working to attract tourists. Table 3-3-3 summarizes these efforts.

As shown in the table, each DMO is targeting not only tourists from East and Southeast Asian countries, which are expected to remain stable in the future, but also those from Europe, North America, and Australia. As for visitors from the former regions, an increase in the number of visitors to Japan is

Table 3-3-3   Targets of the DMOs in Kyoto Prefecture

Kyoto by the Sea	Kyoto in Forests	Kyoto Infused with Tea
Targets		
Europe, U.S.A, and Australia: Long stays are expected to increase the amount of tourism consumption.	**Europe, U.S.A, and Australia**: Long stays are expected to increase the amount of tourism consumption. Interest in experiencing the four seasons and nature tours has a high affinity with the characteristics of "Kyoto in Forests."	**Europe, U.S.A, and Australia**: Tourists from Europe, U.S.A, and Australia account for a high percentage of international visitors to the Kyoto City area. Since they tend to stay for long periods of time, the DMO will encourage them to visit the neighboring "Kyoto Infused with Tea" area as well.
East Asia: Tourists from East Asia, mainly from Taiwan, account for about 80% of the international visitors to "Kyoto by the Sea." A stable and further increase in the number of visitors from this region can be expected in the future.	**East Asia**: Tourists from East Asia account for the highest percentage of international tourists visiting "Kyoto in Forests." Visits from East Asia are expected to remain stable in the future as well.	**Repeat visitors to Japan from Asia, mainly Hong Kong, Taiwan, and China**: Tourists from Asia account for approximately 90% of all international visitors to the Yamashiro area. The DMO will continue to encourage them to visit the area.
Southeast Asia: A region where the number of visitors to Japan is increasing due to the launch of LCCs and the increase in the number of flights. Tourists from Thailand, a pro-Japanese country whose people's tastes match the food that is one of the strengths of "Kyoto by the Sea," have a high repeat rate. Tourists from Singapore and other countries who prefer experience-based tourism have a high affinity with the characteristics of "Kyoto by the Sea." Further growth in the number of visitors is expected in the future.		**Tourists (both domestic and international) visiting Kyoto City**: Attract tourists to the Yamashiro area as it is easily accessible from Kyoto City and has a strong affinity with Kyoto City in terms of its resources of Japanese tea culture and history.

Source: Prepared by the author based on the Kyoto Prefectural Government's website and the Plan for Formation and Establishment of Destination Management/Marketing Organization on the Japan Tourism Agency's website

expected due to the launch of LCCs and the increase in the number of flights, and the number of visitors is expected to increase even more in the future. As for the visitors from the latter regions, an increase in tourism consumption by long-stay visitors is expected. Therefore, each DMO is vigorously engaging in promotional activities for both groups.

(ii) Analysis of the Effectiveness of Promotions to Attract Visitors Implemented by DMOs in Kyoto Prefecture

As mentioned above, the tourists targeted in each area are diverse. Therefore, in the following sections, we will discuss the effectiveness of the promotions to attract tourists in each area, mainly focusing on the trends in the number of overnight stays by international tourists.

Figure 3-3-3 shows the changes in the rate of international guests staying overnight to the total number of guests in each area. As shown in the figure, the rate of international guests in Kyoto City increased sharply from 13.4% in 2012 to 38.2% in 2019, reflecting a remarkable increase in the number of international overnight visitors.

Looking at the entire Kyoto Prefecture, the rates of international visitors to Kyoto increased in all regions: specifically, the DMO in "Kyoto by the Sea" (from 1.8% in 2012 to 6.2% in 2019), the DMO in "Kyoto in Forests" (from 0.8% in 2012 to 3.6% in 2019), and the DMO in "Kyoto Infused with Tea" (from 0.9% in

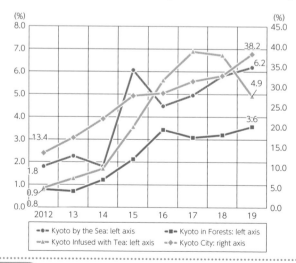

Figure 3-3-3   Trends in the rate of international overnight visitors in each area: Kyoto Prefecture

Source: Prepared based on individual data from the Japan Tourism Agency's Overnight Travel Statistics Survey

2012 to 4.9% in 2019). Especially, the DMO in "Kyoto by the Sea" has shown an increasing trend year by year, which suggests the effectiveness of the measures to attract visitors is becoming evident.

The rates of international visitors in the areas covered by the DMOs by nationality show that the share of East Asian countries such as Taiwan and Hong Kong is high (Figure 3-3-4). Among these, focusing on Taiwan, the share of Taiwan has been dominant since 2014 (12.0% in 2014, 18.5% in 2015, and 22.9% in 2016), and since 2017 it has accounted for about half of the total number of international visitors to Japan (44.2% in 2017, 44.1% in 2018, and 50.3% in 2019). We can say that this is a result of the fact that the DMO in "Kyoto by the Sea" participated in the largest travel expo in Taiwan in 2017 and 2018, as well as due to on-site promotions and other activities.

As shown above, the rate of international overnight visitors in the areas of the DMOs in Kyoto Prefecture has been steadily increasing, but Kyoto City still accounts for an overwhelmingly large portion of the total number of foreign guests. Still, a certain positive impact can be seen as a result of the steady efforts to attract international visitors, such as the promotional activities implemented by the DMO in "Kyoto by the Sea."

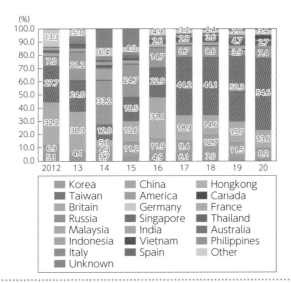

Part I
Part II
Part III
Part IV

Figure 3-3-4   Trends in the rate of international overnight visitors by nationality: "Kyoto by the Sea"

Note: Data are collected from facilities with 10 or more employees.
Source: Prepared based on individual data from the Japan Tourism Agency's Overnight Travel Statistics Survey

(2) Case Study of DMOs in Wakayama Prefecture[10]

(i) Activities of DMOs in Wakayama Prefecture

Table 3-3-4 shows the history and activities of the characteristic DMOs in Wakayama Prefecture.

Table 3-3-4 History of the establishment of DMOs in Wakayama Prefecture

Year	Koya Tourism Association	Tanabe City Kumano Tourism Bureau	Nankishirahama Tourism Association
		2006 Established 2010 Incorporated and began the travel business in the region	
2012			
2013			
2014			
2015	July Established		
2016		**February Registered as a regional DMO (candidate corporation)**	May Launched preparatory council for the establishment of DMO Shirahama **July Registered as a regional DMO (candidate corporation)** **(DMO Shirahama (General Incorporated Association))** **(tentative name)**
2017	**August Registered as a regional DMO (candidate corporation)**	Established Kumano Travel, a travel support center Launched Kumano Kodo Women's Club	
2018	October Established iKOYA, Koya Town Tourist Information Center		April Established Nankishirahama Tourism Bureau (General Incorporated Association)
2019		**March Re-registered as a regional DMO**	**March Re-registered as a regional DMO**
2020	**January Re-registered as a regional DMO**	Developed content based on the keywords 'single trip' and 'women's trip' Organized crowdfunding for the preservation of Kumano Kodo	Registered as a travel agent (Type 3)
2021			April Nankishirahama Tourism Bureau (General Incorporated Association) and Shirahama Tourism Association merge to form Nankishirahama Tourism Association (General Incorporated Association).

Source: Prepared by the author based on the Plan for Formation and Establishment of Destination Management/Marketing Organization on the Japan Tourism Agency's website

10) Please refer to Yoshihisa Inada, Kenta Koyama and Ryosuke Nomura (2022-b) for a detailed analysis of DMOs in Wakayama Prefecture.

In particular, the activities of the Tanabe City Kumano Tourism Bureau are unique. The DMO was established in 2006 following the reestablishment of Tanabe City through a merger. It became a corporation and registered as a travel agency in 2010 to start a travel business in the area. It was registered as a regional DMO in March 2019 and selected by the Japan Tourism Agency as a priority support DMO in FY 2021.

In 2014, Tanabe City and Santiago de Compostela City in Spain signed a tourism exchange agreement to disseminate information. Since then, they have successfully attracted inbound visitors by conducting joint promotions and common pilgrimages. In terms of the environment to receive visitors, the City has implemented measures for inbound tourism from an early stage and has accumulated a large amount of data on inbound travelers by integrating language expressions and by its own company conducting travel business transactions. In terms of refining tourism resources, it has established Kumano Travel, a travel support center, and Kumano Kodo Women's Club, and it has developed content based on the keywords 'single trip' and 'women's trip.'

Next, we will examine the tourists that are the targets of each DMO (Table 3-3-5).

The Koya Tourism Association, based on its own survey, targets the younger generation among domestic tourists in particular. While approximately 80% of inbound tourists have come from Europe and North America, the Association intends to create new value and demand in anticipation of a major change in travel patterns in the future.

Based on its past results, while the Tanabe City Kumano Tourism Bureau will continue to target tourists from Europe, North America, and Australia, it will also emphasize domestic tourists in the context of the COVID-19 pandemic. Mainly focusing on the Tokyo metropolitan area and Kansai area, the Bureau is developing and promoting travel products for each generation, such as specific to women in their 20s to 40s who live and work in the Tokyo metropolitan area.

The Nankishirahama Tourism Association is focusing on the Tokyo metropolitan area to increase its name recognition domestically, while also targeting the East Asian region for inbound tourism based on its past results.

(ii) Analysis of the Effectiveness of Promotions to Attract Visitors Implemented by DMOs in Wakayama Prefecture

The activities of the characteristic DMOs in Wakayama Prefecture show that they are making good use of the tourism resources in their respective areas and appealing to the targets set by each DMO. The following is an analysis of the effectiveness of each DMO in attracting foreign visitors to Koya Town,

Table 3-3-5   Targets of the DMOs in Wakayama Prefecture

The Koya Tourism Association	Tanabe City Kumano Tourism Bureau	The Nankishirahama Tourism Association
	Targets	
Domestic tourists	**Individual travelers from Europe, U.S.A, and Australia**	**Attract visitors from the Tokyo metropolitan area**
(Young adults and seniors mainly from the Tokyo metropolitan and Kansai areas) The Association will focus on the age groups that showed unfavorable results in the voluntary survey conducted in FY 2020 and work on the development of travel products, etc.	Based on the past results and the belief that the Kumano area's characteristics of "the syncretism of Shinto and Buddhism" and "nature worship" stimulate the intellectual curiosity of travelers from Europe, U.S.A, and Australia who are accustomed to traveling, the Bureau is targeting inbound travelers from these countries.	Implement promotions targeting the Tokyo metropolitan area, where the name recognition of Nankishirahama is low. Increase awareness of tourist resources such as hot springs, pandas, and white sand beaches.
Toward a recovery of inbound travel	**Domestic tourists from the Tokyo metropolitan and Kansai areas**	**Inbound visitors (East Asia and others)**
Until now, about 80% of the tourists have been from Europe and U.S.A. However, the Association will create new value and demand in anticipation of a major change in travel patterns after COVID-19. It is continuing to develop infrastructure and an environment that enable individual travelers to visit safely.	The area is within a short distance from the Kansai region and can be accessed within an hour by air from the Tokyo metropolitan area. Since many people are attracted to Kumano as a sacred place, the Bureau will refine the contents unique to the region and promote the creation of new experience plans combined with local industries.	Verify overseas promotion implemented during the pandemic of COVID-19. Collect information from Japan National Tourism Organization (JNTO) and the prefectural government.
Attract training programs and camps	**Women in their 20s to 40s, mainly in the Tokyo metropolitan area**	**Attract tourism trough MICE (anacronym of Meetings, Incentives, Conferences, and Exhibitions) and sport camps**
Taking advantage of having many lodging facilities (shukubo) in the area, the Association will propose high value-added contents, such as experiences that allow visitors to experience the religious nature and spirituality unique to Koyasan.	Since many people living in the Tokyo metropolitan area, especially women, are attracted to the Kumano area for its spiritual appeal, the Bureau has targeted this demographic. It established the Kumano Kodo Women's Club to promote the charms of the Kumano Kodo from a female perspective, leading to an increase in the number of domestic tourists.	Examine new contents to attract visitors and conduct sales activities to universities and travel agents. Specifically consider the possibility of attracting tourism through MICE.

Source: Prepared by the author based on the Plan for Formation and Establishment of Destination Management/Marketing Organization on the Japan Tourism Agency's website

the Kumano area in Tanabe City (hereafter referred to as TKTB area)[11], and Shirahama Town (Figure 3-3-5).

Looking at the rate of international overnight visitors to total overnight visitors in each area, the current rate of international visitors in Koya Town approached approximately 50% in 2019. Koya Town is a unique area where half of all visitors are non-Japanese. Next, looking at the Kumano area in Tanabe City, the number of international visitors has been steadily increasing, reflecting the upward trend in the rate of international visitors (from 2.4% in 2012 to 8.5% in 2019). Finally, looking at Shirahama Town, the rate of international visitors showed an upward trend toward 2017 and has trended at 7 to 8% since then.

As mentioned above, while the number of Japanese overnight visitors has been flat or declining in each area, the number of non-Japanese international overnight visitors has been steadily increasing. In the following sections, We will analyze the effectiveness of the measures taken to attract visitors, paying particular attention to the TKTB area.

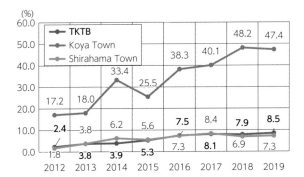

| Figure 3-3-5 | Trends in the rate of international overnight visitors in each area: Wakayama Prefecture |

Source: Prepared based on individual data from the Japan Tourism Agency's Overnight Travel Statistics Survey

Figure 3-3-6 shows the characteristics of accommodation facilities located along the Kumano Kodo route in the TKTB area[12]. The rate of visitors from the East Asia region[13] is about 30 to 40% (from 41.7% in 2012 to 30.9% in 2019) and

---

11) Please note that the Kumano area of Tanabe City consists of Shingu City and Nachikatsuura Town in addition to Tanabe City, and it includes the areas related to the Kumano Kodo route.

12) Based on the Kumano Kodo route and the zip codes of the related facilities, we extracted the lodging facilities from the Kumano area in Tanabe City obtained from the individual data of the Overnight Travel Statistics Survey.

13) The East Asia region here refers to South Korea, China, Taiwan and Hong Kong.

the rate of visitors from Europe, North America, and Australia[14] is about 40 to 50% (from 36.9% in 2012 to 48.3% in 2019). It is clear that the rate of visitors from Europe, North America, and Australia, who are the targets of the Tanabe City Kumano Tourism Bureau as shown in Table 3-3-5, has been steadily increasing. In particular, visitors from Australia (3.4% in 2012 to 14.5% in 2019) and visitors from Spain (6.6% in 2015 to 10.1% in 2019) have a relatively large share of the total number of visitors. For Spain, this indicates that the co-promotion with Spain has had a positive impact.

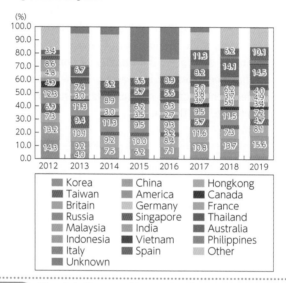

Figure 3-3-6　Trends in the rate of international overnight visitors by nationality: Kumano area of Tanabe City focusing on the Kumano Kodo route

Source: Prepared based on individual data from the Japan Tourism Agency's Overnight Travel Statistics Survey

(3) Case Study of DMOs in Nara Prefecture[15]

(i) Activities of DMOs in Nara Prefecture

Table 3-3-6 shows the history of the establishment of DMOs in Nara Prefecture and their activities.

In terms of refining tourism resources, all of the DMOs are trying to attract

---

14) Europe, North America, and Australia here refer the United Kingdom, Germany, France, Italy, Spain, U.S.A., Canada, and Australia.
15) Please refer to Inada and Nomura (2022) for a detailed analysis of DMOs in Nara Prefecture.

tourists by creating experience programs that make the most of local resources. In terms of improving the environment to receive visitors, each DMO is promoting measures such as the multilingualization of its website, the installation of Wi-Fi, and the establishment of tourist information centers. Finally, in terms

| Table 3-3-6 | History of the establishment of DMOs in Nara Prefecture |

Year	Ikaruga sangyo	Yoshino Visitors Bureau	Nara Prefecture Visitors Bureau
			2009 Established
2012			
2013		February Established	
2014	January Incorporated		
2015			
2016	February Registered as a regional DMO (candidate corporation)	Conducted a marketing survey on tourism in Yoshino Town	April Registered as a regional cooperation DMO (candidate corporation)
2017	[Enhancement of tourism resources] - Creation of experience contents, development of secondary transportation (round-trip cabs, baby carriages, rental bicycles) [Information dissemination] - Creation of brochures, participation in exhibitions and business meetings, multilingualization of website, and creation of promotional videos		[Information dissemination] - Promotion to attract international visitors in cooperation with the prefectural government of Nara
2018		[Enhancement of tourism resources] - Certified as a travel agent (Type 2), organized a wide variety of tours [Improvement of the environment for accepting visitors] - Established 11 free Wi-Fi spots in the Yoshinoyama area	March Re-registered as a regional cooperation DMO
2019	January Registered as a regional DMO (candidate corporation) February Launched Nara Ikaruga Tourism Waikaru, a tourist base July Opened Ikaruga Biyori (private residence temporarily taking lodgers), an inn rented out as a whole house [Improvement of the environment for accepting visitors] - Waikaru: Hired English-speaking staff, equipped with Pocket Talk (AI interpreting machine), improved website (multilingualization) and introduced reservation system, etc.	March Registered as a regional DMO (candidate corporation)	[Enhancement of tourism resources] - Creation of experience programs preferred by international travelers, etc. - Creation of programs that make the most of nature in Totsukawa Village
2020		November Re-registered as a regional DMO [Information dissemination] Establishment of an e-commerce site (product sales, hometown tax donation program) Development of own product brand, information dissemination and promotion in cooperation with the prefectural government	[Improvement of the environment for accepting visitors] - The Bureau was entrusted with management of Kashihara Navi Plaza, a tourist information center in Kashihara City
2021	April Established WEST NARA Wide Area Tourism Promotion Council		

Source: Prepared based on individual data from the Japan Tourism Agency's Overnight Travel Statistics Survey

Part I

Part II

Part III

Part IV

of information dissemination, the DMOs are engaged in various activities, including creating promotional videos mainly for non-Japanese and promoting brand-name products through e-commerce sites.

We organized the targets of the DMOs as shown in Table 3-3-7.

Ikaruga Sangyo domestically targets tourists in their 50s to 70s in the Tokyo metropolitan area, three-generation groups (parents, children, and grandchildren), and day-trippers from the Kinki and Chubu regions. It internationally targets tourists from Europe, North America, and Australia. The

Table 3-3-7   Targets of the DMOs in Nara Prefecture

Ikaruga sangyo Co., Ltd. Town Development Division	General Incorporated Association Nara Visitors Bureau	Yoshino Visitors Bureau
Targets		
(Domestic) Overnight visitors in their 50s to 70s or three-generation groups from the Tokyo metropolitan area	Domestic and international individual tourists who love Nara	(Domestic)
Unlike the cities of Kyoto and Nara, the area offers a relaxed atmosphere and a taste of history and culture. Attract visitors to hot springs such as Totsukawa Onsen in the southern part of the prefecture.	By communicating new attractions that are not yet known to those who are already interested in Nara, the Bureau will further promote repeat visits and sightseeing tours within the prefecture.	Independent spiritual but not religious (SBNR) tourists (sometimes urban women) Nature-oriented family households Retired couple households
(Domestic) Day-tourists from the Kinki and Chubu regions	Individual tourists (especially the wealthy) mainly from the Tokyo metropolitan area	Non-Japanese (especially Europeans, Americans, and Australians) who understand Japanese culture, have a certain level of education, and are intellectually curious
Areas suitable for travel by private vehicles.Create plans making use of the Go To Campaign.	Due to the annual tourism campaign conducted by JR Tokai since 2006 in the Tokyo metropolitan area, awareness and interest in Nara are relatively high. In addition, since many of the tourists from the Tokyo metropolitan area involve overnight stays, the unit consumption price is relatively high.	Non-Japanese who have visited historical sightseeing spots, including Kyoto, and who are authentic-minded and wish to learn more about Japanese spirituality and religious beliefs have a high affinity with historical sites that are the origins of the faith of mountain priests.
(Overseas) Europe, U.S.A, and Australia	Individual tourists (especially the wealthy), mainly from Europe, U.S.A, and Australia	Non-Japanese who admire Japan's natural landscape and love walking on long trails in the mountains
With excellent access from Osaka, Kyoto, and Kansai Airport, lodging in the Horyuji area can be used as a base to travel to various destinations.	Due to the geographical location of Japan, the length of their trips is longer, and their total consumption is correspondingly higher. In addition, the wealthy are highly intellectually curious and Nara Prefecture is a good match for them as its strengths include its cultural and historical background.	The town's natural landscape can attract non-Japanese visitors who love walking on long trails in the mountains and promote them revisiting the town throughout the year. In light of the high rate of active young people, the town can also benefit from the spreading power of social media.

Source: Prepared based on individual data from the Japan Tourism Agency's Overnight Travel Statistics Survey

Yoshino Visitors Bureau domestically targets individual travelers (females living in urban areas), nature-oriented families, and retired couples, taking advantage of the historical heritage and natural resources of the area. It internationally targets non-Japanese travelers who understand Japanese culture and who are intellectually curious, as well as those who enjoy walking on long trails and the natural scenery.

The Nara Visitors Bureau is domestically trying to attract visitors by targeting Nara-loving individual travelers and wealthy individual travelers mainly from the Tokyo metropolitan area. It internationally targets mainly wealthy individual travelers from Europe, North America, and Australia.

As shown above, all the DMOs are working on attracting inbound travelers, mainly from Europe, North America, and Australia, but they are also targeting domestic travelers. In the following sections, we will examine the trends in international overnight visitors in the municipalities related to each DMO.

(ii) Analysis of the Effectiveness of Promotions to Attract Visitors Implemented by DMOs in Nara Prefecture

Figure 3-3-7 shows the trend of the rate of international overnight visitors in the municipalities and areas related to the DMOs mentioned above.

First, we will look at the area[16] of the municipalities that are covered by the WEST NARA Wide Area Tourism Promotion Council established by Ikaruga Sangyo. The rate rose from 1.5% in 2012 to 4.8% in 2015, and it has remained at around 4% since then. Next, looking at Yoshino Town, the rate trended upward

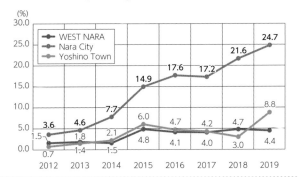

Figure 3-3-7 Trends in the rate of international overnight visitors in each area: Nara Prefecture

Source: Prepared based on individual data from the Japan Tourism Agency's Overnight Travel Statistics Survey

16) The WEST NARA area consists of the following cities, towns and villages. Yamato Koriyama City, Heguri Town, Sango Town, Ikaruga Town, Ando Town, and Oji Town.

Part I

Part II

Part III

Part IV

from 0.7% in 2012 and had risen to 6.0% in 2015. After 2016, the rate trended downward, but then rose to 8.8% in 2019.

Finally, looking at Nara City, the rate of international overnight visitors has been on the rise from 3.6% in 2012 to 24.7% in 2019, indicating a steady increase in the number of international overnight visitors compared to other areas.

Therefore, we will look at the rates of international overnight visitors by nationality, focusing especially on Nara City, which has a high rate of international overnight visitors. Figure 3-3-8 shows the rate of international overnight visitors by nationality in Nara City. As the figure shows, the rate of tourists from East Asia has been increasing year by year since 2012 (from 30.1% in 2012 to 65.4% in 2019). Among these, the rate of visitors from China increased by 16.8 percentage points from 32.9% in 2014 to 49.8% in 2015, partly due to the impact of shopping sprees.

The rate continued to trend upward, reaching 56.0% in 2019 and accounting for more than 50% of the total. On the other hand, it is clear that the rate of tourists from Europe, North America, and Australia is not as large as that of tourists from East Asia.

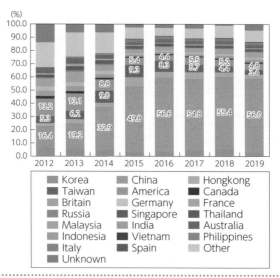

| Figure 3-3-8 | Trends in the rate of international overnight visitors by nationality: Nara City |

Note: Data are collected from facilities with 10 or more employees.
Source: Prepared based on individual data from the Japan Tourism Agency's Overnight Travel Statistics Survey

3. Implications of the Analysis and Future Issues

In the previous sections, we analyzed the tourism policies of DMOs in Kyoto, Wakayama and Nara prefectures using basic statistics. We organized the above analysis and summarized the implications and issues obtained as follows.

<Kyoto Prefecture>
Looking at the total number of overnight visitors before the pandemic, it is clear that the total number of international overnight visitors has consistently contributed to the overall growth of the number of visitors. However, most of the international overnight stays are concentrated in Kyoto City. Therefore, it is necessary to promote round-trip tours that involve an overnight stay in the wider area of Kyoto Prefecture.

It will be important to develop the tourism promotion projects undertaken by the DMOs. In particular, the DMO in "Kyoto by the Sea" has exhibited at one of the largest travel Expos in Taiwan and put a lot of effort into local promotions, which has resulted in a significant increase in the rate of visitors from Taiwan.

In addition to conventional promotion activities, it is necessary to develop a more attractive structure so that users will want to extend their trips from Kyoto City to the greater Kyoto area for sightseeing.

<Wakayama Prefecture>
Let's look at the number of overnight visitors and the rate of international overnight visitors in each area. In Kowa Town, the number of Japanese visitors has remained about the same, while the rate of international visitors has been steadily increasing and reached approximately 50% in 2019. In the Kumano area of Tanabe City, the number of Japanese overnight visitors peaked in 2016 and has been declining since then, while the rate of international overnight visitors has been rising, reflecting an increase in the number of international overnight visitors. In Shirahama Town, the number of Japanese overnight visitors has been decreasing since 2012, but it bottomed out in 2016 and has been increasing since then. On the other hand, the rate of international overnight visitors rose toward 2017 and has remained in the 7 to 8% range since then.

Looking at the rate of international overnight visitors by nationality in the Kumano area of Tanabe City by narrowing down the scope to the Kumano Kodo route, the rate of visitors from Europe, North America, and Australia is around 40 to 50% compared to that of those from East Asia. The rate of Spain, in particular, is increasing year by year, suggesting that the impact of the joint promotions is steadily appearing.

Part I

Part II

Part III

Part IV

\<Nara Prefecture\>

Comparing with Kyoto and Wakayama prefectures, the number of day-trippers always exceeds the number of overnight stay travelers. Therefore, promoting stay-over tourism involving an overnight stay is an issue.

The trend of overnight visitors in each area shows that the rate of international overnight visitors is steadily increasing, especially in Nara City where the rate is around 25.0%, while the number of Japanese overnight visitors is stagnant. Looking by nationality, the share of East Asia (especially China) is increasing. On the other hand, most of the overnight visitors are confined to Nara City. Therefore, it will be necessary to create programs to encourage visitors to visit and stay in other areas in Nara Prefecture in the future.

As mentioned above, in the pre-pandemic period when inbound demand was steadily increasing, the characteristic DMOs in the three prefectures mentioned above steadily developed tourism promotion measures. However, the spread of COVID-19 has forced not only DMOs, but also local governments to make major changes to their tourism strategies. In such cases, the role expected of DMOs is to refine the tourism resources possessed by each municipality. In the next Column, we will discuss the strength of the brand in Kansai region.

References

Asia Pacific Institute of Research, Kansai and the Asia Pacific Economic Outlook (2020)

Asia Pacific Institute of Research, Kansai and the Asia Pacific Economic Outlook (2021)

Japan Tourism Agency (2022), White Paper on Tourism in Japan, 2022

Inada, Y., Koyama, K., and Nomura, R. (2022-a), DMO's Efforts to Attract Inbound Visitors and Their Effectiveness: An Analysis Focusing on the Marketing Management Area: A Case Study of Kyoto Prefecture (Japanese title: *Diiemuoo no Inbaundo Yuukyaku no Torikumi to Sono Kouka—Maaketingu manejimentoeria ni Chakumokushita Bunseki: Kyoutofu no Jireikara—*), APIR Trend Watch No. 76, January 7, 2022, https://www.apir.or.jp/research/10533/, last checked on November 24, 2022

Inada, Y., Koyama, K., and Nomura, R. (2022-b), DMO's Efforts to Attract Inbound Visitors and Their Effectiveness (2): An Analysis Focusing on the Marketing Management Area: A Case Study of Wakayama Prefecture (Japanese title: *Diiemuoo no Inbaundo Yuukyaku no Torikumi to Sono Kouka—Maaketingu manejimentoeria ni Chakumokushita Bunseki: Wakayamaken no Jireikara—*), APIR Trend Watch No. 79, March 28, 2022, https://www.apir.or.jp/research/10533/, last checked on November 24, 2022

Inada, Y. and Nomura, R. (2022), DMO's Efforts to Attract Inbound Visitors and Their Effectiveness (3): An Analysis Focusing on the Marketing Management Area: A Case Study of Nara Prefecture (Japanese title: *Diiemuoo no Inbaundo Yuukyaku no Torikumi to Sono Kouka—Maaketingu manejimentoeria ni Chakumokushita Bunseki: Naraken no Jireikara—*), APIR Trend Watch No. 82, September 7, 2022, https://www.apir.or.jp/research/11256/, last checked on November 24, 2022

Column B   Place Branding in Kansai

OSHIMA, Hisanori; INADA, Yoshihisa; NOMURA Ryosuke

Revenue from regional tourism, which had relied heavily on inbound tourism, has been seriously impacted by the COVID-19 pandemic. Now that post-COVID-19 measures are gradually being taken, it is necessary to seek out attractions that appeal to domestic tourists, not just to wait for the recovery of inbound tourism.

The previous section discussed that enhancing brands, such as those of Destination Marketing Organizations (DMOs), is important for tourism-related parties among the determinants of tourism consumption. As branding strategies become increasingly important for the future, "place branding" will emerge as a key factor.

1. What is Place Branding?

The concept of place branding means building the idea of the region with any related element, such as culture, nature, history, industry, and regional life. Although its meaning is not limited to tourism-specific, the term "place branding" is often used in association with it, because tourism accounts for a major portion of the elements that create a brand.

(1) Its Definition and Movements toward Practical Implementation

In 2009, the United Nations World Tourism Organization (UNWTO) prepared the Handbook on Tourism Destination Branding, which is a practical handbook for place branding for tourism-related parties. The Handbook defines place branding as "the process of branding a place in a holistic way that encompasses a country's, a region's or a city's overall political, cultural and business image. This also includes a tourism dimension."[1] In addition, according to the Handbook, brand attributes include differentiation and competitiveness. Furthermore, "place" can refer to a nation, region, or city regardless of the geographic size, and place branding initiatives are supposed to be carried out in the entire place.

---

1) UNWTO (2009), p. 161.

From this, it is understood that place branding is a comprehensive concept that combines various factors such as culture, nature, history, industry, and regional life, including tourism (but not limited to the so-called tourism industry) to create an image (brand) of a country or region. Therefore, when promoting place branding in a region, it is necessary to work from the perspective of growing the economy of the entire region without focusing only on tourism, although it occupies an important position in place branding.

Place branding is a concept that has been studied in Europe since 2000, and therefore early examples of practices can be observed in Europe. Regarding the practices of place branding targeting places in Japan, Wakabayashi et al. (2018) provided some examples and the website of the Japan National Tourist Organization (JNTO) provides an example in Gifu Prefecture.

At the policy level in Japan, the Phase-II Town, People, Job Creation Comprehensive Strategy (2020 Revised Edition) by the Cabinet Secretariat and the Cabinet Office advocates the strengthening of regional earning power through collaborations between tourism and other fields, such as traditional industries, by positioning tourist resources as a source of regional attractiveness alongside aspects like culture and sports. In addition, the Strategy also discusses touristic regional development and branding promotion by placing DMOs at the core. Thus, DMOs are expected to play leading roles in place branding in Japan.

(2) Stakeholders and Leadership in Place Branding

Regional brand power is affected by the activities of all stakeholders, such as local governments, organizations, various industries, and residents. Therefore, there is no decisive answer to the question as to who should take the lead in improving regional brand power (place branding). However, a brand image is strongly formed through tourism in the region, while improving the brand image has a positive impact on regional tourism. Therefore, one approach is for tourism players to take the lead in place branding and for all stakeholders involved in the region to participate in the branding process.

DMOs can strengthen regional earning power through place branding and bring benefits to the local economy. Therefore, relationships

Part I

Part II

Part III

Part IV

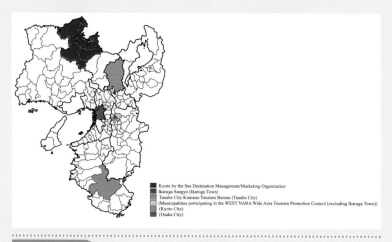

Kyoto by the Sea Destination Management/Marketing Organization
Ikaruga Sangyo (Ikaruga Town)
Tanabe City Kumano Tourism Bureau (Tanabe City)
(Municipalities participating in the WEST NARA Wide Area Tourism Promotion Council (excluding Ikaruga Town))
(Kyoto City)
(Osaka City)

Figure 3-CB-1   Activity areas of three DMOs

Source: The marketing/management target area mapped onto the six prefectures in the Kinki region
based on the DMO Formation and Establishment Plan in the "Plan for the Formation and
Establishment of Candidate Destination Marketing Organizations" published on the Japan
Tourism Agency's website.

with stakeholders who are involved in local economic development, such as the Chamber of Commerce and Industry, are inevitably important for determining branding policies. In areas where temples and shrines are important tourist resources, their intentions are also important. If there are no influential tourism leaders and the local government is leading tourism policies, the local government's views should also be valued.

For DMOs, who are at the center of these stakeholders, it is important that they grasp and adjust their intentions from the perspective of overall optimization and to steer them toward policy making.

Above, we outlined place branding, while in the next subsection, we will discuss place branding initiatives in three areas in Kansai.

2. Examples of Place Branding by Three DMOs

The Asia Pacific Institute of Research (APIR) held a symposium in March 2022, inviting three DMOs in the Kansai region. There it was discussed how DMOs should be after COVID-19 based on the characteristics and differences of place branding in each region. Here we provide a summary from two perspectives: "how DMOs engage in value creation and regional development through collaboration across the boundaries between industry, government, and the private sector" and "the advantages and difficulties of being a DMO in leading a region."

(1) Kyoto by the Sea Destination Management/Marketing Organization (abbreviated name: Kyoto by the Sea DMO) (Kyoto Prefecture)

The Kyoto by the Sea DMO, established in 2016, sets its franchise territory in seven cities and towns in the northern area of Kyoto Prefecture. And it runs promotion and branding or them, based on the concept of "Another Kyoto" that aims to attract visitors from Kyoto City to other areas in the Prefecture.

i) Value Creation and Regional Development through Collaboration across Industrial and Regional Boundaries

This DMO promotes the appeal of the area's history, culture, industry, and lifestyle, which are its common strengths, to visitors, including inbound tourists, under the concept of "the origins of Japanese culture still seen in the whole fields, mountains and seas." As initiatives that make use of these strengths, the DMO has formulated measures that cover a wide area of seven cities and towns, such as a tasting tour of 12 breweries in the northern area of Kyoto Prefecture and an e-BIKE tour that compensates for the area's lack of secondary transportation.

The DMO is also working on fostering local businesses and has been promoting area development that includes tourism as well as accommodation and immigration under "sustainable area development with tourism as a gateway," its new mission. To put the mission into practice, it established the Chiikizukuri Kyo Fund in March 2021 in collaboration with other DMOs[2] and financial institutions in Kyoto Prefecture and launched support for start-ups in the region. Also, the Kyoto by the Sea DMO has individually launched a project called the

Part I

Part II

Part III

Part IV

---

2) Other than the Kyoto by the Sea DMO, two other DMOs, General Incorporated Association Mori no Kyoto Regional Development Agency (Mori no Kyoto DMO) and General Incorporated Association Kyoto Yamashiro Regional Development Agency (Ocha no Kyoto DMO), have invested in the Fund.

"Corporate Proposal-Based Sustainable Regional Development Project" for the joint implementation of selected project proposals. Specifically, it is promoting projects in collaboration with local business operators, such as tours combining multiple modes of transportation, tours combining hunters and gibier (wild game) cuisine, and locally-brewed sake set gifts in return for hometown tax donations.

This DMO also experienced slowdowns in both its inbound and domestic travel businesses due to the COVID-19 pandemic, so it is working on online promotions, information sharing with agents, and developing new agents to attract visitors after COVID-19. To lead regional tourism, this DMO will proactively work to develop commercial products that will encourage tourists to stay two or three nights in the Kyoto by the Sea area so that local businesses can earn money through tourism.

ii) Advantages and Difficulties of Being a DMO
The DMO considers that it should take on the role of a producer to connect areas and give directions, and it is determined to continue to play its role.

As a semi-governmental DMO that steers tourism over a wide area, its public qualification as a registered DMO is an advantage when conducting activities. Another of the DMO's advantages is faster communication and decision-making are faster than in local governments, due to staff from various organizations,.

On the other hand, one of the difficulties for this DMO is its restricted freedom in implementing measures to some extent, because of high dependence on businesses entrusted from and subsidized by local governments. In addition, it finds it difficult to coordinate among the different areas because this DMO is an area-collaboration DMO that covers a wide area, specifically the northern area of Kyoto.

Also, the DMO wants to demonstrate its contribution by disseminating information inside and outside the organization, implying its difficulty to demonstrate its achievement.

(2) Ikaruga Sangyo (Nara Prefecture)
Ikaruga Sangyo is a relatively new DMO whose corporate status is a stock company. The Company, being engaged in the real estate business, has

established the Urban Development Business Division, which is considered the "second founding" of the Company, with the aim of revitalizing the area. The Urban Development Business Division is in charge of the Company's DMO activities and regional tourism business. It also serves as the Secretariat to the WEST NARA Wide Area Tourism Promotion Council described later.

i) Value Creation and Regional Development through Collaboration across Industrial and Regional Boundaries

A buggy tour around the three towers in Ikaruga Town has gained an excellent reputation among foreigners on YouTube, and it has been one method of branding Horyuji Temple. Currently, these circular tours using various vehicles are provided as new Horyuji Temple tours. The use of secondary transportation has also been enhanced to promote the circular tours, and a one-day unlimited ride pass for Nara Kotsu buses is offered to visit nearby tourist spots.

The new approach to the Ikaruga three towers tour, including the Horyuji Temple, has created a new brand image for the Horyuji Temple and Ikaruga, that have traditionally attracted only school excursions and the elderly. This new brand image has quickly spread across a wide audience on YouTube.

Also, in order to stimulate tourism demand beyond the Ikaruga town municipality level, the WEST NARA Wide Area Tourism Promotion Council was established in 2021 through a collaboration with one neighboring city and five towns (Ikaruga Town, Yamato Koriyama City, Heguri Town, Sango Town, Ando Town, and Oji Town). Utilizing its locational advantage of being close to Osaka, the Council will create tours by combining tourist spots in various locations in the area, aiming to increase the number of tourists from 3.9 million in 2019 to 5 million in 2025. During FY 2022, the Council is working to certify regional brands in cooperation with the Chamber of Commerce and Industry, and furthermore, to achieve commercialization of regional brands in cooperation with METI and other government agencies, as well as companies such as JR, Kintetsu, and JAL.

While supporting restaurants and retailers with coupons and other incentives during the prolonged COVID-19 pandemic, the Council is strengthening cooperation to support local temples and shrines that are less likely to obtain subsidies. It is also encouraging local shops to change their mindset to collaborate in developing products and new businesses that will promote tourism.

ii) Advantages and Difficulties of Being a DMO

The reason for registering Ikaruga Sangyo as a DMO is to revitalize the area. For this, the first priority is to increase the number of visitors and related populations in the area. To work on tourism, the Company first established the Urban Development Business Division and then registered it as a DMO. The DMO considers the question whether a DMO is really needed in the area as an issue relating to its raison d'être. The Company believes that the organizations in charge of matters should be the government before the trip, the tourism association and the private sector during the trip, and the private sector after the trip, and that the DMO should be responsible for the overall management of the trip. It is important to divide the roles and work as one team for the area.

(3) Tanabe City Kumano Tourism Bureau (Wakayama Prefecture)

The Tanabe City Kumano Tourism Bureau was established upon a merger of municipalities and registered as a DMO in 2019. It started a destination-oriented travel business in 2010 to attract tourists from overseas, and from that time sales steadily rose but then fell sharply in 2020 due to the COVID-19 pandemic. The Bureau, which is active in the Kumano Kodo area spanning three prefectures, was established as a bottom-up organization on the occasion of the registration of the Kumano Kodo as a UNESCO World Heritage site and the merger of municipalities, and it was subsequently registered as a DMO.

i) Value Creation and Regional Development through Collaboration across Industrial and Regional Boundaries

As a result of focusing on walking tours on the Kumano Kodo and developing food, lodging, and transportation services together with local people, ancillary services have expanded and the number of guesthouses has increased. With the sharp decline in inbound tourism demand due to

COVID-19, it is difficult to increase the number of Japanese tourists only by promoting visits to the Kumano Kodo, so they are trying to balance inbound and domestic travel by utilizing the forests that form the cultural landscape.

Judging that the Kumano Kodo alone has limited appeal to the Japanese, the DMO has expanded the sources of brand power to the mountains, forests, and the sea surrounding the Kumano Kodo, and is working to create a new brand image for a new customer base of Japanese tourists by developing forest education tours that take advantage of the above-mentioned surrounding areas.

In addition to the survival of the DMO, the challenge is to ensure the survival of small accommodation facilities and businesses along the Kumano Kodo and to maintain the local supply chain. From the current inbound sales ratio of 88% to the entire travel industry's sales, the DMO aims to make the ratio of domestic to inbound tourism sales 50:50 in the future.

In order to pass on the 1,000-year-old Kumano Kodo and pilgrimage culture to the next generation through tourism, it is necessary to promote tourism and regional development and to increase demand from Japanese tourists even during COVID-19 conditions by utilizing all of the mountains, rivers, and the sea that make up the Kumano Kodo. The DMO is working with elementary schools in Tanabe City, the Board of Education, and the Forestry Bureau to implement forest tourism education, and going forward, it is aiming to accept elementary and junior high school tours from outside the prefecture, using the entire forests of Kii Peninsula.

ii) Advantages and Difficulties of Being a DMO

This DMO considers that it is necessary to constantly ask themselves whether they are really needed as a DMO and always keeps in mind whether they are having a positive economic impact on the region.

As a semi-governmental organization, it is important that they have a public mindset and a business mindset at the same time. The most difficult aspect is to maintain the organization while striking a balance between the two mindsets.

The DMO has contributed to regional development by focusing

Part I

Part II

Part III

Part IV

on generating its own financial resources through destination-oriented tourism, but the sharp decline in inbound demand has had a significant impact that has forced the DMO to review its direction.

(4) Differences in Strategies and Challenges of the Three DMOs

So far, reviewing the place branding activities of the three DMOs has revealed differences in their contents depending on the conditions of their location. These differences can be identified based on the two axes summarized below.

i) Differences in the Size of the Activity Area

The first axis of comparison is the "size of tourism and regional development."

The Kyoto by the Sea DMO conducts its activities in seven cities and towns in the northern area of Kyoto Prefecture. It creates story-based narrative tourism experiences by identifying the "common strengths of the area" and connecting tourist resources in the area in line with the identified strengths. While the common strengths create a common brand image for the area, the challenge is to coordinate the intentions of the seven municipalities that cover a wide area.

On the other hand, the Tanabe City Kumano Tourism Bureau and Ikaruga Sangyo are both local DMOs based in basic municipalities. Presenting the core tourist resources of the municipality in different ways will be the key to broadening and strengthening their respective brands.

The Tanabe City Kumano Tourism Bureau is a local DMO that covers Tanabe City. Since this DMO focuses on the promotion of the Kumano Kodo, its activities naturally take place mainly in the areas along the Kumano Kodo. Therefore, it is essential to coexist and co-prosper with accommodation facilities and other businesses in the areas, and it will be a challenge for the DMO to formulate measures to ensure the survival of these businesses as its important stakeholders. Going forward, the DMO plans to expand the scope of its activities to include the nature of the Kumano Kodo, and the major focus will be whether it can uncover attractive tourist resources other than in the areas along the Kumano Kodo.

Ikaruga Sangyo successfully implemented new branding by proposing a new way of presenting Horyuji Temple. This DMO, which is developing activities mainly in Ikaruga Town, has expanded its activity area to neighboring municipalities and established the WEST NARA Wide Area Tourism Promotion Council to promote wide-area cooperation. This DMO takes a flexible stance in which it does not limit its activities to those within the basic municipality, and it will spread its activities if synergies can be found with neighboring municipalities.

ii) Differences in Organizational Characteristics

The other axis of comparison is the organizational characteristics of each DMO, especially the background of their establishment and corporate status. The Kyoto by the Sea DMO and the Tanabe City Kumano Tourism Bureau are both general incorporated associations, consisting of personnel seconded from public and private sectors, and they state that they require public support to maintain their stable activities.

Since the Kyoto by the Sea DMO was established from the intention of the Kyoto prefectural government, it can be considered that the prefectural government's intentions are strongly reflected in it, including the public intention to develop local industries. Ensuring the sustainability of the organization has been difficult because it is maintained by employees seconded from public and private sectors who are replaced every few years,. In addition to securing basic financial support, another challenge for the DMO is to create a financial foundation that enables the recruitment and training of career personnel.

The Tanabe City Kumano Tourism Bureau also states that it is impossible to maintain its organization and human resources without financial resources, and it requires measures to secure a certain amount of funds that support the base of DMO operations, rather than selecting DMOs.

Ikaruga Sangyo, a stock company, operates its DMO business through its own departments. As it procures management resources itself, unlike other DMOs, it points to the training of local business owners and the clarification of roles between the public and private sectors in tourism as issues. In particular, it states that the public sector should be responsible for supporting pre-travel promotions that are unlikely to lead to direct revenue, rather than supporting stable DMO operations.

Part I

Part II

Part III

Part IV

3. How to Measure Brand Power

As mentioned above, according to the concept of place branding, the attractiveness of a region as a tourist destination is not formed solely by the so-called tourism industry, but also by fields and factors other than tourism, such as the local landscape, culture, architecture, people's lives, as well as local industries. Therefore, it may be possible to clarify the challenges of regional development by DMOs and other players, and to visualize the results of their efforts by quantifying which factors contribute to regional attractiveness and in what ways.

A precedent for this approach in the Kansai region is provided by Kansai Economic Federation (2009). This report is not limited to tourism, but it identifies the sources of brand power in the Kansai region, regarding it as a single area, by using expert discussions and overseas questionnaire surveys.

On the other hand, there are analyses of how multiple factors contribute to the attractiveness of tourist spots and cities using principal component analysis and other methods. Mizoo et al. (1975) analyzed the attractiveness of tourist attractions based on their scale, composition, and other characteristics, and Kanno and Wakabayashi (2008) and Tanaka (2017) analyzed the factors behind urban attractiveness.

APIR has traditionally focused on "brand power" as one of the determinants of inbound consumption, but the concept is too abstract and difficult to measure. Therefore, APIR aims to measure brand power in order to show the improvement of the region's attractiveness from the perspective of tourism as "improving brand power."

Based on the above preceding studies, APIR aims to conduct a unique analysis targeting tourist attractions.

4. Summary

This column described three DMOs that each play a leading role in their region, which pointed to the importance of brand enhancement and the roles of DMOs in developing strategies for both inbound and domestic tourism after the Osaka-Kansai Expo.

In each of these initiatives, the DMOs themselves are pursuing activities based on the awareness of bringing economic benefits to their region, but their management styles are different.

The Kyoto by the Sea DMO is operated in a way that strongly reflects the prefectural government's intention of encouraging tourists to visit areas in Kyoto. This DMO is working to create a brand image by connecting tourist resources across seven municipalities in the northern part of Kyoto Prefecture based on their common strengths and creating story-based narrative tours. It is also engaged in regional development to promote not only tourism but also immigration, and it is working to foster local businesses through funding.

Ikaruga Sangyo originated as a new business from a real estate company, and its purpose is to bring vitality to the town. This DMO is unique in that it is a stock company, and it takes a rational approach to its goal of strengthening regional earning power by revitalizing temples such as Horyuji Temple, which are absolute tourist resources in the region.

The key stakeholders of the Tanabe City Kumano Tourism Bureau are local accommodation businesses and other supply chain players. After the recovery of inbound tourism, in order to seek an optimal portfolio with domestic tourism, the DMO is seeking to ensure its future survival with its stakeholders by developing new contents such as educational tours.

Although the activities of the three DMOs are different, what they all have in common is that they consider contributing to the local economy to be an important reason for their existence.

References

Ishii, Y., Okubo, A., Suzuki, D. (2019), "A Proposal for New Analysis Method in Tourism Marketing—A Case Study of Text Mining Analysis on Tourism Attractiveness in Izu Peninsula—," *Journal of Japan Society for Fuzzy Theory and Intelligent Informatics*, Vol. 31, No. 4, pp. 745–753.

Japan National Tourism Organization (JNTO), "Introducing Gifu Prefecture's Efforts as an Advanced Example of Sustainable Tourism in Japan (Part 1)" (Japanese title: *Sasutenaburu Tsurizumu no Kokunai Senshin Jirei to Shite, Gifu-ken no Torikumi o Goshokai (Zenpen)*), (https://action.jnto.go.jp/casestudy/2689, Last viewed on December 7, 2022)

Japan National Tourism Organization (JNTO), "Introducing Gifu Prefecture's Efforts as an Advanced Example of *Sustainable Tourism in Japan (Part 2)" (Japanese title: Sasutenaburu Tsurizumu no Kokunai Senshin Jirei to Shite, Gifu-ken no Torikumi o Goshokai (Kohen))*, (https://action.jnto.go.jp/casestudy/2690, Last viewed on December 7, 2022)

Japan Tourism Agency (2013), "Basic Research Work Report on Tourist Site Evaluation Methods" (Japanese title: *Kanko Chiiki ni Okeru Hyoka no Arikata To ni Kakaru Kiso Kento Gyomu Hokokusho*), (https://www.mlit.go.jp/common/001051089.pdf, Last viewed on December 7, 2022)

Kanno, S., Wakabayashi, H. (2008), "Branded City Building Strategies and Assets—Development of a Value Assessment Model" (Japanese title: *Burandedo Shiti Kochiku Senryaku to Shisan—Kachi Hyoka Moderu no Kaihatsu), Japan Marketing Journal* 27 (3), p. 82–96.

Kansai Economic Federation (2009), "Hanayaka Kansai—Proposals on Creation/Dissemination of the Kansai Brand and Promotion of Tourism" (https://www.kankeiren.or.jp/material/pdf/090401-1.pdf, Last viewed on December 7, 2022)

Ministry of Land, Infrastructure, Transport and Tourism (2015), "PRILIT Research Report No. 126: A Study on The Brand Image of Japan as a Travel Destination" (https://www.mlit.go.jp/pri/houkoku/gaiyou/pdf/kkk126.pdf, Last viewed on December 7, 2022)

Tanaka, K. (2017), "Analysis of Elements of Regional Attractiveness Based on Regional Brand Research," E-journal GEO, Vol. 12 (1), pp. 30–39.

UNWTO (2009), Handbook on Tourism Destination Branding.

Wakabayashi, H., Tokuyama, M., Nagao, M. (2018), Compiled by Dentsu abic project, *Place Branding: A Shift from Regional to Place Branding (Japanese title: Pureisu Burandingu: Chiiki kara Basho no Burandingu e)*, Yuhikaku Publishing Co., Ltd.

Website of the Japan Tourism Agency, "Plan for the Formation and Establishment of Candidate Destination Marketing Organizations" (Japanese title: *Kankochiiki-zukuri Koho Hojin "Koho DMO" no Keisei/Kakuritsu Keikaku*), (https://www.mlit.go.jp/kankocho/page04_000055.html, Last viewed on June 30, 2022)

Chapter 4

THE ECONOMIC IMPACT OF THE EXPO 2025 OSAKA-KANSAI: AN ANALYSIS USING THE 2015 KANSAI INTER-REGIONAL INPUT-OUTPUT TABLE

The purpose of Chapter 4 is to examine the economic effects of the Osaka-Kansai Expo using the tentative 2015 Kansai Inter-regional Input-Output table newly prepared by APIR. In Chapter 6, Section 4 of the "Asia Pacific and Kansai: The Kansai Economic White Paper 2019," we have already presented the prospects for the Osaka-Kansai Expo/MICE/IR and analyzed its economic effects using the 2011 Interregional Input-Output Table for the Kansai Region. New points in this analysis are as follows. First, final demand was reviewed by dividing it into consumption and investment expenditures to reflect the progress of Expo-related projects in Osaka and Kansai. Second, a new concept of the development of the Greater Expo (pavilionization of the Kansai region) was introduced. In addition, the possibility of a virtual Expo is discussed. Third, the input-output table used in the analysis was revised to the 2015 table (provisional version).

The development of this chapter is as follows. Section 1 presents a discussion of the possibility of using the Osaka-Kansai Expo and IR as leverage to turn the Kansai economy around, given that an insufficient investment is the cause of the long-term stagnation of the Kansai economy. Section 2 presents the current status of infrastructure development in anticipation of the Osaka-Kansai Expo and IR, and summarizes the economic effects caused by infrastructure development. Section 3 will discuss the economic effects of the Osaka-Kansai Expo based on the assumption of new final demand, using a new 2015 Kansai Inter-regional Input-Output table. Column 4-A, "Expansion and Co-creation Innovation of Osaka-Kansai Expo," explains the basic concept of the Greater Expo.

Section 1
HOW THE EXPO 2025 OSAKA-KANSAI AND THE OSAKA INTEGRATED RESORT CAN HELP REVITALIZE THE KANSAI ECONOMY

INADA, Yoshihisa

The aim of this section is to analyze the causes of the subsidence of the Kansai economy over the 50 years since 1970, and to explore the possibility of reversing the stagnant Kansai economy. The author believes that the Kansai economy is ready for a turnaround, and that the possibility of a turnaround by taking advantage of the Osaka-Kansai Expo and IR has increased. Section 1 begins with a chronological account of the stagnant Kansai economy; Section 2 shows that the sinking of the Kansai economy is due to a relative lack of investment; Section 3 discusses the argument that the Osaka-Kansai Expo and subsequent integrated resort (IR)-related investment will be the catalyst for a Kansai economic turnaround; and Section 4 discusses the challenges to realize a Kansai economic turnaround[1].

1. Kansai Economy in Subsidence

(1) Kansai's share of the economy declined rapidly in the 20 years after the Osaka World Exposition

First, let us compare the size of the Kansai economy (the sum of the nominal Gross Regional Products (GRP) of the six prefectures in the Kansai region) with that of the nation as a whole (nominal Gross Domestic Products (GDP))[2]. The share of the Kansai economy is calculated as the share of the national economy over the long term since FY1955.

The share of the Kansai economy peaked at 19.3% in FY1970, the year of the Osaka Expo, and then declined rapidly to 16.2% in 1989 after two oil crises. Due in part to the bubble economy, the share of the Kansai economy once reversed to 17.1% in 1991, but the increase was only temporary. In the late 1990s, the share again declined, falling below 16% in FY2000, and has remained stagnant at

---

1) The discussion in this paper is based on Inada (2022).
2) Time series of real and nominal GRP are constructed as follows. In the case of overlapping years, the latest base year was used as the official series. The values of the first year of the available official series are compared with the values of the previous base year counts to create a link coefficient. The link coefficients are multiplied to obtain an extended series of GRP for the most recent base year. For making the long term GDP series, we link the 1980-1994 GDP series at 2015 prices to the 1955-1998 GDP series at 1990 prices. See Reference Table 4-1-1 below for the revision of the prefectural and national accounts.

Figure 4-1-1　　Share of the Kansai Economy

Source: Prepared by the author based on the System of Prefectural Accounts and the System of National Accounts published by the Cabinet Office

around 15% to date (Figure 4-1-1).

(2) Signs of a turnaround

Since 2015, the Kansai economy has been supported by two types of exports: strong goods exports to China and service exports (including consumption by foreign visitors to Japan), but in 2018, the the economy showed signs of a slump. Behind this was dark news centered on natural disasters, such as the June 18 earthquake in northern Osaka and the closure of Kansai International Airport due to Typhoon No. 21 on September 4, in addition to the worsening trade friction between the U.S. and China.

However, Japan(Osaka) was selected as the host country of the 25th International Exposition at the General Assembly of the BIE on November 23 changed the depressed atmosphere about the future of the Kansai economy. On July 20, the Integrated Resort (IR) Law, which includes casinos, was enacted[3], raising expectations for a possible economic turnaround in the Kansai region through the Osaka-Kansai Expo and IR-related investment. Subsequently, the Japanese and Kansai economies were forced to make major adjustments due to the Corona disaster of 2020-2022, but the possibility of an economic turnaround in the Kansai region has become a reality with the Osaka-Kansai Expo in 2025 just around the corner.

2. Lack of investment is the cause of subsidence

In this section, we first present the determinants of the growth rate and explain

---

3) See Part III EXPO 2025 Chronology for a time series of events related to the economy in 2018.

that the cause of the subsidence of the Kansai economy is an insufficient investment.

(1) Determinants of Growth Rate

A continued downtrend in the share of the Kansai economy means that the growth rate of the Kansai economy remains below that of the rest of the economy. This section explores the causes of the decline in the growth rate of the Kansai economy.

Harrod's basic equation for economic growth is expressed as follows. That is, the economic growth rate in period t ($\Delta Y_t / Y_{t-1}$) is explained by the investment rate in period t-1 and the marginal capital coefficient in period t.

$\Delta Y_t / Y_{t-1} = (\Delta K_{t-1} / Y_{t-1}) / (\Delta K_{t-1} / \Delta Y_t)$

=Investment Rate / Marginal Capital Coefficient

Y_t : real GDP in period t, K_t: capital stock at the end of period t, and

$\Delta Y_t = Y_t - Y_{t-1}$, where $\Delta K_t = K_t - K_{t-1} = I_t$ (investment)

This growth equation implies that the higher the ratio of investment that goes to capital accumulation (investment) through savings, the higher the rate of economic growth.

(2) Economic growth rate and investment rate move proportionally

Figure 4-1-2 shows the relationship between the real (GRP) growth rate and the investment rate in the Kansai economy. Here, the investment rate is defined as the ratio of non-residential fixed capital formation (= private-sector business facilities + public-sector business facilities + general government) to GRP. The

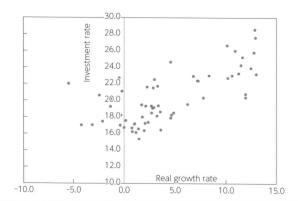

| Figure 4-1-2 | Real growth rate and investment rate |

Source: Prepared by the author based on "Prefectural Accounts," Cabinet Office, Government of Japan

Table 4-1-1	Relationship between economic growth rate and nonresidential investment rate

	Cofficient	t value
Constant term	-6.62314	2.04
SRN(-1)	0.463165	2.74
D74	-9.22254	-3.37
D75	8.392434	3.08
D09	-5.51446	-2.04
Determinant coefficient	0.45	

Note: SRN (-1) is the nonresidential investment ratio in Kansai a year earlier, and D74, D75, and D09 are dummy variables that are set to 1 for 1974, 1975, and 2009, respectively, and 0 for other years.

figure shows that except during periods of major economic shocks (oil crisis and global financial crisis), the growth rate of the Kansai economy is proportional to the investment rate[4] .

Next, Table 4-1-1 shows the regression results of the non-residential investment rate on the economic growth rate of the Kansai economy based on the growth equation. The estimation period is from 1971 to 2018. As shown in the estimation results, in Kansai, a 1 percentage point increase in the investment rate (SRN(-1): non-housing fixed capital formation/nominal GRP) in the previous year would result in a 0.46 percentage point increase in the GRP growth rate (GRPH) in this period[5] . In estimating the growth rate equation, dummy variables are used for the periods of major economic shocks (1974, 1975, and 2009).

Let us explain the meaning of this formula with numerical example: Since the nominal GRP of Kansai in 2018 was 86.13 trillion yen, an additional investment of 1 trillion yen will boost the investment ratio by 1.16 percentage points (1/86.13*100). This means that the economic growth rate of the Kansai region in the next fiscal year will increase by 0.54 percentage points (0.46*1/86.13*100). The relationship between the real (GDP) growth rate and the nonresidential investment rate in the Japanese economy was estimated. The coefficient of the investment rate explaining the Japan's GDP growth rate is 0.479, which is almost the same as that of the Kansai region. This means that the difference in the investment rate explains that in the growth rate well in between Kansai and Japanese economies.

---

4) When the marginal capital coefficient is stable, the level of the investment rate almost always determines the growth rate. The marginal capital coefficient was stable up to 1990, but unstable from 1990 to 2010.
5) Here, we use the investment rate not in real terms, but in nominal terms, which shows a more stable relationship with the growth rate.

(3) Sinking of the Kansai economy and insufficient investment

Next, let us compare the investment rate between Kansai and the nation as a whole. First, let's look at the investment rate on a nonresidential basis (Figure 4-1-3). Partly due to the impact of the two oil crises, the investment rates of the Kansai and the Japanese economy showed a downward trend after peaking in the high-growth period (Japan: 26.8% in 1969, Kansai: 25.8%), but bottomed out in the mid-1980s. In the latter half of the 1980s, the investment rate once turned upward due to the bubble economy, but after the burst of the bubble economy, it showed a downward trend again. In 2000, the downward trend bottomed out, followed by a sign of reversal in 2013. See reference Figure 4-1-1 and Figure 4-1-2 below for a breakdown of the nonresidential investment rate by private and public sectors.

Until 1996, the investment rate in Kansai was consistently lower than the national rate. The gap widened from 1 percentage point at the peak to a maximum of 3.6 percentage points. This means that the Kansai region has been consistently underinvested. Since then, the gap between the national and Kansai investment rates has remained below 1 percentage point, and the gap was reversed in FY09-10. This means that the economic growth rate of Kansai was consistently lower than that of the nation as a whole, based on the relationship between the investment rate and the growth rate confirmed above. Table 4-1-2 shows the average difference in investment rates between the nation and Kansai by period: 2.27 percentage points for FY1965-89, 1.72 percentage points for FY1990-92, and 0.33 percentage points for FY1993-18. After the collapse of the bubble economy, the

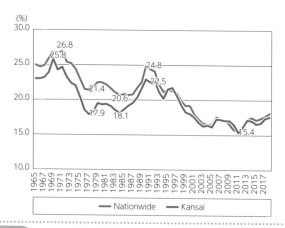

| Figure 4-1-3 | Comparison of investment rates: non-housing |

Source: Prepared by the author based on "Prefectural Accounts," Cabinet Office, Government of Japan

| Table 4-1-2 | Breakdown of the average investment rate gap between Japan and Kansai | | |

Period	Non-residential	Breakdown	
		Private corporate sector	Public sector
1965-1989	2.27	0.54	1.74
	100.0	23.6	76.4
1990-1992	1.72	0.81	0.90
	100.0	47.5	52.5
1993-2018	0.33	-0.35	0.67
	100.0	-107.1	207.1

Note: Units are percentages and percentage points. The upper panel shows the period average of the disparity in investment rates between Japan and the Kansai region. The lower panel shows the contribution.

investment rate gap between Japan and the Kansai region has narrowed significantly, and the growth rate gap between Japan and the Kansai region has also narrowed considerably. In other words, it can be said that the deceleration of growth rates in regions other than Kansai has become relatively conspicuous.

Let us analyze the disparity in the non-housing investment rate by dividing it into the private corporate sector (private corporate facilities) and the public sector (public corporations + general government). In FY1965-FY1989, the gap in non-residential investment (100%) between Kansai and the nation as a whole is mainly due to the public sector (76.4%), other than the private sector (23.6%). This period was characterized by underinvestment in the public sector. Kansai's share of public investment is lower than that of the nation as a whole. In FY90-92, the gap in the non-housing investment rate was about the same for the private sector and the public sector, while in FY93-18, the gap was exclusively caused by the public sector (207.1%). In the private sector (-107.1%), the gap between the nation as a whole and that of the Kansai region has reversed, unlike in the past. In addition to the fact that the gap in the public sector investment rate between the nation as a whole has narrowed over the entire period, and that public works in Kansai in 2021 exceeded the growth of the nation as a whole, there is a strong possibility that the public sector investment rate in Kansai is currently higher than that of the nation as a whole.

3. Osaka-Kansai Expo and IR to Reverse the Kansai Economy

(1) Average growth rates of the Kansai economy and the Japanese economy

As discussed in Section 1, the share of the Kansai economy peaked (19.3%) in the year of the Osaka Expo. In Section 2, it is assumed that the cause of the sinking of the Kansai economy is the relative underinvestment of the Kansai economy based on the growth equation. Therefore, if the underinvestment can be resolved (i.e., if the investment rate rises), we can expect a turnaround in the Kansai economy.

Before considering the future, let us look back at the past (Table 4-1-3). The average growth rate of the Kansai economy exceeded that of the nation as a whole during the high-growth period, and the share of the Kansai economy increased as shown in Figure 4-1-1 above. In the 1980s and 1990s, both Kansai and national average growth rates declined while Kansai slowed down even faster. The average growth rate for the 2000-2021 period was 0.6% for the nation as a whole, and 0.3% for the Kansai economy, which is almost zero growth[6].

According to the Cabinet Office, the potential growth rate of the Japanese economy will slow to 0.5% in FY2021[7]. Compared to the case in which the national economy grows at a potential growth rate of 0.5%, two cases were assumed for the growth rate of the Kansai economy, in which the rate accelerates by 0.5 percentage points and 1 percentage point from the assumed national potential growth rate. Behind this assumption is the estimation that an additional investment of about 1 trillion yen would raise the economic growth rate of the Kansai region by about 0.54%, as shown in Section 2 (2). The increase in investment in the Osaka/Kansai Expo and subsequent IR will lead to further growth in the Kansai region, both domestically and internationally.

If further investment can be attracted from within and outside Japan, including increased investment in the Osaka-Kansai Expo and subsequent IR, a turnaround in the Kansai economy will be possible. The following section presents the results of a simulation of a Kansai economic turnaround based on an

| Table 4-1-3 | Comparison of real growth rates (annual average): Kansai vs. Nationwide |

	Nationwide	Kansai region
1956-1969	9.8	10.6
1971-1979	5.0	5.7
1980-1989	3.8	3.7
1990-1999	1.6	1.0
2000-2021	0.6	0.3

Note: Unit: %.
Source: Prepared by the author based on the Cabinet Office's "Prefectural Accounts" and "National Accounts."

6) The Kansai economy is based on actual results through FY2018 and APIR forecasts for FY2019-2021.
7) The latest GDP gap and potential growth rates are available from the Cabinet Office. (https://www5.cao.go.jp/keizai3/getsurei/2211gap.xls)

acceleration of the growth rate in Kansai.

(2) Simulation of Kansai Economic Reversal

In creating the baseline, we set the benchmark (FY2021) nominal GDP of Japan at 541.6 trillion yen and the nominal GRP of the Kansai region at 84.2 trillion yen. The nominal GDP for Japan is actual through FY2021, but the nominal GRP for the Kansai region is available only through FY18, so the advanced estimates presented in Chapter 2, Section 2 were used.

For FY2022 and beyond, we assume that the Japanese economy will grow at a potential growth rate of 0.5%. Real GDP and nominal GDP are assumed to grow at the same rate. Compared to these baselines, Case 1 assumes that the Kansai region grows at a rate 0.5 percentage points faster than the nation as a whole (1%), and the shares of Kansai and the nation as a whole were calculated. According to this assumption, the share of the Kansai economy will increase to 16.2% in FY2030 and 17.1% in FY40. As a result, the Kansai economy will recover its share from the early 1980s (Figure 4-1-4).

Next, we calculated the share of the Kansai economy and the nation as a whole assuming Case 2 (additional investment of approximately 2 trillion yen/year), in which the growth rate of the Kansai region (1.5%) exceeds that of the nation by 1.0 percentage point relative to Case 1 (additional investment of approximately 1 trillion yen/year). In this case, the share of the Kansai economy would increase to 17.0% in FY2030 and to 18.7% in FY40, which means that the Kansai economy would recover its share in 1973 (Figure 4-1-5).

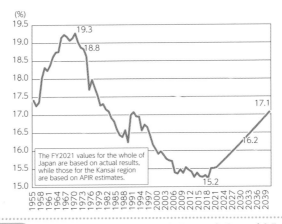

Figure 4-1-4   Scenario for Kansai Economic Reversal: Case of 0.5 percentage point growth acceleration in Kansai

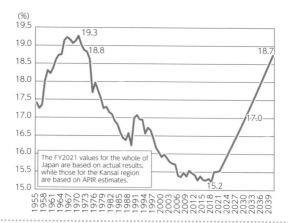

Figure 4-1-5   Scenario of Kansai Economic Reversal: Case of 1.0 percentage point growth acceleration in Kansai

4. Implications of the analysis

In this section, we have identified a lack of investment relative to the nation as the cause of the Kansai economy's 50-year slump. In addition to the underinvestment in the private sector, we found that in the public sector it was particularly large.

Based on the relationship between the growth rate and the investment rate, an additional investment of about 1 trillion yen would raise the growth rate of the Kansai region by about 0.54 percentage points. In addition, simulations showing that the Kansai economy will grow 0.5 percentage points faster than the Japanese economy (potential growth rate) indicate that the share of the Kansai economy in FY2030 could increase from a current 15.2% (FY18) to 16.2%, and to 17.1% in FY40.

The investment for the Osaka-Kansai Expo in 2025 and the accompanying transportation infrastructure development, as well as the IR-related investment expected to follow, is well in excess of JPY 1 trillion. The simulations presented in this paper show the impact of increased investment based on a reasonable basis.

The issue is the sustainability of the large increase in investment triggered by the case such as, the Osaka-Kansai Expo and IR. The key to guaranteeing this is how to attract investment from both inside and outside the country. Another important point is how to attract "profitable industries" and how to envision a shift to "profitable industries". Now that the infrastructure of the Kansai economy is in place and the conditions for a turnaround have been created, it is

important that the world recognize the attractiveness of Kansai as a legacy of the Osaka-Kansai Expo, resulting in a virtuous cycle of human resources and funds.

References

Inada, Yoshihisa (2022) "Toward a Reversal of the Kansai Economy: Leveraging the Osaka-Kansai Expo and IR Expo, using IR as leverage", APIR Trend Watch No. 81. (https://www.apir.or.jp/research/11106/, last checked on July 5, 2022)

Part I

Part II

Part III

Part IV

Reference Chart

Reference Table 4-1-1 Revision status of Prefectural Accounts and National Accounts

System of Prefectural Accounts

Period	1955-1974	1975-1999	1990-2003	1996-2009	2001-2014	2006-2018	2011-2019
Compliant SNA	1968SNA	1968SNA	1993SNA	1993SNA	1993SNA	2008SNA	2008SNA
Base year	1980 base	1990 base	1995 base	2000 base	2005 base	2011 base	2015 base
Substantiation method	Fixed base year method	Fixed base year method	Fixed base year method	Fixed base year method	Fixed base year method	Chain method	Chain method
Period of formal series		1975-1989	1990-95	1996-2000	2001-2005	2006-2018	
Period of reference series	1955-1974						

System of National Accounts

Period	1955-1998	1980-2003	1980-2009	1994-2012	1994-2020	1994-
Compliant SNA	1968SNA	1993SNA	1993SNA	1993SNA	2008SNA	2008SNA
Base year	1990 base	1995 base	2000 base	2005 base	2011 base	2015 base
Substantiation method	Fixed base year method	Fixed base year method	Chain method	Chain method	Chain method	Chain method
Period of formal series						1980-1994
Period of reference series	1955-1998					

Source: Prepared by the author based on "Prefectural Accounts" and "National Accounts" by the Cabinet Office

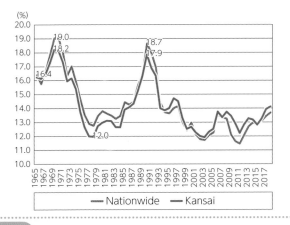

Reference Figure 4-1-1   **Comparison of Investment Rates: Private Sector**

Source: Compiled by the author based on "Prefectural Accounts" and "National Accounts," Cabinet Office, Government of Japan

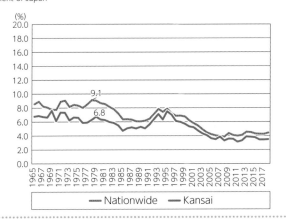

Reference Figure 4-1-2   **Comparison of investment rates: Public sector**

Source: Prepared by the author based on "Prefectural Accounts" and "National Accounts," Cabinet Office, Government of Japan

Section 2
EXPO 2025 OSAKA-KANSAI: INFRASTRUCTURE DEVELOPMENT IN VIEW OF THE OPENING OF THE OSAKA INTEGRATED RESORT

IRIE, Hiroaki; KINOSHITA, Yusuke; INADA, Yoshihisa

Expo 2025 Osaka, Kansai, Japan is scheduled to be held at Yumeshima Island in Osaka City. With less than three years to go before the Expo, infrastructure improvements are underway around the venue and in the center of Osaka City. In the previous section, it was pointed out that the reason for the long-term stagnation of the Kansai economy over the past 50 years was the lack of investment relative to the rest of Japan. The infrastructure development that is underway for the Osaka-Kansai Expo is expected to make up for the lack of investment in Kansai and to contribute to a positive turnaround in the growth of the Kansai economy.

This section discusses infrastructure development in Kansai in preparation for hosting the Expo. First, we summarize the economic effects of infrastructure development, and then we review the state of social infrastructure and public investment in Kansai prefectures. Next, we outline the Expo, the largest infrastructure development project in the Kansai region, and the attraction of IR (Integrated Resort) facilities to Yumeshima, the proposed site of the Expo. Finally, we estimate of the economic impact of the Expo based on the costs of hosting the Expo and related projects.

1. The Economic Effects of Infrastructure Development and the Current Situation in Kansai

(1) The Economic Effects of Infrastructure Development

As shown in Figure 4-2-1, infrastructure development has two types of economic effects: a flow effect and a stock effect. The flow effect refers to the short-term expansion of the economy due to the induced economic activities such as production, employment, consumption, etc., during the period of investment in the construction, maintenance, and renewal of the relevant infrastructure. The economic effects estimated in the next section are flow effects.

The stock effect, on the other hand, is realized in the medium-to-long term as infrastructure is accumulated and starts functioning as social infrastructure. The stock effect can be further classified into three types: safety and security effects; quality of life effects; and productivity effects. The safety and security effects improve disaster safety against earthquakes, tsunamis, floods, etc., to

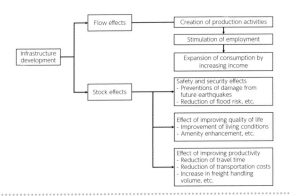

Figure 4 - 2 - 1   The Economic Effects of Infrastructure Development

Source: Prepared based on the White Paper on Land, Infrastructure, Transport and Tourism published by the Ministry of Land, Infrastructure, Transport and Tourism (MLIT)

ensure safety and security. The quality of life effects enhances the quality of life by improving living standards, such as hygiene and amenity conditions. The productivity effects increase productivity by reducing travel time, lowering transportation costs, etc., which leads to economic growth.

As a concrete example of infrastructure development, let us consider the economic effects of the development of transportation networks such as railroads and roads. Transportation infrastructure provides a means of transportation for people, goods, and money, which contributes to improving the quality of life and productivity by reducing travel time and transportation costs. It also provides evacuation routes to protect people from disasters and increases the number of visitors from outside the region. In other words, the development of transportation infrastructure produces all of the three stock effects mentioned above. APIR has conducted a study to estimate the economic effects of reducing travel time associated with the development and expansion of expressway networks on the prefectures and industries in Kansai (see the box below entitled "APIR Research Projects on the Economic Effects of Infrastructure Development").

(2) The state of Infrastructure Development in Kansai

Next, we will look at the status of infrastructure development in Kansai from the perspective of flow and stock effects.

To analyze flow effects, we look at the weight of public gross fixed capital formation (hereinafter, "public investment") in the economy of each prefecture. Figure 4-2-2 compares the ratio of public investment to nominal GRP in the prefectures of the Kansai region. The share of public investment is high in Wakayama and Nara prefectures, indicating that the economic structure

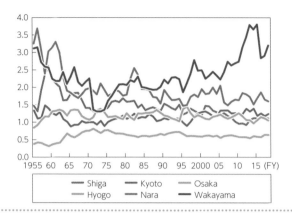

Figure 4-2-2　Public Investment Relative to Economic Size in Each Kansai Prefecture

Note: Share of public gross fixed capital formation in Kansai/nominal GDP share
Source: Prepared by the author based on the System of Prefectural Accounts published by the Cabinet Office

is relatively tilted toward public investment. In Osaka Prefecture, the share of public investment has remained low for a long time. This indicates that in Kansai, the importance of public investment is unbalanced between urban and rural areas.

Next, we look at stock effects. Figure 4-2-3 shows the share of social infrastructure (total and roads) of the six prefectures in Kansai relative to the national level. After peaking at 16.6% in FY 1975, the share declined to 14.2% in FY 2014.

When focusing on roads only, the share of social infrastructure relative to the national level rose to 17.7% in 1969. This is due to the road development projects related to the Osaka Expo (EXPO'70). According to Sumitomo Mitsui Trust Realty, of the total Expo-related project costs of JPY 650 billion, road-related projects accounted for JPY 334.2 billion, or 51.4% of the total. After the Kinki Expressway and Suita IC opened to traffic in 1970, the Expo-related road development effects declined, and so did Kansai's share of road infrastructure – it declined to 13.8% of Japan's in FY 2014.

As mentioned earlier, after the Osaka Expo in 1970, the Kansai economy entered a prolonged period of stagnation due to a lack of investment, partly because of the loss of the effects of roads development. We hope that the infrastructure developed for the upcoming Expo and the opening of IR facilities will be the legacy of Expo 2025, so that Kansai can reap the benefits of the stock effects of infrastructure development.

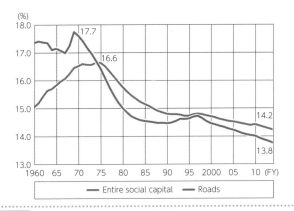

(%)

Legend: —— Entire social capital   —— Roads

Figure 4-2-3   Changes in Shares of Social Infrastructure in Kansai

Note: Kansai = six prefectures in the Kansai region
Source: Prepared by APIR based on Social Infrastructure Statistics published by the Cabinet Office

2. Expectations for the Osaka-Kansai Expo and Integrated Resorts

The Osaka-Kansai Expo 2025 will be the largest ever infrastructure development project in Kansai in recent years. Below, we first provide an overview of the Osaka-Kansai Expo based on the Expo Master Plan presented by the Japan Association for the 2025 World Exposition. We also outline the plans to attract IR facilities to Yumeshima Island where the Expo site will be located.

(1) Overview of the Osaka-Kansai Expo 2025 in the Master Plan

The Osaka-Kansai Expo will be held for about half a year from April 13 to October 13, 2025. The site for the Expo is located in Yumeshima, an artificial island on the waterfront of Osaka City. The venue area is 155 hectares, which accounts for approximately 40% of Yumeshima's total area of 390 hectares.

On December 25, 2020, the Japan Association for the 2025 World Exposition formulated and announced the Master Plan in preparation for the Expo. Table 4-2-1 summarizes the overview of the Osaka-Kansai Expo shown in the Master Plan.

Below is an overview of the Osaka-Kansai Expo according to the Master Plan. The Master Plan summarizes the site plan, the operation plan, the financial program, etc., including diverse forms of participation and projects and the site design that embody the theme of the Osaka-Kansai Expo, "Designing Future Society for Our Lives." Based on this Master Plan, activities will be promoted to invite participating countries and international organizations and to

Part I
Part II
Part III
Part IV

Table 4-2-1	Overview of the Osaka-Kansai Expo 2025
Title	Expo 2025 Osaka, Kansai, Japan (abbreviated name: Osaka-Kansai Expo 2025)
Theme	Designing Future Society for Our Lives
Sub-themes	Saving Lives Empowering Lives Connecting Lives
Concept	People's Living Lab
Venue	Yumeshima (Konohana-ku, Osaka City)
Period	Sunday, April 13 to Monday, October 13, 2025
Projected number of visitors	Approx. 28.2 million

Source: Prepared based on the Master Plan of the Japan Association for the 2025 World Exposition

encourage the participation of and co-creation between businesses, organizations, grassroots bodies, etc. Also, an implementation plan for each project will be formulated and specific initiatives will be promoted.

The projected number of visitors is approximately 28.2 million based on the results of past international expositions, the location of the venue, etc., and the breakdown is as follows: approximately 15.6 million from Kansai, approximately 9.1 million from other regions of Japan, and approximately 3.5 million from abroad. The projected number of visitors from abroad is based on the registration applications submitted to the Bureau International des Expositions (BIE). It should be noted that the applications were submitted at the end of 2019 before the COVID-19 pandemic and that the estimates assume that Japan would welcome 50 million inbound travelers in 2025.

For the success of the Osaka-Kansai Expo, it is essential to ensure smooth access for the expected 28.2 million visits to the Expo venue. To access Yumeshima during the Expo, the plan is to secure transport routes by making the most of rail, land, sea, and air transport. As railways will be the main means of transport, the Osaka Metro Chuo Line is being extended and Yumeshima Station (provisional name) will be newly built. Railways are expected to carry approximately 40% of visitors to the venue. For access via road, shuttle buses will run directly from major railway stations and airports to the Expo venue. Phase 2 construction of the Yodogawa Left Bank Line, which Osaka City originally planned to complete by the end of FY 2026, will be brought forward for its early completion to tentatively use the line as an access route from Osaka Station, Shin-Osaka Station, and other stations. In addition, a park-and-ride system will be adopted, whereby general private car users will transfer to buses at off-site parking sites that will be installed within 15 km of the Expo site. Entry of general private cars into the site will be prohibited, in principle.

Next, we look at the financial program in the Master Plan. The financial program includes two expense items: site construction expenses and operating expenses. The total amount of site construction expenses is JPY 185 billion, consisting of JPY 118 billion for facility construction and JPY 67 billion for infrastructure construction. Site construction expenses have been agreed to be borne one-third each (JPY 61.7 billion) by the national government, Osaka Prefectural and City governments, and funds from the business community. Operating expenses are estimated to be JPY 80.9 billion, which will be covered by the organizer's own financial resources, such as admission ticket sales.

When the Government, local governments, foreign governments, international organizations, and private companies hold exhibitions at the Expo, the construction expenses and project cost of pavilions, etc., will be borne by the exhibitors. For this reason, the specific amounts are unknown at this time and are not recorded in the financial program in the Master Plan. The project costs for the Osaka Pavilion at which Osaka Prefecture and Osaka City and the economic world in Kansai will hold exhibitions are estimated to be approximately JPY 16 billion, which will be covered by private sponsorships and donations, in addition to public funds.

In addition, according to the budget information released by Osaka City, JPY 112.8 billion is expected as related project costs, such as for railway development, road improvement, and additional construction expenses for land reclamation. The details are discussed in the next sub-section.

(2) Plans to Attract Integrated Resort (IR) Facilities

Osaka Prefecture and Osaka City are promoting activities to attract IR facilities to Yumeshima Island where the Expo site will be located. The movements to attract IR facilities are detailed below.

In a Cabinet decision in 2019, the Government announced that the IR facilities should be based on the Act on Development of Specified Complex Tourist Facility Areas (the so-called IR Development Act) to realize internationally competitive and attractive stay-type tourism and to manifest the policy effects as soon as possible. The Government plans to develop up to three IR (Integrated Resort) facilities in Japan, including casinos, which are scheduled to open in the late 2020s, and development plan applications are being accepted.

In Kansai, activities to attract IR facilities are being promoted by Osaka

Table 4-2-2	Outline of Planned IR Facilities in Osaka and Nagasaki	
	Osaka	Nagasaki
Core operators	MGM, Orix	Casino Austria International Japan
Construction site	Yumeshima, Osaka City	Land adjacent to Huis Ten Bosch, Sasebo City
Opening schedule	Autumn to winter 2029	Autumn 2027
Facility floor area	770,000 square meters	640,000 square meters
Initial investment amount	JPY 1.08 trillion	JPY 438.3 billion
Annual target visitors	20 million visits	6.73 million visits

Source: Prepared based on various media reports

Prefecture and Osaka City with Yumeshima as a potential location[1]. In December 2019, the Osaka IR Fundamentals Plan was announced, in which the development of Japan's largest international convention hall and exhibition facilities that combine world-class scale and quality is planned. As of June 2022, Osaka and Nagasaki are planning to attract IR facilities (Table 4-2-2).

3. The Expo-related Infrastructure Development Plan

The infrastructure development that is underway for the Osaka-Kansai Expo is expected to make up for the lack of investment in the Kansai region, and to put the Kansai economy on a positive growth trajectory. In the previous section, we looked at the overview of the Osaka-Kansai Expo based on the Master Plan. The Master Plan provides rough estimates of the amounts, but it does not specify the details of infrastructure development. Therefore, this section discusses the state of infrastructure development related to the Expo based on the materials released by the Ministry of Land, Infrastructure, Transport and Tourism (MLIT), Osaka Prefecture, and Osaka City, as well as information obtained through interviews with related parties.

At the 2nd meeting of the Headquarters for the World Expo 2025 held in August 2021, an infrastructure development plan for the Osaka-Kansai Expo 2025 was decided. According to this plan, infrastructure development will be

1) In Kansai, in addition to Osaka Prefecture and Osaka City, Wakayama Prefecture has also examined development plans to promote IR attraction with Wakayama Marina City as a candidate site. However, at the plenary session of the prefectural assembly held in April 2022, the proposal to submit the plan to the national government was rejected by a majority of opposition votes, making it impossible to apply for the plan by the deadline of April 28. Therefore, the attraction plan was essentially returned to a blank slate.

promoted to support the smooth holding of the Osaka-Kansai Expo and to enhance its effectiveness, as well as to provide a growth platform to support socio-economic activities in the region after the Expo. The five main projects are (1) infrastructure development around the venue, (2) improvement of access to the venue, (3) improvement of safety, (4) improvement of liveliness and attractiveness, and (5) the development of a wide-area transportation infrastructure, the details of which are described below.

Figure 5 in the EXPO 2025 Chronology (Part III) presented later shows the locations of the major development plans on the map.

(i) The infrastructure development around the Expo site aims to support the smooth holding of the Expo by enhancing passenger transportation capacity and facilitating traffic around the Expo site. This includes improving infrastructure such as roads and railways around ports and harbors, including the extension of the Osaka Metro Chuo Line, and improving the efficiency of container logistics functions at Hanshin Port.

(ii) Access to the venue will be improved in order to enhance transportation infrastructure such as railways, roads, air routes, and sea routes. This project covers not only the Yumeshima area, but also access roads from neighboring prefectures to the Osaka area. Specifically, fundamental functional enhancements are planned, including the front-loaded Phase 2 construction of the Yodogawa Left Bank Line and the expansion of international flight capacity of the Kansai International Airport.

(iii) The safety improvement plans include ensuring the safety of access routes to the venue, improving the earthquake resistance of facilities, and developing relief-activity bases in the event of a disaster. Countermeasures for the Nankai Trough Mega-Earthquake are also included.

(iv) The improvement of liveliness and attractiveness aims to facilitate exchanges between visitors in city centers and areas where visitors are expected to stay overnight by developing new water and sea networks centered on Yumeshima. At the time of the Expo, Yodogawa River ship transportation will be revived, and a wide-area transportation network will be formed to connect Osaka and the upper reaches of the Yodogawa. In Osaka City, the Umekita Phase 2 Development project, the creation of an attractive waterside space along the Dotonbori River, and the reorganization of the area around Namba Station, which is the southernmost point of Midosuji Avenue, are included in the plan for the recovery of inbound tourism, which was damaged by the COVID-19 pandemic.

(v) The development of a wide-area transportation infrastructure will promote the development of railways and the formation of a ring expressway network as the foundation for growth of Osaka and Kansai, which is expected to contribute to the revitalization of socio-economic activities and the building of national land highly resilient to large-scale disasters. For example, if the development of Shin-Meishin Expressway progresses, it is expected to shorten the travel time between Osaka and Nagoya and to improve transportation convenience, contributing to revitalizing the local economy. In addition, the Naniwasuji Line will improve access from Shin-Osaka Station, which is connected to the east-west national axis, to Kansai International Airport via Kita-Umeda Station (provisional name), which will be newly constructed in the Umekita Phase 2 Development area.

Table 4-2-3 below provides an overview of the budgets for Expo-related projects based on the Infrastructure Development in Yumeshima, Osaka, announced in February 2022. A total of JPY 192.9 billion has been recorded as related project costs, and the breakdown is as follows: JPY 61 billion for the construction of railways including an extension of the Osaka Metro Chuo Line and to enhance transportation capacity, JPY 25 billion for road improvements including the widening of the Konohana Bridge and Yumemai Bridge, JPY 10.2 billion for land reclamation, and JPY 96.7 billion for others. These projects, however, include some that will continue after 2025 and also IR-facility related projects. Excluding the projects that are specified as those for IR facilities (marked with ◎ in the right column of Table 4-2-3), the project costs amount to JPY 112.8 billion. Table 5 in EXPO 2025 Chronology (Part III) presented later shows the timetable of the infrastructure development plan by Osaka City.

4. Conclusion: Challenges for Infrastructure Development in Kansai over the Medium to Long Term

So far, we have summarized the infrastructure development in the Kansai region in anticipation of the Osaka-Kansai Expo. Table 4-2-4 summarizes the new demand associated with the Osaka-Kansai Expo shown in this section. In the next section, we will estimate the economic effects of the Osaka-Kansai Expo using APIR's Kansai Inter-Regional Input-Output Table based on these expenditure figures.

Finally, we would like to conclude by describing the challenges for infrastructure development in the Kansai region in the medium to long term.

When looking beyond the Expo, one of the challenges for infrastructure development in the entire Kansai region is that it lags behind other regions in terms of developing infrastructure in an efficient manner. As a matter of course, the convenience of infrastructure is essential to improving productivity. No

Table 4-2-3	Overview of Related Project Costs

Expense item	Details	Budget amount (JPY 100 million)	IR project or not (Note)
Railway construction, etc.: extension of the Osaka Metro Chuo Line, transportation capacity enhancement, etc.		610	
	Railroad (southern route)[preliminary survey]	1	
	Railroad (southern route) [infrastructure (road construction-related)]	346	
	Railroad (southern route) [infrastructure (railway-related)]	230	
	Railroad (southern route)[Phase II urban development]	33	○
Roadway improvement: Konohana Bridge and Yumemai Bridge expansion, etc.		250	
	Tourist perimeter road	49	○
	Elevated road	98	
	Station facilities	30	
	Yumeshima trunk road	10	
	Maishima trunk road, Maishima East multi-level intersection	34	
	Konohana Bridge (6-lane roadway, pedestrian walkway)	26	
	Yumemai Bridge (6-lane roadway, pedestrian walkway)	2	
	Sakishima Cosmo North Line	1	
Reclamation costs, etc.		102	
	Reclamation and embankment (Expo)	89	
	Reclamation and embankment (IR)	13	◎
Others		967	
	Sewerage systems (pumping stations, drains, etc.: Expo)	115	
	Water supply systems (pumps, water pipes, etc.: Expo)	34	
	Mooring facilities (floating pier, waiting area, breakwater)	10	
	Firefighting base equipment	20	
	Land improvement (IR land)	788	◎
Total		**1,929**	
(excluding those used primarily for IR)		**(1,128)**	

Note: "○" indicates that the project includes some IR facilities, and "◎" indicates that the project is mainly for IR facilities.
Source: Prepared based on the website of Osaka City

matter how much infrastructure is developed, productivity will not improve unless that infrastructure can ensure convenience and efficiency.

For example, expressways in Kansai have many more missing links

Table 4-2-4   Final Demand Estimates Associated with the Expo

(Unit: JPY 100 million)

Site construction costs (organizers)

Developing the foundation (civil engineering, pavements, landscaping, etc.)	130
Developing infrastructure facilities (electricity, water supply and drainage work, etc.)	285
Parking lots, entrance	171
Pavilion construction and service facilities	1,103
Arrangement of the venue	50
Other (research and design costs, administrative costs)	108
Total	**1,847**

Operating costs

Organizers (total cost only)	**809**

Related business expenses

Railway construction, etc. (extension of the Osaka Metro Chuo Line, transportation capacity enhancement, etc.)	610
Roadway improvement (Konohana Bridge and Yumemai Bridge expansion, etc.)	250
Reclamation costs, etc.	89
Other	179
Total	**1,128**

Source: Prepared by APIR based on the Master Plan of the Japan Association for the 2025 World Exposition and other materials

(undeveloped sections) on roads accessing international airports and harbors than those in the Kanto and Chubu regions. In addition, the construction of ring road networks, which are necessary to alleviate congestion in city centers, has significantly lagged behind other regions. In addition to the problem of domestic logistics, the inconvenient access from Kansai International Airport to tourist destinations such as Kobe and Hyogo also serves as an obstacle to wide-area excursions within the Kansai region. For example, it is reported that the opening of the section between Yawata-Kyotanabe Junction/Interchange (JCT/IC) to Takatsuki JCT/IC of Shin-Meishin Expressway is four years behind schedule and will not open in time for the Osaka-Kansai Expo in 2025[2].

In this regard, it is crucial for the future of the Kansai economy that the Infrastructure Development Plan for Osaka-Kansai Expo 2025 formulated by the Ministry of Land, Infrastructure, Transport and Tourism (MLIT) can actually be implemented. The Development Plan was formulated from a medium- to long-term perspective, looking beyond the Expo, including transportation infrastructure for areas adjacent to the Expo venue, such as Osaka city, as well as

---

2) Reference: Nihon Keizai Shimbun, February 9, 2022

transportation infrastructure covering wider areas. We hope that the realization of a series of development plans will bring about the success of the Osaka-Kansai Expo, and that this will be a major achievement in terms of both flow and stock effects, which will put the Kansai economy, including the private sector, on a trajectory of positive growth.

Box) APIR Research Projects on the Economic Effects of Infrastructure Development

In this section, we outlined the social and economic significance of enhancing infrastructure. The economic effects of infrastructure development have been quantitatively analyzed using various approaches such as production functions, macro-econometric models, input-output analysis, and CGE models. With regard to the Kansai region, APIR conducted a series of research projects on the economic effects of the development and expansion of transportation networks between 2015 and 2017.

Since previous research did not sufficiently examine the impact on the local economy of a more efficient local economic structure achieved through the development of social infrastructure, including expressways, in 2015, APIR estimated the transportation accessibility in the six prefectures in the Kansai region from 2005 to 2014 by focusing on "transportation accessibility" as an indicator that expresses the ease of interaction between living areas through the use of expressways. Then, in 2016, we estimated production functions that incorporate transportation accessibility by prefecture and examined the impact of changes in transportation accessibility due to the development of expressways on gross prefectural product (GRP) of the six Kansai prefectures. In 2017, we expanded the above analysis by examining the effects of improving transportation accessibility by industry.

Based on our analyses, we find that positive economic effects can be observed in five of the six Kansai prefectures (except Nara), that and the economic effects are particularly large in Kyoto Prefecture. The reason for the large effects in Kyoto Prefecture is that the extent of transportation accessibility improvement there is larger, and the positive impact of the transportation accessibility improvement on the economy is greater in Kyoto Prefecture than in other prefectures. On the other hand, in the case of Nara Prefecture, transportation accessibility improvements generate negative spillover effects, which cause translate into negative economic growth.

By industry, we find that the effects of transportation accessibility improvement are not uniformly spread across industries. While a positive impact is observed on the electricity, gas, and water industries, almost no impact can be seen on the wholesale and retail trade, and the transportation and communications industry. A negative impact is observed on the agriculture, forestry and fisheries, manufacturing, construction, and service industries. One possible reason for this is that the use of expressways differs in each industry. Using the Kansai Intra-Regional Input-Output Table, we compare the size of freight-related transportation costs in the total production of each region by industrial sector and we clarify the existence of differences in the cost structure of cargo transportation.

In summary, APIR's research projects analyzed the economic effects brought about by the improvement of transportation accessibility through the development of infrastructure that affects a wide economic area, such as expressways. When the results are broken down by region and industry, the economic effects are far from uniform. In consideration of this, it is necessary to formulate development plans from regional and industrial perspectives when considering the ideal form of wide-area social infrastructure development.

References

Asia Pacific Institute of Research (2015), "Kinki Region Road Network Effectiveness Analysis" Report (Japanese title: *Kinki-ken Doro Nettowaku Koka Bunseki*)

Asia Pacific Institute of Research (2016), "Verification of Infrastructure Stock Effects in the Kinki Region: Estimating Economic Ripple Effects Using Production Functions" (Japanese title: *Kinki-ken no Infura Sutokku Koka no Kensho: Seisan Kansu ni Your Keizai Hakyu Koka no Suikei*), "Projected Improvements in Transportation Proximity and Expected Economic Effects of the Development and Expansion of the Transportation Network" (Japanese title: *Kotsu-mo no Seibi Kakuju ni Tomonau Kotsu Kinsetsusei no Kaizen to Kitai dekiru Keizai Koka no Yosoku*": Project reports

Asia Pacific Institute of Research (2017), "Verification of Infrastructure and Stock Effects of Expressways by Industry" (Japanese title: *Sangyo Betsu ni Mita Kosoku Doro no Infura Stokku Koka no Kensho*), "Economic Impact Analysis for Transportation Infrastructure Development" (Japanese title: *Kotsu Infura Seibi no Keizai Inpakuto Bunseki*): Project reports

Ministry of Land, Infrastructure, Transport and Tourism (MLIT) (2016) "White Paper on Land, Infrastructure, Transport and Tourism in Japan, 2016"

Ministry of Land, Infrastructure, Transport and Tourism (MLIT) (2021) "Promoting Infrastructure Development for Osaka-Kansai Expo: Decision on the Infrastructure Development Plan for Osaka Kansai EXPO 2025" Press Release, August 27, 2021

Nikkei Inc. (2021) "The Opening of Shin-Meishin Expressway's Section between Yawata-Kyotanabe and Takatsuki Will be Postponed by 4 Years to FY2027" (Japanese title: *Shin-Meishin no Yawata-Kyotanabe-Takatsuki Kaitsu 4-nen Enki 27-nendo ni*), Nihon Keizai Shimbun (morning edition), February 9, 2022

The Institute of Behavioral Sciences (IBS) (2012) "A Study on Measuring the Economic Ripple Effects of Expressway Improvements" (Japanese title: *Kosoku Doro Seibi no Keizai Hakyu Koka Keisoku ni Kansuru Kenkyu*)

Website of Sumitomo Mitsui Trust Real Estate (https://smtrc.jp/town-archives/city/senri/p07.html, Last viewed on June 28, 2022)

Part I

Part II

Part III

Part IV

Column A   The Legacy of Expo 2025 Osaka-Kansai and Co-Creation Innovation

ISHIHARA, Yasuyuki

1. The World Expo 2025 Is Coming to Osaka-Kansai

What will the Osaka-Kansai Expo 2025 bring to Kansai, the host region of the Expo, as well as to Japan? This report discusses the methodology of how the Kansai region as a whole should take advantage of the once-in-a-lifetime opportunity of hosting the Expo, and the future social and business possibilities that can be expected from the event[1].

(1) Outline of the Osaka-Kansai Expo

The Osaka-Kansai Expo (official name: Expo 2025 Osaka, Kansai, Japan) is a large-scale registered Expo (formerly certified Expo) that is to be held in Osaka for the first time in 55 years, and its outline (theme, concept, goals, etc.) is as follows (Figure 4-CA-1).

It can be said that the theme, concept, and other features of this Expo should not be merely for the period of the Expo, but rather they are the very direction that Kansai should aim to take.

Expo 2025 Osaka, Kansai, Japan
Abbreviated name: Osaka-Kansai Expo 2025 (registered Expo)

Expo logo

Title: Expo 2025 Osaka, Kansai, Japan
(Abbreviated name: Osaka-Kansai Expo 2025)
Venue: Yumeshima Island on the waterfront of Osaka City
Period: Sunday April 13 to Monday October 13 2025
Number of visitors: Approx. 28.2 million people (projected)

▶Theme
"Designing Future Society for Our Lives"

▶Concept
"People's Living Lab"

▶Goals
Achieving the SDGs
Achieving Society 5.0

Figure 4-CA-1   The Outline of EXPO 2025 Osaka, Kansai, Japan

Source: Materials from the Japan Association for the 2025 World Exposition

---

1) The content of this report is based on the author's personal views and does not represent the official views of the organization, etc., to which the author belongs.

(2) Challenges after Festivals Like the Expo

For example, when looking at the economy during the two 10-year periods before and after the Osaka Expo in 1970, the ratio of Osaka Prefecture's GDP relative to the national level increased until the Expo's end and then dropped sharply immediately after its closure (relative to the national level).

A similar phenomenon was evident after the 1975 Okinawa Ocean Expo, when many lodging facilities and retail stores that expected to attract Expo visitors experienced difficulties. In addition, many of the Expos that were held after the 1975 Expo, such as the 1990 Osaka Flower Expo and the EXPO 2005 Aichi, Japan (Exposition of Global Harmony), experienced declines in the host regions' economies relative to the national level after the end of the events, albeit with some time lag.

Although phenomena, such as a decrease in construction investment, may be unavoidable as "the silence after festivals," for this coming Osaka-Kansai Expo, it is important to devise regional strategies so that the Expo can have a significantly positive impact on the local economy over the long term, while minimizing these declines as much as possible.

In particular, tourism and other strategies that expect to attract Expo visitors should consider measures in advance, such as strategies to promote repeat visits and regional brand strategies, to avoid a depression of the local economy even after the end of the Expo.

(3) Thinking about the Expos' Soft Legacies

The Expos, which began with the first London Expo in 1851, have been held in many countries and regions to date, and they have greatly impressed many people with their respective country's architectural heritages, such as the Eiffel Tower, and exhibitions of cutting-edge technologies, such as Bell's telephone and Edison's phonograph.

In particular, the 1970 Japan World Exposition (1970 Osaka Expo) in Japan, which the first time it was held in Asia, left a strong impression on people. I myself visited the 1970 Osaka Expo 13 times as a child, and the exhibitions of cutting-edge science and technologies, including the Tower of the Sun and the Moon Stone, are deeply etched in my mind.

What is also noteworthy is that, in the past Expos, mechanisms and rules that would be useful to future generations after the Expos, such as

Part I

Part II

Part III

Part IV

the wine grading and international patent systems, were also examined. At the 1970 Osaka Expo, pictograms were presented.

It is no exaggeration to say that at the Osaka Expo in 1970, many boys and girls began to enthusiastically dream about the future and some aimed to become technologists while others yearned to conduct overseas business, and their later performances in the real world became the driving force behind the stable growth of the Japanese economy in the 1980s.

I call such mechanisms that could contribute to the perpetual development of industries in Kansai "soft legacies (intangible heritages)" and consider them to be one of the most important factors for the achievements of the Expo 2025.

2. The Greater Expo—a New Concept beyond the Conventional Expo

(1) Extension of the Three Axes and a New Expo Concept

The Osaka-Kansai Expo will not be large scale in comparison to the previously held 1970 Osaka Expo or the Dubai Expo. Considering the physical restrictions such as the venue area, holding exhibitions and events only within the Expo venue may not be very impactful.

Expos are large-scale global events that have great potential to change society, and in order to maximize the effects, the Osaka-Kansai Expo requires a completely different and more realistic approach than previous Expos.

Concerning this proposition, the author would like to propose the idea of the Greater Expo that extends the concepts of "theme, time, and space" of the conventional Expo.

Specifically, the strategy focuses on (i) the development of new actions from the perspective of the Expo's theme and goals, such as SGDs and Society 5.0, (ii) long-term actions over the periods before and after the Expo, (iii) and the expansion of the space for activities that are highly compatible with the Expo to include the entire Kansai region (and even the whole country), in addition to the Yumeshima venue where the Expo will be held.

In other words, this new concept is to extend the conventional

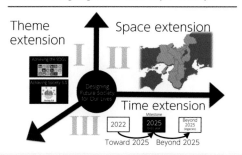

Strategy for Utilizing the Expo
Axes for Designing the Greater Expo Concept

Theme extension

Space extension

Time extension

2022 2025 Beyond 2025 (legacy)

Milestone
Expo year

Toward 2025   Beyond 2025

Figure 4 -CA- 2   Concept of the Greater Expo

(Prepared by the author)

Expo's concept from various perspectives such as the theme, time, and space, and to implement the Expo in an extended way to include projects that are difficult to implement at the Expo site, such as trade markets and activities outside the Expo period in particular, by regarding the entire Kansai region as a virtual pavilion.

From such a point of view, the Greater Expo has already started and will continue even after the Expo itself is over. While previous Expos exhibited only within the Expo venues, the Expo 2025 could regard all activities over an entire vast area as exhibits, in addition to those within the Expo venue, and by calling them collectively the Greater Expo, more people will be able to become involved in the event and it can be expected to be far more attractive than previous Expos, providing ripple effects to local communities.

In fact, by demonstrating many economic activities, new markets, and events in Kansai that are in line with the Greater Expo's concept while associating them with the Expo, it would be possible to revitalize industries by maximizing the geographical advantages of the host region.

Incidentally, I would like to add that for the Expo 2025 to break with the conventional concept, it is necessary to change the mindset from the past successful experience of the 1970 Osaka-style Expo.

Part I

Part II

Part III

Part IV

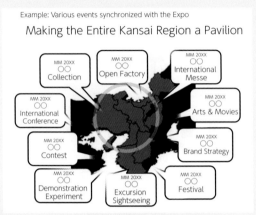

Example: Various events synchronized with the Expo

Making the Entire Kansai Region a Pavilion

Figure 4-CA-3   Making the entire Kansai region a pavilion

(Prepared by the author)

(2) Edinburgh Fringe

The Edinburgh International Festival is a reference case when considering the Greater Expo. As many of you may know, this Festival is a world-class cultural event that began in Edinburgh, Scotland, UK in 1947 and that includes opera, theater, classical music, and other events.

During the Edinburgh International Festival, unique events such as comedy performances and musicals were voluntarily started in the surrounding areas. This was called the Edinburgh Festival Fringe and gradually grew to surpass the main international festival.

After that, self-organized events like those in the Fringe gradually increased to more than 15, covering a wide variety of genres such as international film, jazz and blues, and art and entertainment festivals, and even Internet-related events. These are collectively called the Edinburgh Festival and it attracts many tourists from around the world.

If the Expo 2025 itself is compared to the Edinburgh International Festival, it is very important that many fringe projects (the Greater Expo) are implemented in Kansai, which will be one of the factors for the success of the Expo 2025.

(3) Specific Examples and Fringe Map

So what are the activities of the Greater Expo? The following can be considered examples of activities.

(i) Opening of various sites: Various sites and facilities that have not so far been deemed tourist-worthy can become pavilions, such as small and medium-sized factories (open factories), hospitality service sites, and universities and research institutes.

(ii) Expansion of international activities: Invite international conferences, international academic meetings, etc., to Kansai and hold them on a regular basis. Promote youth exchanges with sister cities and cities with which there has been little interaction so far, as well as promote trade with overseas companies.

(iii) Markets (marts): While the Expo venue is the center of exhibitions, many markets (marts) can be opened outside the venue so that Kansai can continue to function as an international business center even after the Expo.

(iv) Attracting visitors to various places in Kansai: Attract business people visiting the Expo venue both from Japan and overseas to various places in Kansai. Measures to encourage repeat visits after the closure of the Expo and regional cooperation are also important.

(v) Co-creation activities: Implement the Expo's concept of "People's Living Lab" in the entire Kansai region. In order for Kansai to continue to function as a co-creation space in the world even after the Expo, start co-creation activities in various places before the Expo.

When implementing Greater Expo activities in various regions, if there was a list (a fringe activity map) that systematically illustrates the activities and highlights their characteristics, visitors from Japan and overseas could easily access such activities.

In fact, the Kansai Bureau of Economy, Trade and Industry has created and released a list of activity data called the 360-degree EXPO Extension Map as a prototype.

(4) Connection with the Expo

The Greater Expo is a group of activities conducted in Kansai. By associating them with the original Expo in some way, they can be easily recognized as part of the Expo's activities.

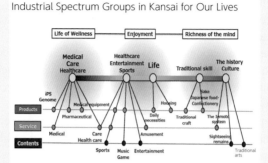

Industrial Spectrum Groups in Kansai for Our Lives

Figure 4-CA-4 Industrial Spectrum Groups in Kansai

(Prepared by the author)

The main theme of the Osaka-Kansai Expo is "Designing Future Society for Our Lives," which can be understood as a very broad concept. If various industry groups in Kansai are mapped onto a spectrum under the theme of "Industries for Our Lives" from the aspects of hardware, services, and content, many industries in Kansai can be arranged seamlessly with a very high affinity with the Expo.

It is also important to demonstrate that the Greater Expo activities outside the venue are connected with the Expo under a common theme.

In addition, as the organizer of the Osaka-Kansai Expo, the Japan Association for the 2025 World Exposition is promoting the TEAM EXPO 2025 program to register activities outside the Expo venue that are in line with SDGs. This new approach is very close in concept to the Greater Expo that has not been seen at previous Expos, and it can also be a way to show the connection between the Expo and the activities registered in the program.

3. Next-generation Co-creation Innovation Brought About by the Expo

(1) Changes in the Business Environment

During the COVID-19 pandemic, teleworking and meetings using communication tools have become widespread, and many seminars and

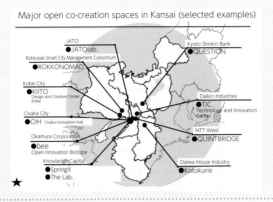

Major open co-creation spaces in Kansai (selected examples)

JATO
● JATOlab.
Rokkosan Smart City Management Consortium
● ROKKONOMAD

Kobe City
● KIITO
Design and Creative Center
Kobe

Osaka City
● OIH Osaka Innovation Hub

Okamura Corporation
● bee
Open Innovation Biotope

Knowledge Capital
● SpringX
● The Lab.

Kyoto Shinkin Bank
● QUESTION

Daikin Industries
● TIC
Technology and Innovation
Center

NTT West
● QUINTBRIDGE

Daiwa House Industry
● Kotokurie

Figure 4-CA-5   **Major open co-creation spaces in Kansai**

Source: 360-degree EXPO Extension Map created by the Kansai Bureau of Economy, Trade and Industry

events are being held via the Internet.

Facebook changed its name to Meta and Microsoft announced its Metaverse strategy, which became hot topics, so XR[2] and the Metaverse have been the focus of much attention since last year.

The rapid penetration of cyberspace and the "improved adaptability of people" to it have eliminated the sense of discomfort and resistance to interactions through cyberspace.

Thus, cyberspace is expected to be used extensively at the Osaka-Kansai Expo and will continue to advance along with the spread of 5G and 6G, becoming an indispensable part of people's lives and business.

For example, Okamura Corporation developed exchange activities in its own co-creation space as part of the TEAM EXPO 2025 program activities and NTT West established a vast co-creation space. In this way, co-creation activities in real co-creation spaces have been actively developed by various companies in recent years.

(2) From industrial clusters to theme-based co-creation activities

The concept of the Osaka-Kansai Expo 2025 is "People's Living Lab."

---

2) XR is a generic term for VR (Virtual Reality), AR (Augmented Reality), MR (Mixed Reality), and other technologies that integrate the real and the virtual worlds.

This concept represents the Expo's approach of co-creation activities through open innovation in which users and other various players participate. I hope that the Greater Expo mentioned above will function as a living laboratory and become a permanent device for creating innovation for the entire Kansai region even after the closure of the Expo.

The concept of an "industrial cluster," which is similar in the sense that it refers to a region where industries are revitalized, is a state in which a group of enterprises mainly in the same industry are located in proximity to each other and "compete and cooperate" with each other to revitalize themselves based on the theory of spatial economics, etc.

With the aforementioned development of cyberspace, it is quite possible that in the near future, not only proximity co-creation that allows face-to-face interactions (i.e., the conventional industrial cluster concept), but also interactions and co-creation activities in cyberspace transcending physical distance will become commonplace (the liberation from physical space constraints).

While conventional industrial clusters are often areas of concentration of specific industries that have emerged due to historical or geopolitical factors, such as "production areas," co-creation in cyberspace will make it easier for players from diverse industries to participate simultaneously and for which the "attractiveness of co-creation themes" will become even more important. For example, under the theme of "future sports," a

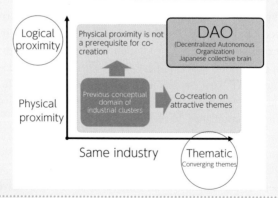

Figure 4-CA-6   Theme-based co-creation activities

(Prepared by the author)

new business through unique co-creation that intersects different industries such as "events," "music," "fashion," "IT/media," and "education" will become possible (the liberation from industry constraints).

However, rather than carrying out all exchange activities in cyberspace, a more realistic and effective methodology would be co-creation activities focusing on "attractive themes" in a hybrid environment by concurrently utilizing cyberspace, free from physical distance and time constraints, and the aforementioned real co-creation spaces that are becoming more and more common.

(3) Developing strong human networks and community activities

In recent years, co-creation activities in which talented individuals gather together to develop new products have been gaining momentum due to the limited mobility of individual companies and the lack of power of individuals. Many SDGs-oriented co-creation teams have registered with the TEAM EXPO 2025 program mentioned above.

The excitement (heightened mood) that people feel about the future through holding the Expo is a very important power, and it is desirable to prepare places for exchanges of ideas and co-creation in which people who are excited about starting something new can gather together.

Part I

Part II

Part III

Part IV

Active Theme-Oriented Communities

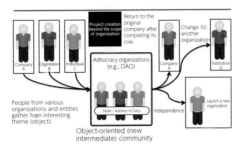

Figure 4-CA-7   **Theme-oriented communities are active**

(Prepared by the author)

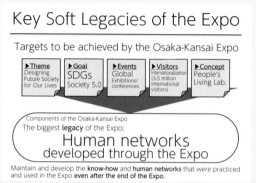

Key Soft Legacies of the Expo

Targets to be achieved by the Osaka-Kansai Expo

▶Theme	▶Goal	▶Events	▶Visitors	▶Concept
Designing Future Society for Our Lives	SDGs Society 5.0	Global Exhibitions/ conferences	Internationalization (3.5 million international visitors)	People's Living Lab.

Components of the Osaka-Kansai Expo

The biggest **legacy** of the Expo:

Human networks
developed through the Expo

Maintain and develop the **know-how** and **human networks** that were practiced and used in the Expo **even after the end of the Expo.**

Figure 4-CA-8   Forming strong human networks through the Expo

(Prepared by the author)

The collective-brain[3] methodology, in which a large number of people come up with ideas together, is well suited to the Japanese. At this moment, if we call the organizational form that acts as an intermediary between individuals and companies and that functions as a "team" that goes beyond the scope of a corporate organization a "new intermediate community[4]," this new intermediate community may play a central role as a new economic entity in the future.

Recently, new forms of organizations such as DAOs (Decentralized Autonomous Organizations[5] derived from Web 3.0, which is being called the next-generation Internet, have also become a hot topic. We should also pay attention to the organizational forms that are undergoing various changes that could become new economic entities.

The themes and goals of the Osaka-Kansai Expo are "the very image of what Kansai aspires to be," and using the Expo as an opportunity to

---

3) A collective brain refers to the wisdom and abilities of a number of individuals that are gathered together to co-create and to evolve. It is said that the human race has prospered because of the collective brain.
4) An intermediate community is an entity that exists between the state and individuals. Since the Meiji era, "companies" have mainly played the role of intermediate communities. Here, intermediate communities are expressed as entities that exist in an intermediate position between companies and individuals.
5) Decentralized communities and organizations using blockchain and other technologies. DAOs are able to promote businesses and projects by connecting people with similar goals, even without a central administrator.

promote co-creation activities both inside and outside the Expo venue will be an important legacy of the Expo, not only in terms of their results, but also in terms of the strong human networks that will be fostered during the process of examining such activities.

(3) The Future We Imagine and The Future We Desire

Using the Expo as a springboard, what kind of mindset should we adopt when developing new businesses in the future?

For example, in the past, when the innovative technology of television was created, it became a catalyst for the birth of content technologies such as TV dramas and sports broadcasts. As such, when a new innovative technology is created, new businesses associated with this new technology are also created one after another.

Now that AI and the Metaverse are evolving dramatically, we should be the first to use our imaginations and explore new businesses that can be derived from the innovative technologies to be developed.

But on the other hand, in the midst of the major changes to technologies and society, it is difficult for many people to accurately understand such changes and it is not easy to predict the future. Rather, it is also important to envision "the desired future" and work backwards (backcast) to explore new businesses.

I look forward to new and further efforts by each and every individual, as well as by various sectors of society, from the opportunity provided by the Expo. Let's begin!

Part I

Part II

Part III

Part IV

Section 3
THE ECONOMIC IMPACT OF EXPO 2025 OSAKA-KANSAI AND THE POSSIBILITY OF A 'GREATER EXPO'

SHIMOYOAMA, Akira; SHIMODA, Mitsuru; TAKABAYASHI, Kikuo

In Section 1, we explained that underinvestment was the cause of the persistent decline of the Kansai economy and concluded that increasing investment in Kansai would boost its economic growth rate. Then, in Section 2, we summarized the progress of infrastructure development related to the Expo, the largest infrastructure development project in the Kansai region, as well as investment related to the project.

In this section, based on publicly available data from the Association for International Expositions and the Osaka City reflecting the progress made for Expo-related projects in Osaka and Kansai, we use the new 2015 Kansai Inter-Regional Input-Output Table (provisional version) developed by the Asia Pacific Institute of Research (APIR) to estimate the economic impact of the Expo from the final demand for consumer spending and investment expenditure. The estimates presented here represent the economic impact when the final demand is generated mainly from the pavilion at the Yumeshima site. In addition, we introduce a new concept of the development of a 'Greater Expo' (turning the whole Kansai region into a pavilion). We estimate the economic impact in the event that the concept of a 'Greater Expo' is realized, and we compare the economic impact of these two scenarios. We also discuss the possibility of a virtual Expo and examine the need to expand demand not only in Osaka but also in the greater Kansai region in order to boost economic growth.

1. The Economic Impact of the Expo 2025 Venue (Yumeshima)

(1) Assumptions about Final Demand
In order to measure the economic impact of the Expo 2025 Osaka-Kansai, first we need to make assumptions about final demand. As discussed in the previous section, the final demand generated by the Expo can be broadly classified into (1) investment expenditure, represented by expenses for constructing venues, exhibiting, and related projects, including railroads and roads, and (2) consumer spending by visitors. For the final demand, we first estimated each demand item by region and industry, and we then assigned it to one of the 108 sectors in the Kansai Inter-Regional Input-Output Table. Table 4-3-1 shows the

Table 4-3-1	Investment expenditure, etc., accompanying the Expo 2025 Osaka-Kansai

1-1. Venue construction expenses (organizer) (JPN 100 million)

Infrastructure development (civil engineering construction, pavement, landscaping, etc.)	130
Infrastructure development (electricity, water supply and drainage, etc.)	285
Parking lot, entrance	171
Pavilion facilities, service facilities	1,103
Rendering at the venue	50
Other (research and design expenses, administrative expenses)	108
Total	1,847

1-2. Venue construction expenses (exhibitors)

Pavilion facilities, service facilities	495
Rendering at the venue	49
Other (research and design expenses, administrative expenses)	106
Total	650

Total construction expenses	2,497

2-1. Operating expenses (organizer)

Planning business, transportation business, etc.	565
Venue management, administrative personnel expenses, etc.	146
Advertising, promotion, etc.	58
Planning, project coordination, etc.	39
Total	809

2-2. Operating expenses (exhibitors)

Venue management, administrative personnel expenses, etc.	876
Advertising, promotion, etc.	350
Planning, project coordination, etc.	234
Total	1,460

Total operating expenses	2,269

3. Related infrastructure development

Railroad development, etc. (extension of the subway Chuo Line and expansion of the transportation capacity)	610
Road improvements, etc. (widening of Konohana Bridge and Yumemai Bridge, etc.)	250
Expense for reclamation, etc.	89
Other	179
Total	1,128

Total related infrastructure	1,128
Total	5,894

Source: Prepared based on the Basic Plan by the Japan Association for the 2025 World Exposition and the website of the Osaka City

estimated breakdown of the expenses for venue construction, operations, and related projects.

Table 4-3-2   Consumer spending by visitors to the Expo 2025 Osaka-Kansai

(JPY 100 million)

	Domestic day visitors	Domestic overnight visitors	Overseas
Transportation expenses	1,196	738	198
Lodging expenses	0	838	562
Food and drinks expenses	540	404	412
Shopping expenses	832	357	633
Entertainment services expenses	777	303	76
Total	3,344	2,640	1,881

	Total	7,866

Source: Based on the Basic Plan by the Japan Association for the 2025 World Exposition and the Travel and Tourism Consumption Trend Survey by the Japan Tourism Agency

Consumer spending by visitors is calculated by first assuming the number of visitors and then multiplying it by the per capita consumption unit price obtained from the Travel and Tourism Consumption Trend Survey published by the Japan Tourism Agency. The total number of visitors is expected to be 28.2 million. Of this total, 15.6 million (55% of the total) will come from the Kansai region, 9.1 million (32%) from other regions of Japan, and 3.5 million (13%) from overseas. We assume different consumption unit prices for each of these regional categories. We assume that visitors from domestic regions other than Kansai were overnight guests, and that they would stay in Osaka Prefecture where the Expo 2025 Osaka-Kansai is to be held. We included transportation, lodging, food and drinks, shopping, and entertainment services in the consumer spending category. Table 4-3-2 shows the estimated consumer spending based on this approach.

Total final demand (JPY 1,376.0 billion), which is the sum of investment expenditure (JPY 589.4 billion) and consumer spending (JPY 786.6 billion), is shown by major industry in Figure 4-3-1. Since final demand is not necessarily generated only in Osaka Prefecture, the venue of the Expo, it is divided into demand inside and outside of Osaka Prefecture. 'Services and others' have the largest share in final demand (JPY 632.5 billion), followed by the construction sector (JPY 331.2 billion), the transportation and communications sector (JPY 235.6 billion), and the manufacturing sector (JPY 95.3 billion).

Most of the final demand is generated in Osaka Prefecture (JPY 1,330.2 billion), but some is generated in Hyogo Prefecture (JPY 11.3 billion) and Kyoto Prefecture (JPY 3.0 billion).

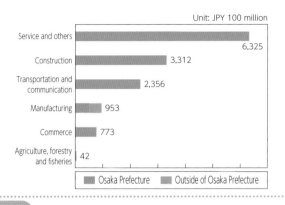

Part I

Part II

Part III

Part IV

Figure 4 - 3 - 1 **Final demand by industry**

Source: Prepared by the authors

(2) The Economic Impact of Expo 2025 is JPY 2.4 trillion

We proceed to examine the economic impact of the conventional form of the Expo 2025 Osaka-Kansai, which will be held mainly on Yumeshima island (hereafter referred to as the 'conventional Expo'), based on (1) the above final demand assumptions and (2) the Basic Plan by the Japan Association for the 2025 World Exposition.

We estimate that the induced production (including direct and indirect impacts) throughout Japan resulting from the Expo 2025 will be JPY 2,375.9 billion, which is larger than the 2.0 trillion yen estimated by the Ministry of Economy, Trade, and Industry (METI). The reason for this is the inclusion of related project expenses for the development of the surrounding area, etc., and the increased number of visitors compared to the initially assumed number. The induced gross value added will be JPY 1,359.9 billion and the employee income impact will be JPY 720.6 billion.

The economic impact of the Expo 2025 Osaka-Kansai will not be limited to Osaka Prefecture. Within the total JPY 2,375.9 billion, the impact on Osaka Prefecture will be JPY 1,770.7 billion, the impact on other Kansai prefectures will be JPY 185.1 billion, and the impact on the rest of Japan (i.e. outside Kansai) will be JPY 420.1 billion. Figure 4-3-2 shows the induced production amount generated outside of Osaka Prefecture by region.

Next, Figure 4-3-3 shows the induced production by industry. The industry that will benefit the most from the Expo 2025 Osaka-Kansai will be 'services and others', with JPY 807.4 billion (Osaka Prefecture: JPY 701.7 billion). This is followed by transportation and communications with JPY 424.3 billion (Osaka Prefecture: JPY 331.6 billion), manufacturing with JPY 341.9 billion (Osaka

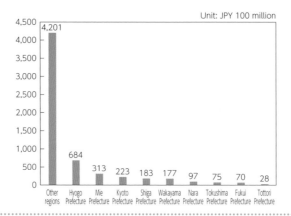

Unit: JPY 100 million

4,201	Other regions
684	Hyogo Prefecture
313	Mie Prefecture
223	Kyoto Prefecture
183	Shiga Prefecture
177	Wakayama Prefecture
97	Nara Prefecture
75	Tokushima Prefecture
70	Fukui Prefecture
28	Tottori Prefecture

Figure 4-3-2   Induced production amount by region (excluding Osaka Prefecture)

Source: Prepared by the author

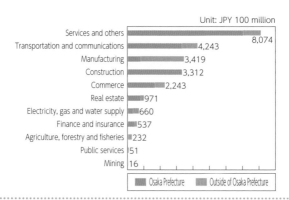

Unit: JPY 100 million

Services and others	8,074
Transportation and communications	4,243
Manufacturing	3,419
Construction	3,312
Commerce	2,243
Real estate	971
Electricity, gas and water supply	660
Finance and insurance	537
Agriculture, forestry and fisheries	232
Public services	51
Mining	16

■ Osaka Prefecture   ■ Outside of Osaka Prefecture

Figure 4-3-3   Induced production amount brought about by holding the Expo by industry

Source: Prepared by the author

Prefecture: JPY 80.6 billion), construction with JPY 331.2 billion, and commerce with JPY 224.3 billion (Osaka Prefecture: JPY 165.9 billion).

2. A 'Greater Expo' with the Whole Kansai Region as a Pavilion

The Expo 2025 Osaka-Kansai will affect not only Osaka Prefecture, where the event will be held. In addition, based on the idea of a 'Greater Expo', various initiatives are expected to be undertaken throughout the Kansai region. As described in Column A, the 'Greater Expo' concept refers to expanding the Expo in terms of theme, time, space, and other aspects, in a way that the entire Kansai region can function as a pavilion. For example, in conjunction with the Expo 2025 Osaka-Kansai, Hyogo Prefecture plans to develop a field pavilion in which the whole of the prefecture will be transformed into a pavilion to attract tourists. In the following section, we explain the economic impact of the various measures taken throughout the Kansai region based on this idea of a 'Greater Expo'[1].

(1) Will a 'Greater Expo' Increase the Number of Overnight Stays?

First, we examine the possibility of increasing the number of overnight stays (extended stays) by implementing initiatives such as the 'Greater Expo' based on several previous cases and studies.

A good example to refer to is the Edinburgh Fringe Festival. In contrast to an official festival that began in 1947 presenting classical and contemporary plays, opera, and classical ballet, the Fringe Festival started as a small and peripheral event. Despite this, it is now known as the largest arts festival in the world. This art festival not only produces economic impact but also fosters pride among local residents by achieving synergies through cooperation and joint promotion by the respective business entities.

Among previous studies, Towse (2010), based on data from Massachusetts, U.S., revealed that tourists who visit for cultural purposes spend USD 62 per day and USD 200 in total during a trip more than other tourists, and they stay half a day more at each destination. In other words, cultural tourism can potentially boost overall tourism in terms of increasing the number of days visitors stay and the amount of money they spend. With respect to Australia, it has been found that the economic impact of cycling tourism is expected to be more than AUD 60 million per year by 2030 due to an increase in the number of days tourists spend[2]. As a Japanese case study, Akasaka and Hirooka (2021) developed a one-day trial tour for foreign tourists with children at the Ocha no Kyoto site in the suburbs of Kyoto, and they found through an empirical analysis of the results of the trial tour that 62% intended to stay longer. Experiential tours, which are representative of the consumption of intangible goods, are believed to have a

1) It is assumed that the Expo 2025 Osaka-Kansai will include not only initiatives in various parts of the Kansai region, but also initiatives through virtual experiences and other online initiatives. The economic impact of these virtual experiences is summarized in the Box.
2) For further details, please refer to the Results of a Survey on Global Intangible Goods Consumption and Overseas Travelers' Attitudes and Actual Situations from the Japan Tourism Agency's Overview of the Experience-based Tourism Content Market.

positive impact on the length of stay[3].

Based on the above, it is expected that the number of overnight stays (extra nights) will increase by providing content sufficiently attractive for tourists to encourage them to stay longer.

(2) Assumptions about Final Demand related to the 'Greater Expo'

As discussed above, we can expect a certain degree of overnight stay extension if we take advantage of the Expo 2025 Osaka-Kansai as an opportunity to provide attractive content in each region and to implement the 'Greater Expo' concept. We assume that domestic visitors would extend their stay by one night for the Greater Expo[4]. For international visitors, we assume that they would stay for three nights and four days, but for the 'Greater Expo', we assume that they would stay two nights longer due to the other additional experiences at various locations[5].

Table 4-3-3 shows the assumed spending by visitors related to the Greater Expo. The assumptions for per capita spending and the number of domestic visitors are the same as for the conventional Expo (discussed above). In addition to lodging expenses, food and drinks and entertainment, services are also assumed to increase proportionally to the number of days spent in Japan. Greater Expo spending by domestic overnight visitors would be JPY 420.1 billion, an increase of JPY 156.1 billion compared to the conventional Expo (JPY 264.0 billion), and spending by international visitors would be JPY 259.9 billion, an increase of JPY 71.8 billion compared to the conventional Expo (JPY 188.1 billion). Total spending by visitors would be JPY 1,014.4 billion.

---

3) On the other hand, not all initiatives necessarily have the effect of extending stays, and there are studies with negative results. A typical example is the research of Rizzo et al. (2016), who found that despite expectations that World Heritage sites would increase stays, such effects were not always apparent based on the results of an analysis of Italian data from 1995 to 2010.

4) Since the overnight guests are considered to be visitors from outside the Kansai region, the impact of offering various additional sightseeing experiences throughout the Kansai region as part of the Greater Expo would be highly effective.

5) As for the destination of the extra night stay, for domestic overnight visitors, the destination of the extra night stay was determined according to the total number of overnight visitors in Osaka Prefecture from Kyoto Prefecture, Hyogo Prefecture, and Nara Prefecture that reported in the Japan Tourism Agency's Lodging Travel Statistics Survey (2019). For overseas visitors to Japan, the first night was assumed to be spent in Osaka Prefecture, and the destination of the second night was determined based on the same approach as that for domestic overnight visitors.

Table 4-3-3	Spending by visitors in the case of a 'Greater Expo'

(JPY100 million)

	Domestic day visitors	Domestic overnight visitors	Overseas
Transportation expenses	1,196	1,107	297
Lodging expenses	0	1,676	937
Food and drinks expenses	540	606	619
Shopping expenses	832	357	633
Entertainment services expenses	777	454	114
Total	3,344	4,201	2,599

	Total	10,144

Source: Prepared by the author

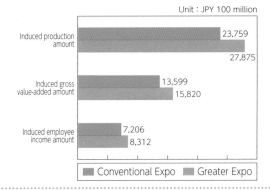

Unit : JPY 100 million

Induced production amount — 23,759 / 27,875
Induced gross value-added amount — 13,599 / 15,820
Induced employee income amount — 7,206 / 8,312

■ Conventional Expo   ■ Greater Expo

Figure 4-3-4	Comparison of the 'Greater Expo' and the conventional Expo

Source: Prepared by the author

(3) The Economic Impact of 'Greater Expo' 2025 Osaka-Kansai

Based on our assumptions about final demand related to the Greater Expo, we calculate the additional amount of induced production, gross value added, and employee income. Figure 4-3-4 is the comparison of the magnitude of each impact with those of the conventional Expo. The induced production would be JPY 2,375.9 billion in the case of the conventional Expo and JPY 2,787.5 billion in the case of the Greater Expo, an increase of JPY 411.6 billion. The induced gross value-added and induced employee income would increase by JPY 158.2 billion and JPY 83.1 billion, respectively. These amounts represent an increase of 13.3 to 14.8%.

Relative to the Gross Regional Product (GRP), we examined the economic impact from the perspective of induced gross value added and we found that it is

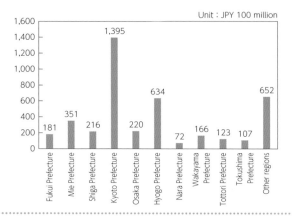

Figure 4-3-5   Differences with the conventional Expo (by region)

Source: Prepared by the author

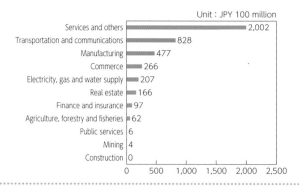

Figure 4-3-6   Differences with the conventional Expo (by industry)

Source: Prepared by the author

expected to increase by approximately 1.6%.

Figure 4-3-5 shows the extent of changes in the economic impacts of the Greater Expo and the conventional Expo for each region. The figure shows an increase in the induced production amount obtained by deducting the figure for the conventional Expo from the figure for Greater Expo. The largest increase was seen in Kyoto Prefecture, at JPY 139.5 billion, followed by other areas at JPY 65.2 billion, Hyogo Prefecture at JPY 63.4 billion, and Mie Prefecture at JPY 35.1 billion. The reason for the large increase in Kyoto Prefecture is thought to be the high ratio of ordinary overnight stays in Kyoto Prefecture.

Figure 4-3-6 shows the increase in the induced production by industry in

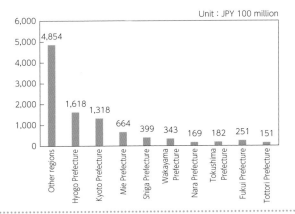

Figure 4-3-7 Induced production amount by region in the 'Greater Expo' (excluding Osaka Prefecture)

Source: Prepared by the author

order to compare the economic impact of the Greater Expo and the conventional Expo. 'Services and others' recorded the largest increase (JPY 200.2 billion), followed by transportation and communications (JPY 82.8 billion), manufacturing (JPY 47.7 billion), and commerce (JPY 26.6 billion). Thus, the impact was found to be significant in a wide range of industries, particularly in the lodging-related industry that is associated with extended stays.

Next, Figure 4-3-7 shows the amount of induced production in Osaka Prefecture versus other prefectures. In the case of a Greater Expo, additional induced production throughout Japan would be JPY 2,787.5 billion, of which, JPY 1792.7 billion would be in Osaka Prefecture and JPY 994.7 billion elsewhere. The total induced amount in regions other than Kansai would be JPY 485.4 billion, while the total induced amount in the Kansai region excluding Osaka Prefecture would be JPY 509.4 billion. Within Kansai, Kyoto Prefecture will receive the largest impact (JPY 161.8 billion), followed by Hyogo (JPY 131.8 billion), Mie (JPY 66.4 billion), and Shiga (JPY 39.9 billion) prefectures.

Finally, Figure 4-3-8 shows the amount of induced production by industry. The industry that would gain the most from the Greater Expo is 'services and others' (JPY 1,007.7 billion). This is followed by transportation and communications (JPY 507.1 billion), manufacturing (JPY 389.7 billion), construction (JPY 331.2 billion), and commerce (JPY 251.0 billion).

The above analysis focused on the economic impact generated by actual visits to the Expo 2025 Osaka-Kansai and the Kansai region, but what has also been attracting attention recently is the economic impact generated by virtual experiences. Although we did not directly analyze the impact of virtual

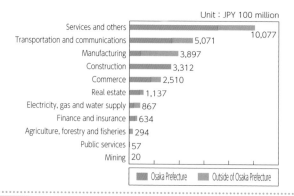

| Figure 4-3-8 | Induced production amount by industry in the 'Greater Expo' |

Source: Prepared by the author

experiences in this article, we emphasize their importance in the Box below.

Box1) The Economic Impact of Virtual Experiences

The outbreak of COVID-19 has brought about various changes in how sight-seeing tours are provided. One of the most representative initiatives of this is virtual sightseeing tours on the Internet[6]. We examine the economic impact of virtual sightseeing tours from two perspectives: the impact of virtual sight-seeing tours themselves, and the impact of virtual experiences leading to real experiences.

Since the outbreak of COVID-19, several studies have revealed the impact of virtual sightseeing tours. Maekawa, Senoo, and Katahira (2022) indicated that the market size of virtual sightseeing tours in Japan (in 2020) is JPY 9.59 billion, with an annual growth rate of approximately 30%, establishing a sepa-rate market from that of real sightseeing tours. JTB (2021) reported that the ratio of people who have experienced virtual sightseeing tours is 2.9%. In the White Paper on Information and Communications in Japan 2021, the Ministry of Internal Affairs and Communications (2021) indicated that the number of people who participated in the virtual sightseeing tours provided by HIS, a travel agency, had exceeded 23,000 (as of October 2020). As a case study, Sasaki (2021) reported that an initiative to send local products in advance to share region-specific experiences online is proving successful.

---

6) Virtual sightseeing tours here refer mainly to the so-called 'online tours'.

However, since the amount of money spent on virtual sightseeing tours alone is small, it is important to consider how virtual experiences lead to actual experiences. For the rationale for virtual experiences leading to real experiences, we can use the increase in electronic commerce (EC) transactions by inbound tourists returning to their home country as a case study. Arai (2019) indicated that for inbound tourists, a trip to Japan itself is an opportunity to try and experience Japanese products, agriculture, forestry, and fishery products, food, drink, and services. He also indicated that, there is a "showroom effect" in that visiting Japan encourages people to purchase Japanese products in their own countries even after returning home.

It is also believed that experiencing virtual sightseeing can induce real experiences. We examine if virtual sightseeing tours can lead to real sightseeing tours and consumption in the region. In the aforementioned case study in Japan, Maekawa, Senoo, and Katahira (2022) report that 88.7% of the respondents answered that they would like to visit the target area after participating in an online tour. They find that young people in particular are inclined to purchase local specialties and visit the area. In a survey on post-tour activities of those who had participated in online tours, JTB (2021) found that 11.7% of the respondents actually visited the region and 19.1% purchased local products. Adding those who answered they would like to do so in the future, nearly 60% of the respondents were stimulated to take action based on their virtual sightseeing experience.

Additionally, the Development Bank of Japan and the Japan Travel Bureau Foundation (2021) found that online tours are highly effective in stimulating the intention to visit Japan. According to a survey by Mizuho Research & Technologies (2022), 27.4% of the respondents answered that participation in virtual tours made them want to actually visit the places for which they were guided, indicating that their intention to travel to the actual sites increased.

In view of the fact that virtual experiences provide impetus for real experiences has been confirmed in various surveys, we believe it will be important to link virtual experiences to actual sightseeing tours in the case of Expo 2025 Osaka-Kansai as well.

3. Revitalizing Kansai's Economy through a Greater Expo and Infrastructure Development

In Section 1 of this chapter, we cited a lack of investment as the main cause for the stagnation of Kansai's economy over the past 50 years, and we suggested the potential for growth in the Kansai region through increased investment leveraged by the Expo 2025 Osaka-Kansai and other events.

In Section 2, we explained the economic impact of infrastructure development in general, and we then outlined the actual state of infrastructure development in the Kansai region in preparation for the Expo 2025 Osaka-Kansai.

In Section 3, we estimated the economic impact of the Expo 2025 Osaka-Kansai, which will be held mainly at the pavilion on Yumeshima island. In addition to this, we estimated the economic impact of a 'Greater Expo' which is the idea of expanding the Expo in terms of theme, time, space, and other aspects, in a way that the entire Kansai region can function as a pavilion. To compare the economic impact of the conventional Expo versus a Greater Expo in terms of the GRP in Osaka, we estimated the additionally induced gross value added. The additional gross value-added amount would be JPY 1,359.9 billion in the case of the conventional Expo and JPY 1,582.0 billion in the case of the Greater Expo, or JPY 222.1 billion (+14.0%) higher. Comparing the impact on the GRP of the greater Kansai region, an increase of +1.6% is expected. Osaka Prefecture's share of the economic impact would be 74.5% (= JPY 1,770.7 billion/2,375.9 billion) in the case of the conventional Expo and 64.3% (= JPY 1792.7 billion/2,787.5 billion) in the case of a Greater Expo.

Clearly, it is undesirable for the economic impact of a large-scale event such as Expo 2025 to be limited to a specific region or a specific period. Our analysis shows that the impact of a Greater Expo would be much larger not only in terms of induced value added, but also in terms of the regions it would affect. If a 'Greater Expo' is implemented, including creating contents that are attractive to tourists and incentives that encourage consumption, visitors will stay longer in Kansai. In consideration of this, medium- to long-term initiatives should be undertaken throughout the Kansai region. It is important to strengthen the link between Expo 2025 and the growth of the Kansai economy through mechanisms such as virtual sightseeing.

We should recognize that the purpose of the Expo is to make the world aware of Kansai's attractiveness and to promote a virtuous cycle of human resources and funds through initiatives, such as implementing a 'Greater Expo,' which will provide economic momentum to the entire Kansai region. We believe that by promoting a virtuous cycle and encouraging investment from Japan and abroad, the Kansai economy will revive and grow.

References

Arai, Naoki (2019), "The Significance, Impact and Challenges of Inbound Tourism," Nara Prefectural University Seasonal Report of Research, Vol. 30, No. 1, pp. 1–34.

Cuccia, T., C. Guccio and I. Rizzo (2016), "The effects of UNESCO World heritage list inscription on tourism destinations performance in Italian regions," Economic Modelling, Vol. 53, pp. 494–508.

Development Bank of Japan, the Japan Travel Bureau Foundation (2021), Survey of Intention of International Travelers from Asia, Europe, U.S.A. and Australia to Japan (The 2nd Special Survey on the Impact of the New Corona).

Fumito Sasaki (2021), "The Textbook of Online Tours, How to Create a New Related Population and Revenue with an Eye to the After-Corona Period," Yamato Gokoro Books.

Ichika Maekawa, Yasushi Senoo and Haruki Katahira (2022), "The Current Status and Market Size of Online Tours," Mitsubishi UFJ Research and Consulting.

Japan Tourism Agency (2019), "Overview of the Experience-based Tourism Content Market, Results of a Survey on Global Intangible Goods Consumption and Overseas Travelers' Attitudes and Actual Situations" (https://www.mlit.go.jp/common/001279555. pdf, last viewed on July 21, 2022).

JTB (2021), Questionnaire Survey of People Who Have Experienced Online Tours.

Miho Akasaka and Yuichi Hirooka (2021), "Development of contents for overseas tourists visiting Japan with children in suburban areas—Japan Tourism Agency, A proof of the state-of-the-art tourism content incubator project—," Tourism Management Review, Vol. 1, pp. 66–77.

Ministry of Internal Affairs and Communications (2021), White Paper on Information and Communications in Japan 2021.

Towse, R. (2010), A Textbook of Cultural Economics, Cambridge University Press, p. 53.

Mizuho Research & Technologies Consulting (2022), "Arousing Travel Intentions through DX-Based Virtual Tour."

Part

III

EXPO 2025 CHRONOLOGY

Table of Contents

About the Editorial Work of the EXPO 2025 Chronology
·This EXPO 2025 Chronology was written by the Chronology Group of the APIR.
·The data below were last checked on November 30, 2022 (exceptions noted).
·EXPO 2025 OSAKA, KANSAI, JAPAN is referred to as "Osaka-Kansai EXPO" and The Japan Association for the International Exposition, 2025 is referred to as "Expo Association" due to space limitation.

1. Chronology

○On November 23, 2018, Osaka is chosen to host the 2025 International Exposition. However, due to the spread of COVID-19 infection in 2020, face-to-face events and other activities were restrained. In 2022, three years before the opening of the Expo, the Expo Association and other organizations outside Osaka have been active in holding events related to the Expo.

Table 1 Movements related to the Expo:2018-22

year		Movements related to the Expo
2018	11/23	Japan (Osaka) selected as the host country for the 2025 International Exposition at the BIE General Assembly
2019	1/30	The Japan Association for the 2025 World Exposition (hereinafter referred to as the Expo Association) is established.
2020	2/14	Announced ambassadors for Osaka-Kansai Expo
	7/13	Osaka-Kansai Expo producer selected
	8/25	Brandnew Expo logo revealed
	12/1	Japan's registration dossier concerning Osaka-Kansai Expo approved by the BIE general assembly
2021	12/25	Master plan for Osaka-Kansai Expo formulated
	12/15	Event planning producer decided for Osaka-Kansai Expo
2022	1/28	Canada announces its participation, and all G7 members decide to join
	2/28	Osaka prefecture and city establish new city-linked metaverse "Virtual Osaka"
	3/22	Brandnew Expo character design revealed
	4/8	Participation reached a total of 100 countries/regions
	4/18	Osaka-Kansai Expo thematic project master plan of the "Brilliance of Life Project"
	4/27	"EXPO 2025 Green Vision" released
	5/13	Tokushima Prefecture opens "Tokushima Virtual Pavilion"
	6/17	Osaka prefecture and city of Osaka released an image of the exterior of the "Osaka Pavilion"
	7/18	Osaka-Kansai Expo Official character nickname "MYAKU-MYAKU" decided at 1000 days to go events
	9/25	Fireworks display held on Yumeshima to promote momentum for Osaka-Kansai Expo
	10/25~26	International Planning Meeting held"

Source: Prepared by APIR based on press materials from various sources

2. Participating Countries, Regions and International Organizations

○As of November 30, 2022, 142 countries/regions and 8 international organizations have announced their participation (Table 2 and Table 3). As shown in Figure 1, many countries and regions in the African region have announced their participation recently.

Table 2   Changes in International Organizations Declaring Participation

cumulative number	Date	corporate body
1	2021/2/10	International Thermonuclear Experimental Reactor (ITER)
2	2/10	International Sorar Alliance (ISA)
3	4/7	International Federation of Red Cross and Red Crescent Societies
4	5/28	African Union Commission (AUC)
5	7/2	European Union (EU)
6	2022/1/7	Association of Southeast Asian Nations (ASEAN) Secretariat
7	4/8	Pacific Islands Forum (PIF) Secretariat
8	7/5	United Nation

Note: As of November 30, 2022.
Source: Prepared by APIR based on Expo Association press release.

Table 3   Countries/regions that have announced their participation

cumulative number	Date	Country&Region
7	2021/2/10	Republic of Yemen, Republic of Greece, Republic of Djibouti, Turkmenistan, People's Republic of Bangladesh, Kingdom of Bhutan, Republic of Mali
14	3/12	Islamic Republic of Afghanistan, Republic of Uzbekistan, Republic of Senegal, Kingdom of Bahrain, Federative Republic of Brazil, Burkina Faso, Kingdom of Lesotho
18	4/7	Qatar, Republic of Guinea-Bissau, Republic of Zimbabwe, Nepal
19	4/13	Kingdom of Thailand
25	4/21	Democratic People's Republic of Algeria, Republic of India, Federal Republic of Germany, French Republic, Jordan, Russian Federation
29	5/14	Republic of Angola, Republic of Zambia, Swiss Confederation, Lao People's Democratic Republic
34	5/28	Islamic Republic of Iran, Republic of Ghana, Republic of Guinea, People's Republic of China, Grand Duchy of Luxembourg
43	6/15	United Kingdom of Great Britain and Northern Ireland, Kingdom of Cambodia, Republic of Cuba, State of Kuwait, Union of the Comoros, Central African Republic, United Mexican States, Republic of Mozambique, Romania
46	7/2	United Arab Emirates, Republic of Kazakhstan, Kingdom of Spain
48	7/16	United States of America, Republic of Korea
49	7/27	Portuguese Republic
54	8/20	Republic of Indonesia, Arab Republic of Egypt, Kyrgyz Republic, Republic of Suriname, Socialist Republic of Vietnam
57	9/28	Argentine Republic, Dominican Republic, Republic of Burundi

58	10/15	Kingdom of Saudi Arabia
63	11/17	Republic of Italy, Republic of Uganda, Republic of Tajikistan, Brunei Darussalam, Republic of South Sudan
64	11/24	Republic of Paraguay
67	12/14	Republic of Austria, Sultanate of Oman, Kingdom of Tonga
72	2022/ 1/7	Republic of Azerbaijan, Republic of Estonia, Commonwealth of Australia, Republic of Serbia, Republic of Turkey
78	1/28	Republic of Armenia, Canada, Saint Lucia, Independent State of Papua New Guinea, Republic of Honduras, Republic of Rwanda
86	3/4	Republic of The Gambia, Democratic Socialist Republic of Sri Lanka, Republic of Equatorial Guinea, Saint Vincent and the Grenadines, Islamic Republic of Pakistan, Kingdom of Belgium, Republic of Madagascar, Republic of Latvia
87	3/11	Republic of Slovenia
100	4/8	Antigua and Barbuda, Republic of El Salvador, Republic of Guyana, Republic of Cote d'Ivoire, Democratic Republic of Sao Tome and Principe, Saint Kitts and Nevis, Tuvalu, Republic of Togo, Republic of Vanuatu, Palestine, Republic of Benin, Plurinational State of Bolivia, Republic of Marshall Islands
105	4/19	Ireland, Eastern Republic of Uruguay, Republic of Guatemala, Republic of Kosovo, Malaysia
106	5/10	Mongolia
115	5/31	Republic of North Macedonia, Republic of Kenya, Independent State of Samoa, Republic of Singapore, Solomon Islands, Republic of Niger, Republic of Haiti, Republic of Bulgaria, Federated States of Micronesia
119	6/7	Federal Democratic Republic of Ethiopia, Kingdom of the Netherlands, Niue, Republic of Poland
120	6/14	Republic of the Philippines
126	7/5	United Republic of Tanzania, Czech Republic, Republic of Trinidad and Tobago, Republic of Palau, Belize, Montenegro
130	7/29	Hungary, Republic of Fiji, Republic of Mauritius, Islamic Republic of Mauritania
137	9/9	Kingdom of Eswatini, Republic of Gabon, Federal Republic of Somalia, Federal Republic of Nigeria, Republic of Nauru, Democratic Republic of East Timor, Republic of Botswana
142	10/25	Slovak Republic, Republic of Tunisia, Republic of Panama, Republic of Malta, Republic of South Africa

Note: As of November 30, 2022.
Source: Prepared by APIR based on Expo Association press release.

■ Countries that have announced their participation for the first time: as of February 10 2021
▨ Over 50 participating countries/regions: as of August 20 2021
☐ Participating countries exceed 100 countries/regions: as of April 8 2022
■ Countries with most recent participation announcement: as of October 25 2022

Figure 1   Map of countries/regions that have announced their participation

Note: As of November 30, 2022.
Source: Prepared by APIR based on Expo Association press release.

Part I

Part II

Part III

Part IV

3. Comparison with Previous International Expositions

○The table below compares the most recent international expositions (registered expositions) . A comparison of the themes of the three Expos shows that they are focused on soft themes such as "Feeding," "Mind," "Future," and " Lives".

Table 4   Comparison with Previous International Expositions

	2020 Dubai International Expo	2025 Japan International Expo(Osaka, Kansai Expo)	2015 Milano International Expo
Holding period	October 1, 2021 ~ March 31, 2022	April 13, 2025 ~ October 13, 25	May 1, 2015 ~ October 31, 15
Number of days	182 days	184 days	184 days
main theme	Connecting Minds, Creating the Future	Designing Futur Society for Our Lives	Feeding the Planet, Energy for Life
logo mark	EXPO 2020 DUBAI UAE	EXPO 2025	≡XPO MILANO 2015
Total Visitors Target Number	25 million people	28.2 million people	20 million people
Total number of visitors	24.1 million people	—	21.5 million people
Venue Scale	438 ha	155 ha	110 ha
Number of participating countries, regions and international organizations	192 countries/regions, 10 organizations	150 countries/regions, 25 organizations (target)	145 countries/regions, 3 organizations
ticket price	1-day pass (adult) ¥2,850 Multi-pass (30 days) ¥5,850 Pass during the exhibition ¥14,850 Free for Under 18, students, over 1 dirham = ¥30	1-day pass (18-64 years old) ¥6,000 1-day pass (12-17 years old) ¥3,300 1-day pass (4-11 years old) ¥2,000 1-day pass (65-80 years old) ¥5,000 Free for children under 3 and over 80	1-day pass Adult (14-64 years old) ¥5,300 1-day pass students (14-25 years old) ¥4,420 1-day pass (4-13 years old) ¥2,140 1-day pass (Over 65) ¥3,750 Free for children under 3 1 Euro = ¥134
Logo and Symbol of the Japan Pavilion	JAPAN EXPO 2020 DUBAI	—	JAPAN EXPO 2014 MILANO
Theme of the Japan Pavilion	Where ideas meet	Between Lives	Harmonious Diversity

* Nihon Keizai Shimbun, "Osaka-Kansai Expo admission fee considered at 6,000 yen" (June 20, 2022).
Source: Prepared by APIR based on press releases from various sources.

4. Introduction of the initiatives for hosting the EXPO 2025

○In addition to Yumeshima, the site of the Expo, various activities are underway in the Kansai region with the aim of building momentum for the Expo and revitalizing local communities in the wake of the Expo. The following is an introduction to some of the most characteristic activities.

○There are programs and events organized by the Expo Association to promote the momentum of the Expo (①~⑤), and programs focusing on regional revitalization supported by the METI-Kinki Bureau (⑥,⑦) .

① Junior EXPO 2025

This educational program is designed to encourage children, who will be responsible for the future, to participate in the Osaka-Kansai Expo before the event is held, and to increase their interest in the event so that they will want to visit the Expo site.
In 2020, the program will be implemented in elementary and junior high schools in Osaka Prefecture, in 2021 in the Kansai region, and in 2022 and thereafter, the program will be expanded to cover all of Japan.
Implementing entity: Expo Association
https://www.expo2025.or.jp/overview/education/

② TEAM-EXPO 2025

A participatory program in which a diverse group of people team up to take on the challenges of the Osaka-Kansai Expo and the future through a variety of activities.
Co-Creation Challenges: Activities for an exciting future for all participants, achieving the theme of the Expo "Designing Future Society for Our Lives".
Co-Creation Partners: Corporations and organizations that create and support multiple Co-Creation Challenges.
Implementing entity: Expo Association
https://team.expo2025.or.jp/

③ Cyber Expo

The program is different from the one at the Expo site, and will be presented in an online space. Under the theme of "Action for Lives," this is another Expo that transcends national borders, race, and culture to take action to sustain the lives of humans, living creatures, and the Earth. It aims to build on the legacy of the Osaka-Kansai Expo as a platform that can run on its own even after 2025.
Implementing entity: Expo Association
https://www.expo2025.or.jp/overview/expo_pll_talks/cyber/

④ People's Living Lab Promotion Conference

The People's Living Lab (PLL) Promotion Conference was held to promote the participation of a wide variety of companies in "demonstration experiments that can be conducted in the special city of Expo. Experts from various fields were invited to the conference to discuss what can be realized at the Expo site as a "testing ground for the society of the future."
Implementing entity: Expo Association
https://www.expo2025.or.jp/pll/

⑤ **EXPO PLL Talks**

The "People's Living Lab" is a concept for realizing the theme of the Osaka-Kansai Expo, and this online talk event will allow a variety of practitioners and experts to communicate their efforts related to the theme to people in Japan and abroad before the Expo period, and to work together to create the Expo.
Implementing entity: Expo Association
https://www.expo2025.or.jp/pll/

⑥ **Regional revitalization strategy utilizing Expo**

Activities to revitalize the entire Kansai region by expanding the concept of the Expo and utilizing the power of the Expo. Specifically, the " Project for Creating Future Innovations " will promote the creation and acceleration of innovation, and the "Regional Expo Utilization Project" aims to promote regional development by utilizing the power of the Expo, including regional branding and attracting visitors to the area.
Implementing entity: the METI-Kinki Bureau
https://www.kansai.meti.go.jp/1-2_2025next/index.html

⑦ **360° EXPO Extended Map**

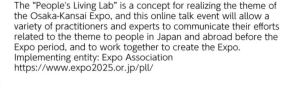

This map summarizes the activities of the Kansai region that are expected to make great strides during and after the Osaka-Kansai Expo in order to convey the attractiveness of the Kansai region to the many people and businesses that will visit the Osaka-Kansai Expo, viewing the entire Kansai region as a pavilion.
The map has been updated every six months since 2021.
Implementing entity: the METI-Kinki Bureau
https://www.kansai.meti.go.jp/1-2_2025next/360expomap_detail.html

Source: Prepared by APIR based on the Expo Association and the METI-Kinki Bureau website.

5. Infrastructure Map

○The Headquarters for Promoting International Expositions, Cabinet Secretariat, released an infrastructure development plan on August 27, 2021. The five pillars of the infrastructure development plan are "Infrastructure planning around the venue," "Improvement of accessibility to the venue," "Improvement of safety," "Enhancement of liveliness and attractiveness," and "Development of wide-area transportation infrastructure. Figure 2 is an excerpt from the main development plan. Based on this development plan, Osaka City has requested approximately 450 billion yen for infrastructure projects.[1]

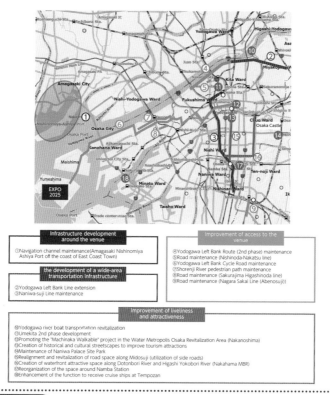

Infrastructure development around the venue	Improvement of access to the venue
①Navigation channel maintenance(Amagasaki Nishinomiya Ashiya Port off the coast of East Coast Town)	④Yodogawa Left Bank Route (2nd phase) maintenance ⑤Road maintenance (Nishinoda-Nakatsu line) ⑥Yodogawa Left Bank Cycle Road maintenance ⑦Shorenji River pedestrian path maintenance ⑧Road maintenance (Sakurajima Higashinoda line) ⑨Road maintenance (Nagara Sakai Line (Abenosuji))

the development of a wide-area transportation infrastructure

②Yodogawa Left Bank Line extension
③Naniwa-suji Line maintenance

Improvement of liveliness and attractiveness

⑩Yodogawa river boat transportation revitalization
⑪Umekita 2nd phase development
⑫Promoting the "Machinaka Walkable" project in the Water Metropolis Osaka Revitalization Area (Nakanoshima)
⑬Creation of historical and cultural streetscapes to improve tourism attractions
⑭Maintenance of Naniwa Palace Site Park
⑮Realignment and revitalization of road space along Midosuji (utilization of side roads)
⑯Creation of waterfront attractive space along Dotonbori River and Higashi Yokobori River (Nakahama MBR)
⑰Reorganization of the space around Namba Station
⑱Enhancement of the function to receive cruise ships at Tempozan

Figure 2   Expo-related infrastructure map

Note: Unfilled numbers indicate the relevant line, filled indicates the relevant spot.
Source: Prepared by APIR based on the Infrastructure Development System Plan of the International Exposition Promotion Headquarters, Cabinet Secretariat

1) Nihon Keizai Shimbun, "Expo-Related Infrastructure, Osaka City's Project Cost 450 Billion Yen" (September 2, 2021)

5. Infrastructure Map

STATISTICAL ANNEX

The definitions of the geographical regions used in the annex are as follows unless otherwise noted.

Region	Prefecture
Kansai	Type A: Shiga, Kyoto, Osaka, Hyogo, Nara, Wakayama
	Type B: Shiga, Kyoto, Osaka, Hyogo, Nara, Wakayama, Fukui
	Type C: Shiga, Kyoto, Osaka, Hyogo, Nara, Wakayama, Fukui, Mie, Tottori, Tokushima
Kanto	Ibaraki, Tochigi, Gunma, Saitama, Chiba, Tokyo, Kanagawa, Yamanashi
Chubu	Nagano, Gifu, Shizuoka, Aichi, Mie
Japan	All prefectures including the Kansai, Kanto and Chubu regions

Figure 1   Total population by region

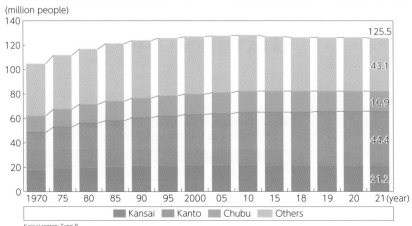

(million people)

Kansai region: Type B
Note: Level as of October 1 for each year.
Sources: Statistics Bureau, Ministry of Internal Affairs and Communications, *"Population Census"* and *"Population Estimates"*

Figure 2   Kansai population by age group

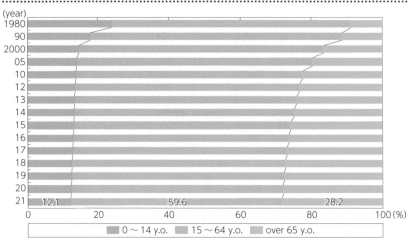

Kansai region: Type B
Note: Does not include persons with unspecified ages.
Sources: Statistics Bureau, Ministry of Internal Affairs and Communications, *"Population Census"*, *"Population Estimates"* and *" Internal Migration in Japan Derived from the Basic Resident Registration (for 2010–21data)"*

Figure 3 Population aging rates

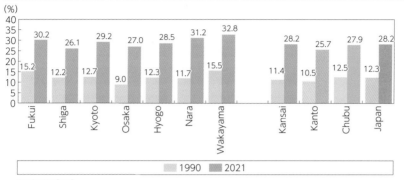

(%)

1990 2021

Kansai region : Type B
Note: Population aging rate (%) = Population aged 65 and above/total population x 100. Level as of October 1 for 1990 and as of January 1 for 2021.
Sources: Health and Welfare Bureau for the Elderly, Ministry of Health, Labour and Welfare, *"Table of Figures for Health and Welfare Services Map for the Elderly(1990)"*
Statistics Bureau, Ministry of Internal Affairs and Communications, *"Population Estimates"* and *"Internal Migration in Japan Derived from the Basic Resident Registers(for 2021data)"*

Figure 4 Gross regional product (GRP) trends

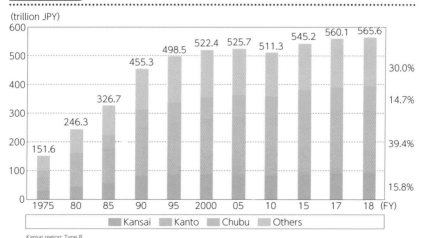

(trillion JPY)

Kansai Kanto Chubu Others

Kansai region: Type B
Note: The 1975-90 period is based on the 1968 SNA, the 1990-2005 period on the 1993 SNA, and the 2006-18 period on the 2008 SNA.
Source: Cabinet Office, *"Annual Report of Regional Accounts Statistics"*

Figure 5 — Trends in the GRP shares of economic sectors

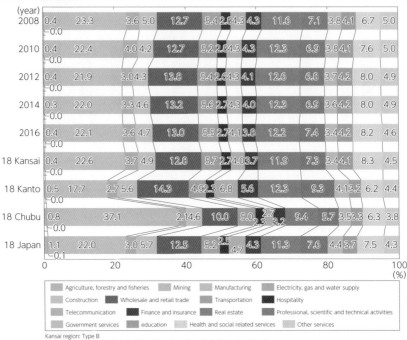

Kansai region: Type B
Note: The values used for the calculation of the shares do not include imputed interest.
However, we used the GDP figures by industry to calculate the total GDP.
Source: Cabinet Office, "Annual Report on Prefectural Accounts"

Figure 6 — GRP per capita

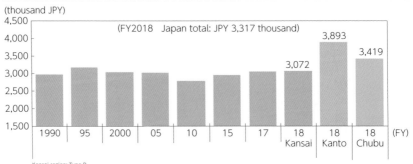

Kansai region: Type B
Source: Cabinet Office, "Annual Report on Prefectural Accounts"

Figure 7 Kansai's GRP and sovereign states' nominal GDP (2019)

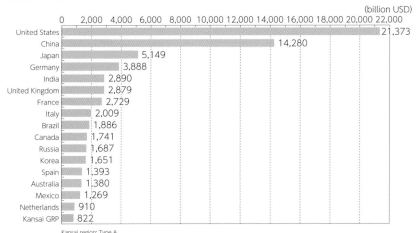

(billion USD)

United States	21,373
China	14,280
Japan	5,149
Germany	3,888
India	2,890
United Kingdom	2,879
France	2,729
Italy	2,009
Brazil	1,886
Canada	1,741
Russia	1,687
Korea	1,651
Spain	1,393
Australia	1,380
Mexico	1,269
Netherlands	910
Kansai GRP	822

Kansai region: Type A
Note: Nominal GDP in 2019. The figure for Kansai is based on its nominal GRP for FY2018 (April 2018–March 2019)
The 2019 exchange rate was JPY 109. 05 to the US dollar.
Sources: UN, "National Accounts Main Aggregates Database" , Cabinet Office, "Annual Report of Regional Accounts Statistics"

Figure 8 Value of manufactured goods shipments

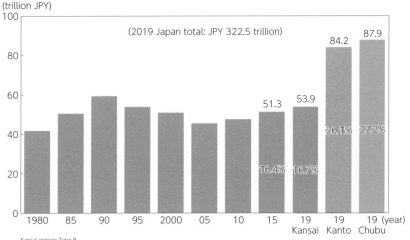

(trillion JPY)

(2019 Japan total: JPY 322.5 trillion)

Kansai region: Type B
Note: Figures represent total values of manufactured goods shipments by firms with 4 or more employees.
Source: Ministry of Economy, Trade and Industry, "Statistics Table on Census of Manufactures"
The Ministry of Internal Affairs and Communications and Ministry of Economy, Trade and Industry, "2016 Economic Census for Business Activity (for 2015 data)"

Part I

Part II

Part III

Part IV

Figure 9   Capital investment in Kansai

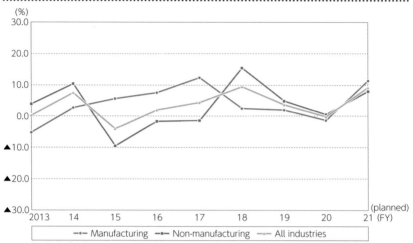

Kansai region: Type B
Note: YoY. Figures for FY2021 are the planned values as of December 2020.
       Includes investments in land, but does not include investments in software.
Source: Bank of Japan, Tankan (Short-Term Economic Survey of Enterprises in Japan)

Figure 10   Capital investment in Japan

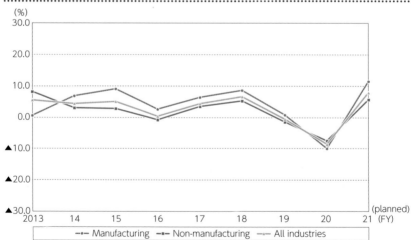

Note: YoY. Figures for FY2021 are the planned values as of December 2020.
      Includes investments in land, but does not include investments in software.
Source: Bank of Japan, Tankan (Short-Term Economic Survey of Enterprises in Japan)

Figure 11 Index of industrial production (IIP)

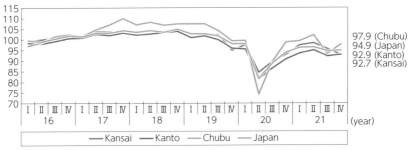

97.9 (Chubu)
94.9 (Japan)
92.9 (Kanto)
92.7 (Kansai)

—— Kansai —— Kanto —— Chubu —— Japan

Kansai region: Type A
Note: 2015 = 100. Seasonally adjusted.
　　The Kansai, Kanto, and Chubu regions are under the jurisdiction of the Kansai, Kanto, and Chubu Bureaus of Economy, Trade and Industry, respectively.
Source: Ministry of Economy, Trade and Industry, "Production, Shipments and Inventories"

Figure 12 Employment by industry (2021)

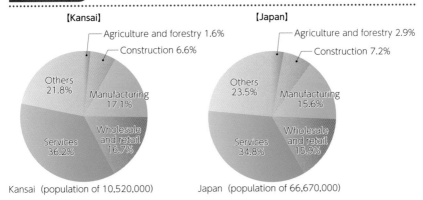

[Kansai]

Agriculture and forestry 1.6%
Construction 6.6%
Others 21.8%
Manufacturing 17.1%
Wholesale and retail 16.7%
Services 36.2%

[Japan]

Agriculture and forestry 2.9%
Construction 7.2%
Others 23.5%
Manufacturing 15.6%
Wholesale and retail 15.9%
Services 34.8%

Kansai (population of 10,520,000)　　　Japan (population of 66,670,000)

Kansai region: Type A
Note: "Services" represents the total employment in the following industries: Hotels and Restaurants, Entertainment, Health and Social Work, Education, Mixed services, and Other services(services that cannot be categorized).
Source: Statistics Bureau, Ministry of Internal Affairs and Communications, "Annual Report on the Labor Force Survey"

Figure 13   Exports by product category (2021)

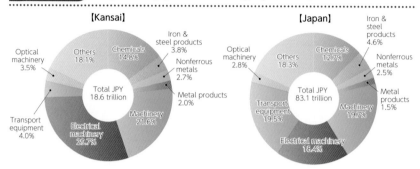

Kansai region: Type A
Source: Ministry of Finance, *"Trade Statistics for2021"*, Osaka Customs, *"Trade Statistics of the Kinki Region for 2021"*

Figure 14   Imports by product category (2021)

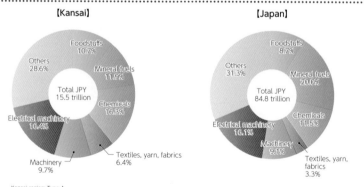

Kansai region: Type A
Source: Ministry of Finance, *"Trade Statistics for2021"*, Osaka Customs, *"Trade Statistics of the Kinki Region for 2021"*

Figure 15　Destination of exports from Kansai

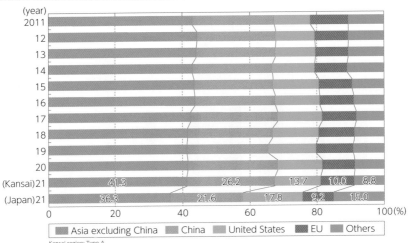

(Kansai)21: Asia excluding China 41.3 | China 26.2 | United States 13.7 | EU 10.0 | Others 8.8
(Japan)21: 36.3 | 21.6 | 17.8 | 9.2 | 15.0

■ Asia excluding China　■ China　■ United States　▨ EU　■ Others

Kansai region: Type A
Note: The figure for 2021 are definite.
Source: Ministry of Finance, "Trade Statistics for2021", Osaka Customs, "Trade Statistics of the Kinki Region for 2021"

Figure 16　Origin of imports into Kansai

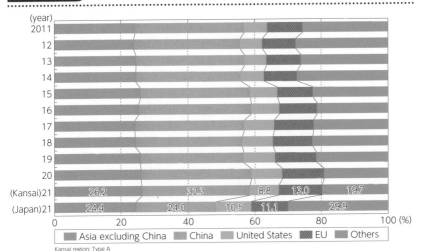

(Kansai)21: 26.2 | 32.3 | 8.8 | 13.0 | 19.7
(Japan)21: 24.4 | 24.0 | 10.5 | 11.1 | 29.9

■ Asia excluding China　■ China　■ United States　▨ EU　■ Others

Kansai region: Type A
Note: The figure for 2021 are definite.
Source: Ministry of Finance, "Trade Statistics for2021", Osaka Customs, "Trade Statistics of the Kinki Region for 2021"

Figure 17 — Number of universities, junior colleges and enrolled students

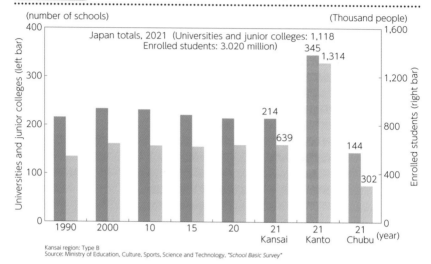

(number of schools)   (Thousand people)

Japan totals, 2021 (Universities and junior colleges: 1,118
Enrolled students: 3.020 million)

Universities and junior colleges (left bar) / Enrolled students (right bar)

1990 2000 10 15 20 21 Kansai 21 Kanto 21 Chubu (year)

345 / 1,314 (Kansai)
214 / 639 (Kanto)
144 / 302 (Chubu)

Kansai region: Type B
Source: Ministry of Education, Culture, Sports, Science and Technology. *"School Basic Survey"*

Figure 18 — Number of national treasures and important cultural properties (2022)

	National treasures	Important cultural properties	National treasures, domestic share (%)	Important cultural properties, domestic share (%)
Fukui	6	114	0.5	0.9
Shiga	56	825	5.0	6.2
Kyoto	237	2,200	21.0	16.5
Osaka	62	683	5.5	5.1
Hyogo	21	472	1.9	3.5
Nara	206	1,328	18.2	10.0
Wakayama	36	395	3.2	3.0
Kansai	624	6,02	55.2	45.1
Kanto	340	3,754	30.1	28.1
Chubu	44	1,100	3.9	8.2
Japan	1,131	13,331	100.0	100.0

Kansai region: Type B
Note: Values are as of April 1, 2021
Source: Agency for Cultural Affairs, "List of National Treasures and Important Cultural Properties Designated by Prefecture."

Figure 19 International overnight visitors

(Total number of overnight visitors: 10 thousand people)   (Ratio of international overnight visitors: %)

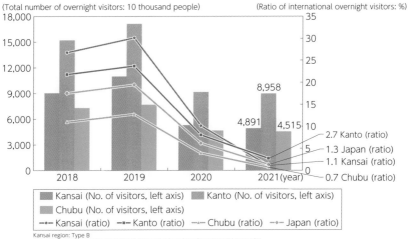

2.7 Kanto (ratio)
1.3 Japan (ratio)
1.1 Kansai (ratio)
0.7 Chubu (ratio)

■ Kansai (No. of visitors, left axis)   ■ Kanto (No. of visitors, left axis)
■ Chubu (No. of visitors, left axis)
—●— Kansai (ratio)   —■— Kanto (ratio)   —▲— Chubu (ratio)   —◆— Japan (ratio)

Kansai region: Type B
Note: Ratio of international overnight visitors = Total number of international overnight
   visitors)/ (Total number of overnight visitors) x 100
Sources: Ministry of Land, Infrastructure, Transport and Tourism, "Overnight Travel Statistics Survey"
   (The figures for 2021 are preliminary).

Figure 20 Visit rates of international visitors by prefecture

(%)

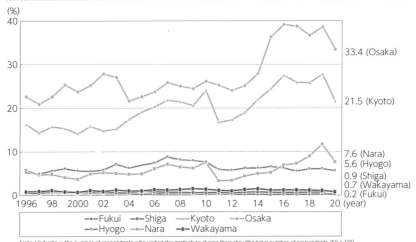

33.4 (Osaka)

21.5 (Kyoto)

7.6 (Nara)
5.6 (Hyogo)
0.9 (Shiga)
0.7 (Wakayama)
0.2 (Fukui)

—◆—Fukui   —■—Shiga   —▲—Kyoto   —◆—Osaka
—▼—Hyogo   —✕—Nara   —■—Wakayama

Note: Visit rate = the number of respondents who visited the prefecture during their stay/the total number of respondents (N) x 100
   The figures of 2020 are average for Jan-Mar as the survey was cancelled after the onset of the COVID-19 pandemic in April.
   The survey was cancelled in 2021 due to the impact of the COVID-19 pandemic.
Sources: Japan National Tourism Organization (JNTO), "Destination Survey of Overseas Visitors to Japan". From 2011, Japan Tourism
   Agency "Consumption Trend Survey for Foreigners Visiting Japan"

Figure 21   Average expenditure per visitor by nationality (2021)

(thousand yen)

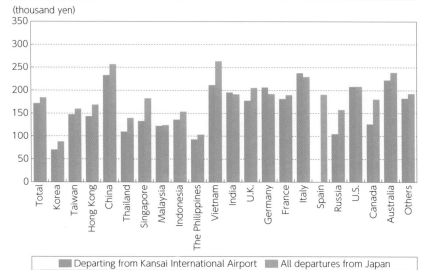

Note 1) Travel spending per person departing from Japan. The figures of 2020 are average for Jan-Mar as the survey was cancelled after the onset
of the COVID-19 pandemic in April.
Due to the impact of the COVID-19 pandemic, nationality-specific values for the 2021 average were not published.
Note 2) No data country shows no respondents.
Source: Japan Tourism Agency, "Accommodation Survey"

About Us

Organization Name: Asia Pacific Institute of Research (APIR)

Date of Establishment: December 1, 2011

Research Director: MIYAHARA, Hideo

Address: 7th Floor., Knowledge Capital Tower C, GRAND FRONT OSAKA
3-1 Ofuka-cho, Kita-ku, Osaka 530-0011 Japan

Kansai and the Asia Pacific
Economic Outlook 2022-23

2023 年 4 月 28 日　初版発行

編　著	ASIA PACIFIC INSTITUTE OF RESEARCH （一般財団法人アジア太平洋研究所）	©2023

発行所　日経印刷株式会社
〒102-0072　東京都千代田区飯田橋 2-15-5
電　話 (03) 6758-1011
https://www.nik-prt.co.jp/

発売所　全国官報販売協同組合
〒100-0013　東京都千代田区霞が関 1-4-1
電　話 (03) 5512-7400
https://www.gov-book.or.jp/

組版・印刷・製本／日経印刷株式会社

ISBN 978-4-86579-359-8　C0033